CW01522152

Palestine in the Interwar Period

Palestine in the Interwar Period

Between Internationalization and Revolution (1918-1939)

Dr. Labeeb Ahmed Bsoul

LEXINGTON BOOKS
Lanham • Boulder • New York • London

Published by Lexington Books
An imprint of The Rowman & Littlefield Publishing Group, Inc.
4501 Forbes Boulevard, Suite 200, Lanham, Maryland 20706
www.rowman.com

86-90 Paul Street, London EC2A 4NE

Copyright © 2023 by The Rowman & Littlefield Publishing Group, Inc.

All rights reserved. No part of this book may be reproduced in any form or by any electronic or mechanical means, including information storage and retrieval systems, without written permission from the publisher, except by a reviewer who may quote passages in a review.

British Library Cataloguing in Publication Information Available

Library of Congress Cataloging-in-Publication Data

Names: Bsoul, Labeeb Ahmed, author.
Title: Palestine in the interwar period : between internationalization and revolution (1918-1939) / Dr. Labeeb Ahmed Bsoul.
Description: Lanham : Lexington, [2023] | Includes bibliographical references and index. | Summary: "The author examines Palestine's interwar political, social, and cultural landscape. The book sheds light on the complex forces at play in the region during this period, including colonial powers' support for the Zionist movement, the Balfour Declaration and Sykes-Picot Secret Agreement, the Peel Commission, the White Papers, the rise of Palestinian nationalism, the Palestinian revolution, and the internationalization of the Palestine question"-- Provided by publisher.
Identifiers: LCCN 2023023744 (print) | LCCN 2023023745 (ebook) |
  ISBN 9781666933680 (cloth) | ISBN 9781666933697 (ebook)
Subjects: LCSH: Palestine--History--1917-1948.Classification: LCC DS126 .B76 2023
  (print) | LCC DS126 (ebook) | DDC 956.94/04--dc23/eng/20230613
LC record available at https://lccn.loc.gov/2023023744
LC ebook record available at https://lccn.loc.gov/2023023745

Dedicated to my beloved late brother Ibrahim Ahmed Bsoul,
students, friends, teachers, and justice seekers.

Contents

Acknowledgments

In the Name of Allah (God), the Most Gracious, the Most Merciful.

Many people should be thanked for their contributions to the completion of this monograph. I'd like to start by thanking my colleagues at Khalifa University, as well as other colleagues and role models, for their advice, encouragement, and many direct and indirect discussions on a variety of topics related to my personal research interests. I would like to express my sincere appreciation to the following professors: Devin Stewart, Tarek Ladjal, Anas Alazamm, Maisam Wahbah, Ayman Abulail, Manal Abu-Al Haja, Ashraf al-Khattib, Muhamad S. Olimat, and Mohammad Bataineh. Their invaluable assistance and guidance have played a crucial role in my academic journey. Their dedication to scholarship, both as exemplary role models and as supportive mentors, has left a lasting impact on me. I am truly grateful for their unwavering moral support and encouragement throughout our studies together. My heartfelt appreciation goes to the following colleagues and doctors: Baker Mohammad, Khaled Salah, Heba Abunahla, Hani Saleh, Sami Bachir Mejri, Yehya Farhoud, Mohammad Awad, Belal Irshaid, Shaju Badarudeen, Abdul Rafi, Shahd Emad Hardan. Their friendship and engaging conversations about my research topics have been invaluable. I am also grateful to Rasha, Ruba, and Aya Nasser for their companionship and insightful discussions. I would like to extend my thanks to the dedicated staff of the Khalifa University librarians, particularly Khawlah Al Hadhrami, Suaad Al Jneibi, Alia Al-Harrasi, Muna Ahmad Abdulla, and Patricia Jamal. Their continuous assistance and support throughout my research journey have been greatly appreciated.

Furthermore, I'm thankful for all of my friends who have been there for me emotionally and helped me understand what's going on. To give my gratitude to everyone who has been in my life and who has been a true and dear friend for a significant amount of time would require many pages and a lot of space. They include my late best friend Muhammed, Nimer Bsoul, and Abbas and Ghanim Yaacoubi. I would also like to thank many friends and students whose names are not mentioned here but who have contributed in one way or another to the completion of this study.

I would also like to express my deep gratitude and thanks to my colleagues in the HSS (Humanities and Social Sciences) department at Khalifa University for their friendship and encouragement. I am grateful to Dr. Curtis D. Carbonell, Lejla Kucukalic, Mutasim Al-Deaibes, Robert Tylor, and all others who have been supportive in various ways. Their contributions have enriched my academic experience. Many thanks also to my students at McGill University, Saint Mary's University, Dalhousie University, United Arab Emirates University, and Khalifa University, with whom I was inspired to share my knowledge and from whose interesting discussions I benefited immensely.

I would like to express my gratitude and appreciation to Dr. Robert Tyler and Ibrahim Aoude, who read the entire monograph and offered valuable suggestions for improvement. A special thanks and gratitude go to the team at Lexington Books for their professionalism and dedication in bringing this book to completion. In particular, I would like to thank most heartily chief editor Josepth Perry and Anna Debiec for their professionalism and understanding. I would like to extend my special thanks to Taylor Breeding, Assistant Production Editor, and Jennifer Kelland, for their exceptional work, professionalism, and meticulous attention to detail. Their dedication and efforts in ensuring that the fluent reading, formatting and measurements of this book meet the highest professional standards are truly commendable. Their contributions have played a significant role in enhancing the overall quality of the book. I am grateful for their expertise and commitment to excellence.

Finally, I am especially grateful to my wife, Sana Ashour, for being beside me throughout the difficult period while I was working on this monograph and other research, as well as for providing the atmosphere to do research. Her patience with me, while I was spending so much time doing research in libraries and traveling, was exemplary. The same goes for my beloved children, Ahmed, Muhammed, Yousef, and Saeed, may Allah be pleased with them always. My special gratitude and thanks go to my beloved family, the Bsouls in Reineh/Nazareth-Palestine, and Ashours in Canada, my brothers and sisters and their families. Lastly, I pray that Allah will bless those people who have assisted me in any way with my research or studies, as well as those who have devoted their lives and education to helping people who are in the greatest need of assistance. Last but not least, I'd like to thank the academics and other individuals who have worked and continue to work toward the goal of improving people's lives and increasing their understanding in order to make the world a better place for all. AMEEN!

Introduction

The interwar period played a major role in shaping the rest of the twentieth century and watered the seeds of the conflicts that occurred at that time. Undoubtedly, one of the most known conflicts is the Arab-Israeli one. The origins of this conflict go back to before 1918; however, what happened as of this date gave the conflict in question an international character and even caused a huge anomaly in the general course of the interwar period. Therefore, it is necessary to draw the theoretical and practical framework of the international system of the interwar period in order to grasp the course of the Arab-Zionist conflict at that time and to reveal some of the known established characteristics of the century. For this reason, it is necessary to devote the introduction of this study to analyzing the period in question. First, it is important to emphasize that despite the idealistic atmosphere and practice of the interwar period, it is necessary to view the history of both the interwar period and the period of the Arab-Zionist conflict realistically, due to the fact that the Arab-Zionist conflict was the primary conflict that constituted an exception to the idealism that prevailed throughout the era between the two wars.

In international relations, the interwar period is referred to as the period when the practices of idealist theory were dominant but still unsuccessful. In this period, the most fundamental development that caused the idealist theory to rise was World War I. First, it is common when developments create epistemic breaks in political history to also find a response in the theoretical framework. In this context, World War I with its consequences is a milestone in world history, and the arguments supporting this claim will be revealed throughout this book. Second, the only situation that triggers theoretical thinking is the framing of facts with an anomaly. To explain this with an example, it is absurd to construct a theory on why firefighters enter a burning building because this is in line with the normal course of life. However, the question of why someone enters a burning building will trigger theoretical thinking. In this context, this person could be the owner, a looter, someone wanting to save belongings, or someone who simply left a pet inside. Considering this example, the results of World War I showed that the war was no longer a

1

rational foreign policy tool; in other words, it was an anomaly, and this case caused the idealist theory to rise. In order to clarify both points, it is necessary to consider the results of World War I. When this war started, it was thought that it would last four to five months at most, but the war lasted four years. The damage caused by the war created great changes in the social structure that can be considered radical. First, the war-winning states, after cost-benefit analyses, understood that they did not gain much out of the war. Second, the developments in weapon technology caused by the Industrial Revolution had increased the destructive power of war. Third, the settlements known as the back of the front and where civilian citizens were located started to be the battlefield of the war. Fourth, the war was fought not only on land but also in the air as well as on and under the sea. Fifth, chemical weapons were used for the first time. All these developments caused epistemic breaks in political history and caused the war to become an anomaly. Before the twentieth century—that is, before World War I—war was seen as one of the legitimate foreign policy tools of states. The most basic argument that supports this claim is that thinkers such as Hugo Grotius put forward approaches such as the Just War Doctrine, noting that the main aim for such thinkers is not to prevent wars but to legitimize them. However, taking into consideration the results of the war, the perception of the war as an anomaly and incompatible with rational human behavior paved the way for theoretical and practical developments to prevent war.

In this context, we need to examine the basic axioms of the idealist theory, idealism being a theory that builds all its assumptions on human nature. According to this—with a theological assumption—man carries a part of God in his soul is good, in essence, but environmental conditions lead him to evils. Idealism believes in the Enlightenment idea of progress and development and that man is also a rational being. Based on this assumption, the way to preserve states, which are human-made historical-social formations according to idealism, from the evil of wars is to get rid of the environmental conditions leading to war. According to idealism, factors such as secret diplomacy, misperceptions of leaders, deficiencies in establishing international law, inadequate international relations education, selfish ideas such as national interest, and the absence of international organizations create these environmental conditions. Based on this point, idealism predicts several mechanisms with the point of preventing war. First of these, an international organization based on collective security understanding, should be established with the aim of preventing war. Such an organization would enable states to think about peace and security together instead of thinking selfishly of national interest and national security.

Second, instead of secret diplomacy, using open diplomacy and having public talks dominating the interstate environment would prevent the outbreak of war. Secret diplomacy jeopardizes the peace of the international system, while open diplomacy is subject to public scrutiny, and this will create public pressure on states to establish peace, because societies are pro-peace based on idealism. Third, and according to idealism, from the end of the nineteenth century, international conflicts have generally been triggered by peoples who are not self-determined, which is why the establishment of the right of nations to determine their own destinies would ensure international peace. At this point, states' right to self-determination is important because it leads us to the fourth mechanism that self-determination secretly points to: democratic governments. Fourth, according to idealism, the proliferation of democratic republics would prevent war in international relations, because—as emphasized before—societies are in favor of peace, and democracy is a form of government where the people determine their own destiny. Similarly, democratic states see other states as rivals rather than enemies. At this point, the main difference between hostility and rivalry is that the first is destructive, and the second is bound by rules.

According to idealism, the number of democratic states should increase, since a declaration of war in democratic states is a time-consuming process depending on long constitutional procedures. Finally, the leader who decides to go to war despite all democracies would pay the price in the next elections because the people favor peace. Fifth, the dissemination of international law and international relations education would help to establish international peace and security. Finally, based on idealism, the gradual reduction of armament also may prevent war, because weapons are invented for use. Therefore, fewer weapons would first prevent the arms race between states and then wars. These assumptions of idealism, which prevailed in the interwar period, were also seen in the practice of world politics. The first of these was published by President Woodrow Wilson, who listed the so-called fourteen principles in his speech to the US Congress on January 8, 1918, and it was emphasized that these principles should dominate the new order after the war. The most important principles were as follows:

1. After peace agreements have been reached in full openness, no special international agreement should be reached, and diplomatic activity should always be conducted sincerely and openly.
2. With the exception that the seas can be closed completely or partially under international agreements, absolute freedom of navigation should be ensured in all seas except territorial waters in war and peace.
3. All economic barriers between countries that approve and agree to maintain peace should be removed as far as possible, and trade should be carried out based on equality.

4. Sufficient safeguards should be given mutually in each country to reduce armaments to the lowest level sufficient to ensure internal security.

5. All demands of the colonies should be handled with a free, open-minded, and completely impartial approach, and in the solution of such sovereignty problems, the interests of the relevant peoples and the fair demands of the state whose sovereignty is discussed should be strictly adhered to.

6. A union that includes all nations should be formed with special agreements in order to give mutual assurance of the political independence and territorial integrity of all states, big and small.

Another development that enabled idealism to be put into practice in the interwar period was the establishment of the League of Nations. The League of Nations is an organization that can be considered the forerunner of the United Nations today. It was established in Switzerland on January 10, 1920, after World War I. The organization aimed to solve through peaceful means the problems that may arise between countries. At the beginning of the League of Nations' contract, the general objectives of the League and the responsibilities of its members were determined as follows: "To accept certain obligations in order not to resort to war in order to develop international cooperation and to ensure international peace and security, and to maintain international relations that are far from confidentiality, just and honorable; To strictly abide by the rules of international law, which are now accepted as the rule of action by governments; To protect justice in the mutual relations of organized peoples and to respect all obligations arising from treaties." The text of the agreement, consisting of twenty-six articles determining membership and the structure of the organization, ensuring the continuity of peace, treaties, international cooperation, and international management, and changing the provisions of the contract, includes the following assertions: the members of the League accepted the necessity of minimizing national weapons in order to ensure the continuity of peace; the League would be able to arbitrate disputes between its members or examine them in the council; international obligations such as arbitration treaties that ensure the continuity of peace and regional treaties such as the Monroe Doctrine were not to be considered incompatible with any provision of the convention; and the countries inhabited by peoples who had gained independence after the war and yet lacked the ability to govern themselves could select a mandate for their governments on behalf of the community until they became capable of self-government.[1]

Another example of the practice of idealism in the interwar period is the Washington and London naval disarmament agreements. Among these, the Washington Naval Treaty, or the Five Powers Treaty, was signed at the

Washington conference on the navy between the United Kingdom, the United States, the Japanese Empire, the Third French Republic, and the Kingdom of Italy on February 6, 1922. It aimed to stop the arms race after World War I. The London Naval Disarmament Treaty emerged in 1928 as a result of the peaceful atmosphere created by the Kellogg-Briand Pact. The agreement is divided into two main parts. In the first part, the United States, Britain, and Japan agreed to limit warships of smaller tonnage. The second part contained provisions regarding the organization of naval warfare.

Another development to be evaluated within the scope of idealism in the interwar period is the Kellogg-Briand Pact. This pact is an international treaty prohibiting the use of war as a national policy. The architects of the treaty were US Secretary of State Frank B. Kellogg and French foreign secretary Aristide Briand. It was signed in Paris on August 27, 1928, by representatives of Australia, Belgium, Canada, Czechoslovakia, France, Germany, the United Kingdom, British India, the Irish Free State, the Kingdom of Italy, the Japanese Empire, New Zealand, Poland, the South African Union, and the United States. According to the treaty, the parties declared that they would solve problems with each other peacefully, and if the issue could not be resolved individually, they would accept the arbitration of the League of Nations.

As can be seen in the interwar period, there was an idealistic atmosphere not only from a theoretical perspective but also from a practical point of view. However, if the issue is handled only from an idealistic viewpoint, it is possible to understand neither the path to World War II nor the course of the Arab-Zionist conflict, because this period has a realistic character both systematically and in terms of the Arab-Zionist conflict. To put it concisely, it is possible to argue that, despite the idealistic periphery of the interwar period, its essence is realistic. Wilson's principles cannot be explained by the fact that Wilson was an apostle of peace because the reason that pushed Wilson to declare the fourteen principles was that the Soviet Union presented an alternative world paradigm and put it into practice—so much so that long before Wilson, Vladimir Lenin disclosed the secret agreements between the Entente powers with the withdrawal of Russia from the war after the revolution and started to openly support national liberation movements. Therefore, Wilson's idealist fourteen principles can be seen within the framework of a realist purpose. It is possible to evaluate the League of Nations, which emerged with idealistic motives, in a similar framework. Due to the its isolationist foreign policy at that time, the United States did not join the League and caused it to be stillborn from the very beginning. This situation prevented the organization from operating adequate and necessary mechanisms in the face of developments such as the occupation of Abyssinia by Italy and Japan's occupation of Manchuria. Furthermore, the Washington and London naval disarmament conferences cannot be considered solely within the scope of arms reduction, because these agreements were signed in order to reduce the naval power of Japan, whose effectiveness in the Pacific gradually increased.

In addition to all these realist readings and considering the course of the Arab-Israeli conflict in this period, it is necessary to list more systematic and realistic factors that have a greater impact on the conflict. First, it is possible to talk about a global loss of power, when talking about the European states, especially with the effect of World War I. At this point, the new emerging power was the United States. However, the isolationist atmosphere that prevailed in the United States during this period prevented it from being fully engaged in global politics. This is one of the reasons why the attempts to achieve peace in the interwar period failed or were even stillborn. Therefore, efforts to design global politics in a way that contrasts with the global powers of Britain and France have failed. The counterpart of this for the Arab-Israeli conflict is that Britain and France lost their political weight at the point when the world powers were trying to solve this conflict, which saw the Zionist attacks grow out of control and made the conflict more severe.

Second, during this period, another powerful actor of in global politics emerged: the Soviet Union. Although the October Revolution ended in 1917, the civil war had not ended in the USSR until 1922. For this reason, it is possible to argue that the Soviet Union could not reveal its global weight in the design of the new world, as communism was excluded from the system by Western states as an alternative world paradigm offered by the Soviet Union. This situation affected Britain and France, the two declining powers of the period, which failed to take responsibility in the design of the new world order as well as the Arab-Zionist conflict.

Third, although starting the history of the Cold War after World War II has become an academic orthodoxy (and this is valid), it is possible to see the struggle between the United States and the Soviet Union as starting immediately after 1917, because the United States did not recognize the Soviet Union until 1933 and supported the White Army against the Red Army. However, especially after Adolf Hitler came to power, the US and Western powers saw Hitler (i.e., fascism) as a counterbalance to the Soviet Union (i.e., communism). Therefore, it is possible to date enmity from 1917, affecting other states and world conflicts long before World War II. Consequently, through the interwar period, the Arab-Zionist conflict was also affected by this rivalry.

Fourth, the interwar period contains important developments in terms of the history of the Arab-Zionist conflict itself, because the Middle East became an important theater of war from 1914 to 1918. As a result, the collapse of the Ottoman Empire during World War I led to the emergence of a new Middle East. In this context, with the end the war, new states whose borders were determined by Great Britain and France were established. The end of World

War I marks the beginning of the awakening of Arab nationalism because after five hundred years of Ottoman rule, Arabs everywhere sought ways to gain their independence against the invasion of European powers. However, three main realist goals of Western imperialism emerged in the Middle East that was shaped after World War I. The first was to make sure that, after the Ottoman Empire, the Middle East would remain a suitable place for feeding the interests of European colonial powers. The second realist goal is associated with the Balfour Declaration of November 2, 1917, which promised all Jews around the world a "national homeland" in Palestine. According to this, the indigenous people of the promised national homeland would accept the citizenship rights of the Jews. The third goal was to prevent the Soviet Union from propagating its communist ideology in the Middle East and the Arab world.

The interwar period (1918–1939) caused a polarization of different doctrines on the Middle East in general and on the Arab-Israeli conflict in particular. Socialism against capitalism and Islamism against secularism are the main examples of these polarizations. However, the most important polarization occurred between Arab nationalism and Zionism. Other important developments occurred in the Arab-Zionist conflict in the interwar period following the Balfour Declaration of 1917: the League of Nations' submission of Palestine under British mandate, the immigration of approximately 250,000 Jews to Palestine with the intensification of fascism in Europe, and clashes between Muslims and Jews over the Western Wall that saw 339 Jews and 232 Arabs wounded and 130 Jews and 116 Arabs dead.[2] In the demonstrations led by the mufti of Jerusalem to protest the Jewish immigration to Palestine, five thousand Arabs were killed by British soldiers during this period.[3] At the same time, the Palestinian cause began to gain an international character, and the search for solutions in international platforms intensified. While the British dominance in the region began to weaken, the Arab-Zionist conflicts intensified. Simply, the developments that took place in this period had a huge impact on the future character of the Arab-Israeli conflict. This book deals with the systemic developments of the interwar period in the Middle East in general and the framework of the Arab-Zionist conflict in particular.

NOTES

1. Northedge 1986, esp. chap. 2.

2. Rossides 1977, pp. 70–91; Shlaim 1993, pp. 593–617; for a detailed analysis of the causes and consequences of the violence, see Cohen 2008, chap. 3. Another important study is Segev 2000, chap. 6.

3. Cohen 2008, chap. 5, pp. 89–117; Rogan 2009, chap. 12, pp. 324–357; Shlaim 2001.

Chapter 1

Balfour Declaration and Colonial Strategy

Land Transfer and Judaization Policy

Palestine serves as a link between Asia and Europe. Its history occupies a position of particular significance in the context of comprehending the development of the modern Arab world. The fate of the Arabs has become closely linked to the great challenges of the global Zionist movement: Jewish immigration and settlement since the late nineteenth century to the present. This chapter addresses Zionist policy in the Judaization of the Palestinian Territories, specifically, the Balfour Declaration and its position in the colonial strategy, the beginning of the policy of Judaization in Palestine until 1917, the transfer of land ownership and the policy of Judaization, Jewish immigration to Palestine and the dedication of the Judaization policy, and the effects of the Judaization policy on Palestinian society.

Although the Zionist movement made intense efforts during the war to contact the warring countries of both groups to take advantage of the circumstances of the war, Zionist leaders focused their attention on strengthening ties with the British and American governments.[1] Subsequently, the declaration issued by British foreign secretary Lord Arthur Balfour on November 2, 1917, contained Britain's sympathy for the establishment of a Jewish national homeland on Arab soil in Palestine.[2] The Zionists held it to be an international promise that Britain would assume before the League of Nations and take responsibility for implementing.[3]

The declaration/promise came as an expression of the decision of the colonial states to adopt the idea of the Zionist project that had been put forward by Napoléon Bonaparte at the beginning of the nineteenth century and adopted by Lord Palmerston in the early 1940s.[4] It was part of the colonial governments' aim to secure continuing exploitation of the Arab world through location, resources, markets, and human capabilities, as well as by exacerbating Arab divisions caused by centuries of authoritarian grievances during the Ottoman Empire. Consequently, an understanding of the contents of the Balfour Declaration and its implications necessitates its reading in the light of the colonial scheme of the Arab East and the division of the Ottoman Empire, preceded by the Sykes-Picot Agreement in 1916.[5]

Herbert Samuel, the prominent Jewish figure at the time in 1915, presented a memorandum to the British government titled "Palestine," which evidenced Britain's growing interest in achieving its political and economic goals in Palestine. The memorandum called for the necessity of including Palestine within the British properties and made the issue of Judaizing Palestine by the Zionist movement the effective way to achieve British control. The memo warned that Palestine would fall under French control, fearing it would become a European superpower near the Suez Canal, which constituted a persistent and frightening threat to the British Empire.[6] However, the proposal to form a British protectorate in Palestine was the most important in that memorandum, which was accepted by some British ministers, including David Lloyd George, who became prime minister in December 1916, and his foreign minister, Arthur Balfour. This memo formed an essential basis for British policy on Palestine, as we find in it the first roots of the Balfour Declaration that was issued two years after Samuel presented his memo.[7]

Moreover, the position of Hussein ibn 'Ali, king of the Hijaz, regarding the declaration/promise is an indication of the official Arab policy that was adopted in dealing with the challenge that the colonial powers imposed on the Arab nation by adopting the Zionist project. It is an approach that has often been managed by most Arab regimes for conflict with the Zionist colonial alliance. As Britain continued to reinforce its plans to Judaize Palestine, at the time when the correspondence took place between Sir Henry McMahon, the British high commissioner in Egypt, and the sheriff of Mecca, Hussein ibn 'Ali, known as the Hussein-McMahon Correspondence, Britain promised Sharif Hussein ibn 'Ali to secure the independence of the Arab land, including Palestine, in exchange for the participation of the Arabs in World War I against the Ottoman Empire.

First, it is essential to discuss the Hussein-McMahon Correspondence at the beginning of the twentieth century. There seemed to be features of a German-Turkish accord versus the Anglo-French accord. It was embodied in the 1904 agreement and reinforced by the recommendations of the Campbell-Bannerman Committee, which the experts of the two countries participated in drafting in 1907. In addition to the two main allies, Russia was keen to strengthen its international position, especially in the Levant, as the sponsor of the Orthodox Church. At the same time, the United States was keen to participate in the exploitation of the Ottoman states economically.

The Fertile Crescent appeared to be the scene of economic conflicts, the subject of which was the construction of railways and ports and the acquisition of oil concessions. The competition for this between Britain and Germany intensified, while the American companies were a rising competitor in the field of oil. Britain was showing interest in Palestine because of its proximity to the Suez Canal and securing its transportation routes to Iraq, the Arabian Gulf, India, and its other colonies in Southeast Asia.[8]

It is no secret that the economic-political conflicts of the countries heralded a fierce war between European countries over the Mediterranean Sea. As at the beginning of the nineteenth century, the Mediterranean Sea was the focal point of the international conflict. With Turkey entering World War I alongside Germany, the Committee of Union and Progress would have made the future of the Ottoman Empire dependent on the outcome of the war. If victorious, the German-Turkish Axis could preserve the majority of its possessions. In the event of the victory of the British-led Allies, it would have accelerated the liquidation of Turkish territories.

The issues of emancipation from the domination of foreign powers and their exploitation and degradation of Arab dignity were what preoccupied the political and intellectual elites in various parts of the Arab world during the few years prior to World War I. Since the Arab countries were not subject to a single foreign power but subordinate to the Ottoman Empire, Britain, France, and Italy, the positions of the leading religious elites toward each of the competing international military personnel varied. The two camps were active in contacting these leaders, each trying to attract the elites under the control of the opposing camp, in an attempt to win their support in the intensifying conflict, in exchange for the bestowal of promises to support the independence and liberation of the Arabs.

With the beginning of the war, the distinction between the political elites in the Arab states of the Ottoman Empire became clear. The faction believing in Arab-Turkish cooperation, whether within the framework of the Islamic League or the binational state, was championed by Dr. 'Abd al-Rahman al-Shahbandar and Muhammad Kurd 'Ali, who approached Jamal Pasha—a member of the leadership of the Union responsible for administrative and military affairs in the Levant, who promised to give Arab states independence after the war.[9] Newspapers speaking on the authority of Shahbandar and Kurd 'Ali were published, and an Arab-Turkish front was formed hostile to European countries.[10]

The effectiveness of this trend was limited, and its public impact was declining due to the transgressions perpetrated during the Ottoman era and the Arab reaction to the blatant chauvinism of the Turkish federalists. There were also effects of the exposure of the extent and depth of German influence on the government of the Committee of Union and Progress and the Ottoman army, to the point that Col. Friedrich Kress von Kressenstein looked as if he were the actual commander of the Axis forces in the Levant, not Jamal Pasha, commander of the Ottoman Fourth Army.

The Ottoman sultan, Muhammad Rashad, had declared jihad in October 1914, which was the declaration that Jamal Pasha and the German leaders were counting on in implementing the plan of the attack on the Suez Canal and the transfer of the battlefield to Egypt and the Arab Maghreb, while the Allies calculated the impact of the call to jihad in the Arab and Islamic countries subject to their authority. The issuance of the call for jihad by the Ottoman sultan had not the slightest role in decision making, a ruling that was mostly dominated by secular federalists, many of them hostile to Islam. Neither did it find resonance with peoples who suffered abuse, corruption, and racial discrimination. Moreover, the decision of the companions of the sultans in the Arab states was not free from the influence of colonial interventions, as Sharif Hussein ibn 'Ali did not call for jihad in the Hijaz, citing that the Turkish navy could not protect the shores of the Arabian Peninsula.[11] Likewise, Sharif al-Idrisi in Yemen, Ibn Saud in Najd, and Ibn Rashid in Ha'il declined to declare jihad.[12] Consequently, the jihad call did not achieve the goal that the Turkish federalists sought; nor did it have the effect that the Allies feared.

However, Britain, concerned about the military situation on the eastern front, especially after the Battle of Amara in Iraq, realized the importance of intensifying contacts with Arab and Islamic leaders in an attempt to raise them against the Turkish-German Axis.[13] Britain had links to many of these leaders, particularly Hussein ibn 'Ali, sharif of Mecca, who wished for independence and to be the Arab caliph. Nevertheless, Sharif was cautious at the beginning, since the views of his sons 'Abdullah and Faisal differed about cooperation with the Allies, with Prince 'Abdullah urging cooperation and Prince Faisal warning against European colonial ambitions.

At the beginning of 1915, the Young Arab leaders contacted Sharif Hussein ibn 'Ali to brief him on their program. Prince Faisal was dispatched to Istanbul, on the pretext of a complaint against the Turkish governor in Hijaz and the intention of contacting the activists of the Arab nationalists in Damascus, where it became clear to him that he was meeting with the Young Arabs in their skepticism about the European colonists, especially the French. This had a good impression on the accuracy of the organization of the Jahiyyah of the Covenant. During the arrival of Prince Faisal in Istanbul, the leaders of the two groups, the Young Arab and al-'Ahd, reached agreement on what is known as the Damascus Protocol.[14] After Prince Faisal returned from Damascus, Sharif Hussein ibn 'Ali approved what was agreed upon, and thus Sharif Hussein ibn 'Ali and his sons, Arab leaders, the Young Arabs, and al-'Ahd agreed to join the opposition against the Turkish-German Axis and express their readiness to stand alongside the Allies. They also laid down the nucleus of what could be considered an Arab national front that included intellectuals, officers, elements of the emerging bourgeoisie, feudal leaders, and city elders.

Accordingly, Sharif Hussein ibn 'Ali decided to resume negotiations with the British commissioner in Cairo, Sir Henry McMahon, which Prince 'Abdullah had previously held with his predecessor. Al-Sharif included in his first letter to McMahon in July 1915 the texts of the Damascus Protocol as the basis for an alliance with Britain, in addition to his demand for Britain to recognize an Arab caliph for Muslims when he announced this. However, in his answer letter dated August 30, 1915, McMahon tried to evade the obligations he demanded of Sharif Hussein ibn 'Ali. Sharif replied in a letter in September 1915, stressing the importance of agreeing on the borders of the proposed state, and the Arabs rejected French greed in Beirut and its coasts, explaining that the issue did not concern a person but rather an entire people.[15]

The position of the Allied armies on the eastern front was critical at the time, and Britain felt an urgent need for Arab cooperation. Muhammad Sharif al-Faruqi,[16] one of the al-'Ahd association officers, had fled the ranks of the Turkish army through the front of Gallipoli and taken refuge with the coalition forces, to whom he provided adequate information about both the Young Arab and al-'Ahd associations. This allowed the British intelligence to understand the strength of the Arab front as shared by Sharif Hussein ibn 'Ali. Accordingly, McMahon retreated from his elusive approach, as his letter dated October 24, 1915, included British recognition of the independence of the Arab countries stipulated in the Damascus Protocol except for the following reservations:

1. Excluding the states of Mersin and Iskenderun and parts of the Levant located in the western front of the states of Damascus, Levant, Homs, and Aleppo. McMahon stated, "It cannot be said that it is purely Arab, and therefore it must be excluded from the required limits."
2. The need to take specific measures to protect Britain's interests and status in the states of Baghdad and Basra.[17]

Sharif Hussein ibn 'Ali did not accept that he excluded from what McMahon requested except in the states of Mersin and Adana, as they were not Arab. In his letter dated November 5, 1915, he affirmed that Iraq, the states of Aleppo and Beirut, and their coastlines were purely Arab, and there was no difference between a Muslim Arab and Arab Christian as they are from one descendant. He assured that the independent Arab state would take into account the interests of Arab Christians as citizens who have full rights and obligations of citizenship, similar to Arab Muslims. He also expressed reservations about McMahon's request to accelerate the movement against the Turks in anticipation of its consequences.[18]

According to other reports, Sharif Hussein penned his letter on January 1, 1916, before these areas were subject to special regulations. The British afterward complained that these provisions encompassed Palestine. It should be noted that what is considered in international correspondence, such as that of Hussein-McMahon, is the text contained therein and not what is inherent in the intentions.[19] There is no doubt that McMahon was aware of British intentions regarding Palestine, but he was not able to dictate conditions to Hussein at the time. If he had mentioned Palestine in what he asked to be excluded, he would have destroyed all the British efforts to win Arab support for the Allies, at a time when this was a very urgent necessity, because of the military Allies' cause for concern on the eastern front at the end of 1915 and the urgent need for Arabs to move against the Turkish-German alliance. After the issuance of the Balfour Declaration, there was a sharp debate in British political and media circles about whether Palestine was part of the independent Arab state mentioned in the McMahon pledges to Sharif Hussein.[20]

SYKES-PICOT SECRET AGREEMENT IN 1916

The Sykes-Picot Agreement in 1916, in addition to the Hussein-McMahon Correspondence, witnessed a series of English and French meetings with politically active Arab personalities. In anticipation of the two allies' struggle, Georges Clemenceau, French prime minister, proposed that a joint committee be formed in order to draw up a new map of the Arab Mashreq. Thus a committee was formed by the representative of Britain, Mark Sykes, and the representative of France, Georges Picot. After extensive discussions, the delegates went to the Russian capital, where it was agreed with the Russian foreign minister in March 1916 to sign the Treaty of Petersburg, according to which it was agreed to divide the Ottoman Empire into areas of influence as follows:

Russia specializes in Turkish regions that are located outside Arab countries. These regions include the Bosporus as well as Turkish Armenia.

Britain specializes in Iraq and the Arab regions on the eastern coast of the Mediterranean Sea from the borders of Egypt on this coast in the south to the port of Acre and even Naqura in the north, meaning Palestine with its natural borders and Jordan, as well as the Arab areas that occupy the Arab coast of the Persian/Arabian Gulf from Basra in the north to Kuwait, as well as Bahrain, Qatar, Muscat, Oman, Hadramout, and reserves until the borders of Aden and the end of the Red Sea (i.e., all the coasts of the eastern and southern Arabian Peninsula).

France is concerned with the rest of the Syrian coast on the Mediterranean Sea from Naqoura in the south to Sidon, Beirut, Lattakia, and Iskenderun (i.e., to the borders of Turkey in the north and the Iraqi borders in the east).

The Treaty of Petersburg stipulated that an independent state, or an alliance of Arab states, would be formed in the zone of influence of Britain and France in accordance with an exclusive agreement between France and Britain. It is noted that Mosul was within Syria under this treaty, and the division process did not refer to the Hejaz, Najd, and Yemen.

In the implementation of the contents of the Petersburg Treaty, signed by Britain and France on May 16, 1916, the agreement that was later known as the Sykes-Picot Agreement, according to which the British and French delegates agreed, in addition to what was included in the Petersburg Treaty,[21] on the following:

1. France and Great Britain were ready to recognize and protect an independent Arab state or an alliance of Arab states, under the presidency of an Arab president in Syria's interior and Iraq's interior. France and Britain in their respective areas would have the priority right in local projects and loans. France was the only country in Zone A and Britain was the only country in Zone B to provide advice and personnel to Arab governments that confederated.

2. It is permissible for France in the coastal half of Syria and for Britain in the coastal half of Iraq, from Baghdad to the Persian Gulf; however, the establishment of this was not desired in the form of direct rule, through mediation, or from monitoring after agreement with the government or the alliance of Arab governments.

3. An international administration would be established in Palestine whose shape would be determined after consulting Russia and in agreement with some allies and representatives of the sharif of Mecca.

4. Britain would obtain the port of Haifa and Acre, and the king's government pledged not to enter into negotiations with other countries by giving up Cyprus, except after the approval of the French government in advance.

5. Iskenderun would be a free port for the trade of the British Empire, and Haifa would be a free port for the trade of France.

It should be noted that the agreement made no mention of the Zionist allegations in Palestine, despite the fact that Sykes had received them on

February 27, 1916, and that a note from Herbert Samuel, the head of the British Local Government Council at the time known for his Zionist zeal, reminded him of the matter before his trip to Petrograd to meet the minister of foreign affairs of Russia. He replied that France might accept Belgium taking over Palestine, instead of the international administration, which the Zionists rejected. He also clarified that the important thing was to achieve a national center with more than one border and a regional extension. Despite the fact that the agreement did not address the Zionist complaints, the fact that Samuel and Sykes issued their statement indicates beyond a reasonable doubt that these charges were present in the interests of those in charge of the British colonial authority.[22]

It is also noted that the agreement contradicted what was included in the Hussein-McMahon Correspondence in relation to what was agreed upon to establish an Arab kingdom under British sponsorship, as it was divided between France and Britain, or what related to the situation of Palestine, despite the aforementioned disagreement about what was included in the McMahon letter dated October 24, 1915, and whether Palestine was included or not covered by what was promised to a new Arab kingdom. This was clarified by the British foreign minister, Lord Curzon, at the meeting of the Eastern Committee of the British Council of Ministers on October 12, 1918, where he stated, "Hussein's general pledge in October 1915 included Palestine as one of the regions to which Britain committed itself to be Arab and independent in the future."[23]

Thus, with the signing of the Sykes-Picot Agreement, the British colonial administration took the first steps toward establishing the Zionist project, which had embraced its notion in the 1840s.[24] Its necessity was reaffirmed in 1907 in the report of the Campbell-Bannerman Committee, whose first manifestation was that the representatives of the British and French colonialists reached the status of this agreement to deepen and establish the origin of the reality of Arab fragmentation, underdevelopment, and dependency.

The representatives of the British and French colonialists agreed in their secret meetings in Paris behind all the Arab personalities with whom the representatives of Britain and France had held talks during the two years preceding the meeting of Mark Sykes and Georges Picot, indicating that those meetings and the discussions that they contained were primarily intended to implicate the Arab parties in relations with the two countries' colonial intelligence services. The Allies sought to test those personalities and identify which could be exploited in the future and which were unlikely to commit treason and be exploited.

Sykes and Picot reached an agreement to divide the Arab Fertile Crescent in 1916, as Turkish forces found a complete list of names of figures who were in contact with France when Turkish forces stormed the French consulate in

Beirut. All of them went to military courts, which sentenced fourteen of them to execution by hanging. This led many of the Arab movement figures at that time to believe that the Turks did not find this list of the names of Syrian leaders by chance and that rather it was with a French arrangement intended to get rid of the dynamic national elements of the revolution active in its ranks, opposing the division of Syria and demanding a united Arab state.[25] Jamal Pasha relied on the list in many of the death sentences pronounced in 1915 and 1916.[26]

In this way, the two parties to the conflict in World War I, the German-Turkish-led Axis and the Anglo-French-led Allies, met their interests to liquidate the most prominent Arab national movement and the advocates of Arab national liberation. This was a necessary step before Palestine and the rest of the Fertile Crescent could fall prey to European colonialism. Consequently, the Zionist project secured European sponsorship, particularly British. Arabia became empty of its most prominent figures with a national orientation and military commitment.

Mark Sykes was not just one of the competent British colonial men. He was assigned the task of participating in setting the scheme of fragmentation of the Arab East. He was a Zionist with deep faith in the idea of colonizing Palestine with poor European Jews and very enthusiastic in working to implement it. In his role as chairman of the Executive Committee of the Zionist Congress, Haim Sokolov, Theodor Herzl's successor, wrote about his Zionist role, "It is my duty to pay special tribute to Sir Mark Sykes. He was the inspiring and driving spirit in guiding our work during that delicate and sensitive period. Sykes has become the man who in fact takes care of most of our affairs, and coordinates between the Ministry of Colonies, the Ministry of War, the High Command, the Ministry of Foreign Affairs, and the Executive Committee of the Zionist Congress."[27] Sokolov added, "In the crucial period of our work, Mark Sykes was the one who made all the communications and coordinated all efforts for a clear commitment from the allies after the victory to give us the opportunity and the right to establish our Jewish homeland in Palestine. Sykes did not perform these tasks in London alone, but he took it upon himself to pave the way in Paris with the French government, and in Rome with the Italian government and with the Vatican."[28]

It is reported that Mark Sykes was a Catholic, and therefore he was not concerned with fulfilling the prophecies of the Torah. He was raised with a Zionist upbringing under the auspices of Benjamin Disraeli, the only Jewish prime minister in British history, who was very enthusiastic about the Zionist vocation. However, that was not the only or the most important motivation of Sykes for his Zionist zeal, which was praised by the president of the Executive Committee of the World Zionist Congress. Furthermore, he was ambitious in his work as an official in the British Colonial Ministry, where he was tasked with implementing the most essential component of the Campbell-Bannerman Committee's strategy study.

Mark Sykes's role indicates the depth of the British government's adoption of the Zionist project and the preoccupation of its most important ministries in wartime to work for a clear international commitment from the Allies to establish the Jewish national homeland in Palestine. Sykes coordinated the ministries of foreign affairs, colonies, and war and the general command of the army. He also contacted the governments of France and Italy and the Vatican to secure this. Furthermore, as Sokolov indicated, he prepared the notion for British public opinion by introducing the Zionist Congress's Executive Committee to prominent journalists and politicians under British authority.

ARAB TERRITORIES' WAR RESISTANCE

Three factors interacted in a dialectical manner to push the Arab nationalist elites to participate in World War I alongside the Allies under France and Britain. The Arabs stabbed the Turkish army in the back, which had a high percentage of Arab officers and soldiers. In addition to that, this participation came in contrast to what is stable in popular Arab memory, which is the main contradiction between the Arab nation and Islamic peoples. With the forces of European conquest and colonization in particular, the contradictions with the Asian and African peoples, especially the Islamic peoples, are secondary in their entirety and do not necessitate a clash. Accordingly, Sykes still considered that participation with suspicion, especially as it was rewarded by Britain and its French allies with the Sanmar penalty.

The first thing that these groups had in common was their antipathy toward Arabs and Arabism, which was fostered by Turkish federalists, as well as the racist tactics they used against Arab nationalist elites. This culminated in the state terrorism practiced by the Fourth Army led by Jamal Pasha, who could not develop his relationship with some elites. The Turkish army in the Levant experienced hostility caused by state terrorism against political activists. Thus, the Turkish practices and not the Ottoman Empire per se drove the wedge between the Turks and Arab elites and led the Arabs to call for dependence on the colonial powers in liberation from the yoke of Turkish domination.

It should be noted that twenty months transpired between the declaration of war by Turkey on November 11, 1914, and the proclamation of participation in the revolution by the Young Arab and al-'Ahd associations on October 6, 1916. This is something that should be taken into consideration.[29] This underscores the impact of state terrorism practiced by Jamal Pasha and the abuse by the Turkish army of the Arab people in the Levant. Some sources say that Prince Faisal ibn al-Hussein, commissioned by the Arab leaders of the Young Arab movement and the al-'Ahd, sought with Jamal Pasha to pardon the arrested political activists but did not succeed.[30] During that period, he came to the conclusion that Faisal ought to head back home to Hijaz in order to prepare for the revolution.[31] The Ottoman Empire's treatment of Arabs in general reached a turning point with the terrorist attacks committed against Arabs by leaders of the Union and Progress party, most notably Jamal Pasha. These attacks were a watershed moment. This was the most important driving force behind the Arab revolt.

The toppling of Hussein ibn 'Ali, who had been persuaded to cooperate with the British and reveal his open animosity toward the Turks, was the second element that contributed to the beginning of the Arab revolution. Some sources state that Sharif Hussein was not successful in obtaining recognition as an independent ruler in the Hijaz from the administration of the Union and that his heirs would inherit the position of controlling the region in its entirety. In addition, he was not successful in obtaining amnesty for the Arab celebrities who had been sentenced to death by Jamal Pasha in April 1916. This compelled Sharif Hussein to declare a revolution in order to acquire funds and weapons from the British government.[32]

Accordingly, Sharif Hussein ibn 'Ali dropped the reservations he had expressed in his letter dated November 5, 1915, to McMahon, which were issued primarily from a feeling of self-defense against possible aggression and not only from the point of view of an unknown fate. Consequences based on the pledges of Sir Arthur Henry McMahon, the British viceroy in Egypt, although this does not mean that at all without these pledges and the reassurance of the Sharif Hussein that the revolution that he will announce will have greater support for the current situation, and will lead to the Arabs having their role in negotiations future peace, he will not already know that he will be criticized by the Muslim public which is the greatest insult to their messenger.[33]

The third factor was the position of the British army on the eastern front. Despite its success in defeating the Turkish-German attack on the Suez Canal, it made little progress on the Palestine front. Two years and five months after Turkey declared war, the Allied armies led by the British in April 1917 were unable to break the Turkish-German defensive line between Gaza and Beersheba.[34] Consequently, the armies of the Allies were in urgent need of a move that secured the eastern front while also conducting a guerrilla war behind the Turkish-German lines on that front. The al-'Ahd and Young Arab associations forced McMahon to seriously deal with Sharif Hussein and pledged to him to accept most of what was mentioned in the Damascus Protocol.

On June 10, 1916, Sharif Hussein announced the revolution against the Turks and appointed his four sons, 'Ali, 'Abdullah, Faisal, and Zaid, as the leaders of the Arab factions that were formed of volunteers who answered his call. He sent a telegram to Damascus asking for "blond horse" to be the agreed password/secret code—so the youth of Levant joined the revolution as groups and individuals.[35] In the cities of Hijaz, the revolutionaries surprised the Turkish garrisons, and they isolated the garrisons in Yemen. When the Turks were able to regain the initiative, the tension turned into a guerrilla war, so that the Turks were forced to evacuate the Arabian Peninsula.[36]

British aircraft dropped leaflets on Turkish forces, including British promises to support Arab liberation and independence. Among the most important was the publication issued by Sharif Hussein on June 26, 1916. That propaganda campaign had an active influence on officers and soldiers who quickly fled the Turkish army and joined the revolutionary forces. Some of them came with accurate information about the plans and actions of the Turkish army, which had an impact on the battles on the eastern front.[37]

From the beginning, the British leadership defined the role and capabilities of the Arab forces that joined the revolution, as they did not provide them with modern weapons that the officers requested. The efforts of Sharif Hussein and his sons to obtain the required weapons failed, which led some officers to withdraw from the field and deepened suspicions regarding Sharif's relationship with the British. Moreover, despite the presence of large numbers of experienced Arab officers who were once prominent in the Ottoman and Turkish armies, the British leadership of the Allied armies did not consider the Arab army led by Prince Faisal to be one of the Allied armies participating in the war. This decision was calculated so as not to entitle the Arabs to a role in the peace conference.

The Turkish army was reinforced with German and Austrian forces. It formed a defensive line between Gaza and Beersheba, and it successfully repelled two British attacks in March and April 1916.[38] The British leadership decided to summon the Arab forces that were led by Prince Faisal, accompanied by British intelligence officer T. E. Lawrence, to carry out a guerrilla war along the Hejaz railway. In June 1917, the forces led by Faisal, accompanied by Lawrence, succeeded in occupying Aqaba and liberating the shores of the Red Sea from the Turks, thereby securing the eastern front of the British forces as they prepared to attack Palestine. The Young Arab and al-'Ahd leaders demanded that Prince Faisal come forward to Damascus in order for the revolution to extend to all areas of the Levant and thus liberate the Arabs themselves from Turkish domination and take possession of the strategic initiative in their land and assure their independence. Lawrence, however, prevented him from adhering to the decision that the Arab forces should not go beyond the decree's role, which was guerrilla warfare within the limits of what the British leadership had outlined.[39]

Thousands of Palestinian youths volunteered in the ranks of the revolution, and those who registered their names in the register established by the British forces in 1917 amounted to thousands.[40] Hajj Amin al-Husseini, at the beginning of his youth, had the role of urging young people to volunteer.[41] Several members of the Young Arab and the al-'Ahd had joined the revolutionaries.[42] They played a role in the Palestinian national movement during the mandate period and included, among others, Khalil Sakakini from Jerusalem, Salim 'Abdel Rahman from Tulkarm, and Hamdi al-Husseini from Gaza.[43]

After the British forces had completed the mid-1917 occupation of Sinai up to al-'Arish and secured its security lines from Egypt, and after the Arab forces led by Faisal had secured for them the eastern front, the British forces prepared to start invading Palestine.[44] The plan included that the British army, backed by English and French planes, would occupy Palestine, while the Arab army would occupy eastern Jordan.[45] These forces included the Arab Ansar Brigades and soldiers who had fled the Ottoman army.[46] As a direct consequence of this, the Arab army was denied the opportunity to take part in the liberation of Palestine. Edmund Allenby had also been successful in preventing the participation of French soldiers in the ground forces in Palestine. He had to limit participation to the Jewish Legion, which was formed by the British leadership from among the Jews working in the Allied armies.[47] Allenby moved quickly to take the offensive in order to beat the highly trained and heavily reinforced Turkish and German reinforcements, as well as the commando army Yildrum of the Turkish forces and the German-Asian Legion.[48] The British forces broke through the military line between Gaza and Beersheba on October 31, 1917, two days before the Balfour Declaration was released. This marked the beginning of the liberation of both cities. Jaffa was the first city to fall on November 16, 1917, followed by Jerusalem on December 11, 1917.[49]

Jamal Pasha was removed from the command of the Turkish Fourth Army, which was placed under German command, but the army was in a very miserable position.[50] At this stage of the war, the Arab forces had a critical role, as the revolutionaries benefited from the deteriorating conditions of the Turkish army, and their ideologies were active in Houran, Ghouta, Damascus, and Jabal Baalbek, as well as in the middle and upper Euphrates basins. The Arab and Kurdish units began to abandon their positions and join the Arab army, and the acts of resistance against the Turkish Fourth Army spread in all areas of the country, which contributed to cutting supplies, creating chaos in its ranks, and demoralizing its members.[51] A report by General Allenby addressed to the British Ministry of War on July 18, 1918, included the following: "The Arab army considerably aided the Allies in achieving a definitive victory in the war."[52]

Fourth, there are those who say that the Zionists, through Louis Bernadez's relationship with President Woodrow Wilson and the strong influence of Jewish financial institutions in the United States, are what dragged the United States into war.[53] This statement does not take into consideration the fact that the United States occupied the first place in the world in terms of industrial production at the beginning of the twentieth century, following its national unity at the end of the Civil War and subsequent economic prosperity. As a direct result of this, it harbored the desire to acquire markets, energy sources, and raw commodities. It turned out that the oil reserves in the Arab region were quite desirable; thus American firms were particularly interested in obtaining a share of the oil concessions in that region.

Moreover, those who say that lobby groups guide American policy ignore the fact that the United States is a country of institutions, and its decision making is subject to the interests of the most influential forces in society, not to the mood of the president of the republic and the whispers of his advisers and friends. The Americans had given their attention to the Zionist project before the birth of President Wilson and his friend Judge Louis Brandeis. The American consul established the first colonial settlement in Palestine in Jerusalem in 1852, and the American Society for the Exploration of Palestine was established in 1870.[54]

It is notable that American participation in World Wars I and II began years after the outbreak of war and after the main parties had exhausted their powers, indicating which side was more likely to achieve victory. Therefore, American participation came with the possibility of victory, and when the victor in the war was in great need of American support, the American decision maker and those behind him, who had interests, imposed conditions on the ally while paying the lowest price possible. This was done so that the United States could continue to support the victor in the war.

When the war erupted, Germany was the center of gravity of the Zionist movement, and Jewish capitalism had a more influential presence in Germany than it had in Britain and the United States.[55] The German Zionists had anticipated their counterparts by expressing support for their home country's decision, believing that victory would favor the German-Turkish Axis. They saw this alliance as an opportunity to secure permission for immigration and settlement in Palestine from Turkey's Union and Progress government.[56] Other Zionist groups denied them their early bias, fearing that it would reflect negatively on Zionist work, rather than waiting and making a decision to align in light of a careful study of the balance of power and the potential for immediate and total defeat.[57] Chaim Weizmann was the most critical in this regard, and he proposed the formation of an executive emergency committee to manage the Zionist work until the end of the war.[58] As previously mentioned, the meetings of the World Zionist Congress were not held after the eleventh congress in 1913 and the confusion of Zionist activity in Palestine during the war years.[59]

Vladimir Jabotinsky had traveled to Egypt, where he was active in the formation and training of brigades of the Zionists, in cooperation with Joseph Trumpeldor, a Zionist officer fleeing the tsarist Russian army. When the British leadership refused to accept these brigades into the British army, they formed a mule battalion and sent it to the Gallipoli front. While General Sir John Grenfell Maxwell, the commander of British forces in Egypt, was preparing for the campaign against Palestine in June 1916, he asked Qatawi Pasha, the head of the Jewish community in Egypt, to allow the Jewish battalions that had been trained in Egypt to participate in the campaign, and he agreed to and authorized the placement of the Star of David on their hats to make clear that they were Jewish brigades.[60]

Jabotinsky did not recognize his defeat in Egypt on the Gallipoli front but went to London, where he reconstituted the Jewish battalions, enlisting the help of those he found there, members of the Maiden Battalion (Katibat al-Baghalah). However, Trumpeldor collided with the opposition of many, including the World Zionist Organization. Trumpeldor and his supporters received solidarity from Herbert Samuel, then British home secretary, who facilitated the formation of Jewish snipers' clerks led by Colonel John Henry Patterson in August 1917. The battalion moved to Palestine through France and Egypt to participate in the Allenby campaign.[61]

In the British cabinet session in which the Balfour Declaration was approved, the secretary of state for war, Lord Derby, informed the council that a delegation from the Zionist Conference had visited him asking for the formation of a Jewish legion to share with the Allies.[62] He approved the request of the Zionist Congress but allowed this legion to raise the Zionist flag, so that it participated in the war and also constituted a Jewish military force ready for the future and for the Jews to have a role in achieving victory. The only minister who opposed the decision was the minister of India, Edwin Samuel Montague, who was Jewish; he argued that forty thousand Jews were fighting in the ranks of the British army and that it was not fair to them and to their reputation to distinguish one brigade and name it as the Jewish Legion.[63] It should be noted that Montague, the only minister who opposed the Balfour Declaration, opposed the formation of the Jewish Legion not in principle but because he did not see the formation of a Jewish brigade as in line with the number of Jews in the British army.

After the southern part of Palestine was occupied, General John Hill, the leader of the Scottish contingent, proposed the formation of a battalion to the Zionist settlers. Rachel Beckett, the wife of Ben-Zvi and later of Eliyahu

Golomb, who played a significant role in founding the Haganah, was among those who participated. The battalion was formed and its troops were subsequently sent to Egypt for training. They returned to Palestine only after the war had ended. In the United States, David Ben-Gurion and Yitzhak Bin-Zvi, the president of the State of Israel, later contributed to forming a battalion in January 1918 that included about five thousand. Jewish volunteers from Canada and Argentina joined them, some of whom participated in the Allenby campaign, while the rest of them arrived in Palestine after the war. Of these, there were some five thousand Jewish officers and soldiers among the Allied forces in the Levant during the war.[64]

The Zionists also had their espionage activity, where Aaron Aaronson formed a spy cell named Nelly.[65] He was the manager of an agricultural testing station in 'Atlit, and he approached Gamal Pasha, who appointed him responsible for locust control, which facilitated his movement in all parts of the country.[66] His cell was collecting information about the Turkish army and sending it to the Allies through his sister Sarah and through the American ambassador in Istanbul. Nelly was working on preparing for a British naval landing on the shores of Palestine.[67] When the Turks discovered the cell members, Sarah was arrested and committed suicide in prison; some members of the cell were executed, while others fled.[68] A long time after the Zionist movement declared its nonaffiliation with the cell, in 1967 Israel honored Sarah.[69]

Fifth, the content and relevance of the Balfour Declaration and the Sykes-Picot Agreement did not put an end to the Anglo-French battle for extended influence in the Levant, as both countries (Britain and France) desired to dominate Palestine's resources due to its strategic importance and the existence of Christian holy places. At the same time, Russia was looking to have control of Palestine as the patroness of the Orthodox Church, while Belgium believed that it had more right to do so based on being a small nation that would satisfy the rest of the European countries by controlling Christian sanctuaries.[70] They would represent Catholics and enjoy the Vatican's support for their cause. Germany's objectives were founded on its support for the Zionist community's aspirations. There are others who believe that by issuing the Balfour Declaration, Britain was boosting the mechanization of Belgium's, Russia's, and Germany's demands.[71]

It is inaccurate to claim that the Balfour Declaration was issued in response to Zionist pressure on the British government and the power of Jewish influence in the British and American decision-making departments. On the eve of the declaration, the Zionist movement was not strong enough to be able to impose its will on international powers. The Zionist congresses ceased in 1913, as did immigration to Palestine.[72] A wave of displacement invaded the colonies, and the majority of the world's Jews were still opposed to the Zionist call.[73] Strong Jewish opinions were strongly opposed to various motives and goals, intellectual, religious, political, and social.[74] The majority of eastern and central European Jews, where the Jews suffered the most, preferred immigration to the United States rather than to Palestine. In addition, Arab resistance was on the rise, and Jewish settlement was in decline.[75]

Moreover, the declaration was not an expression of affection for Jews on the part of the British government or the wider British public. In the early years of the nineteenth century, Britain experienced a significant influx of Jewish immigrants from eastern Europe. These people fled persecution in the east of the continent and sought refuge in the West. The streets of London witnessed riots and demonstrations against Jewish refugees.[76] Parliament passed a statute for foreigners to impose restrictions on Jewish immigration.[77] Balfour, then the prime minister, defended the law, which he denounced to the Zionists as explicit anti-Semitism directed against the Jewish people: "It is conceivable that a situation could arise where the presence of a large community of people, regardless of their level of patriotism, ability, and seriousness, might not align with the interests of the country's civilization. These individuals, despite their involvement in public national life, may still be perceived as a distinct category due to factors such as their adherence to a religion different from the majority, and their limited intermarriage with others."[78] Some claim that Balfour's conscience was affected by the reactionary and illiberal texts included in the Aliens Law passed by his government in 1905 and that this was one of his motives for issuing his promise to establish a Jewish nationalist home in 1917.[79]

Adherents of this claim ignore that the Balfour Declaration was not a Balfour self-made decision but rather the British government's decision, just as they forget that the people of conscience who woke up to the plight of the Arab people in Palestine did not work to cancel the restrictions that he put on the immigration of Jews to Britain. Furthermore, he compounded his actions, which troubled his conscience, by committing what some perceive as a crime against the Palestinian Arab people and an excessive influx of Jews. It is also argued that the Balfour Declaration, being a political document, aimed at resolving the Jewish issue through displacement, thus seeking a final solution.[80]

The promise came only to a British colonial strategy to manage the conflict with the Arab nation, which took its first steps in the 1840s and was then elaborated at the Conference of Colonial Experts in 1907.[81] This does not negate its racist motives against the integration of Jews into European countries. The promise brought about a qualitative shift in the status and role of the Zionist movement through the greatest state (i.e., Britain) of that day declaring its formal commitment to establishing the Jewish national identity on Arab soil in Palestine and thus embracing the Zionist movement and imparting to it British care and protection.[82]

In the first year of the war, discussions between the leadership of the Zionist movement and the Allies ended without an agreement because Russia opposed Zionist attempts. Balfour had asked Weizmann and James de Rothschild to present a draft resolution. To this end, the Zionist organization drafted a project titled "A New Programme of Action for Palestine," for Jewish resettlement in line with the aspirations of the Zionist movement.[83] It was codrafted by Sokolov, Weizmann, and Herbert Bentwich with the consultation of Ahad Ha'am and Boris Goldberg.[84] Several senior English Zionist leaders reviewed the final version, among them Herbert Samuel and James de Rothschild.[85]

In October 1916, the program was presented to the British Foreign Office as the basis for the upcoming British-Zionist discussions.[86] When the intention was to start the direct attack by the British armies on Palestine in February 1917, the British government decided to open negotiations with the Zionists officially.[87] Meetings between the British and Zionist leaders continued with multiple proposed projects until the British war government approved the final version on October 13, 1917.[88] The negotiations ended with an agreement on the content of the Balfour Declaration, but it was agreed to delay the announcement until it became clear that General Allenby's march on Palestine was victorious.[89]

On November 2, 1917, the British foreign secretary, Lord Arthur Balfour, addressed, on the official paper of the ministry, a letter to Lord James Rothschild, the leader of the British wealthy elite movement and a patron of the Zionist movement,[90] which included the following: "His Majesty's government view with favour the establishment in Palestine of a national home for the Jewish people, and will use their best endeavours to facilitate the achievement of this object, it being clearly understood that nothing shall be done which may prejudice the civil and religious rights of existing non-Jewish communities in Palestine, or the rights and political status enjoyed by Jews in any other country."[91]

The issuance of the Balfour Declaration on the official paper of the British Foreign Office and the ministry's approval of it immediately upon its issuance express an official British decision. This means that it was the Zionists who dictated it to the British government. It is also inaccurate to say that Chaim Weizmann's development of potassium nitrate had a decisive role in its issuance because the promise was only the formal departure of a strategic decision adopted by British colonial strategists in the 1840s before Weizmann was born or the Zionists had an influential presence. We have already mentioned a complaint by Palmerston about the indifference of the Jews to the project that had been adopted in the wake of the response of the armies of Egypt led by Ibrahim Pasha from the Levant in 1840.[92]

For the purpose of reinforcing the British promise and gaining the acceptance of major nations, Sokolov led an important Zionist group to Paris, where they met with the French administration, while Rothschild made contact with the French government, which was led by Clemenceau.[93] The French government's connections with Zionists came to an end on February 14, 1918, when Foreign Minister Stephen Jean-Marie Pichon sent Sokolov's message, in which he accepted the declaration. This marked the end of the contact. Sokolov's communications with the Italian government came to a close when he received a letter from the Italian ambassador in London, dated May 9, 1918. In the letter, the Italian ambassador confirmed that his government was committed to working toward the establishment of a Hebrew national center in Palestine. Before the Balfour Declaration was issued, Sokolov met with Vatican officials to discuss the situation.[94]

Nahum Goldmann states that Louis Brandeis, a member of the US Supreme Court and a friend of President Wilson, influenced the president who in turn, influenced the British government in issuing the Balfour Declaration, to which the president gave preliminary approval immediately upon its issuance. Nevertheless, despite the pressure from his foreign minister, Robert Lansing, who warned against making a formal commitment to this in his letter dated September 12, 1917, he was late in expressing official support for the plan. On the other hand, on August 31, 1918, the president reversed his order and wrote a letter to Rabbi Stephen Wise, chairman of the Interim Committee for Zionist Issues, adopting the Balfour Declaration. In this letter, the president stated that the United States recognized Israel as a sovereign nation.[95]

In this way, the four Allied states adopted in one way or another what was targeted by the Balfour Declaration and thus became committed to its content. Therefore, it became an international promise representing the commitment of the governments of these countries, not just Britain. The declaration/promise of a text reflects the strategic position of its authors and those who declared their support for it toward the elements of the Zionist colonial settlement grouping. In clarifying this, the content of the Balfour Declaration meant the colonial states agreed on the following:

First, to recognize the Jews as a nation who have political rights embodied in the commitment to work to establish a national homeland for them in Palestine and the commitment of Britain and the countries that support it to do their utmost to implement it. Second, the recognition that the Jews have political and legal rights that may not be violated, including providing all legal and political guarantees to the activists of the Zionist movement wherever they are in the world and facilitating their work to relocate the Jews to Palestine. Donations and other political, social, and media activities are guaranteed by Britain, France, Italy, and the United States. Third, to consider the Arab people in Palestine, who have had a legal right to live there since the beginning of recorded history, to be no more than other non-Jewish denominations that are present in Palestine, without elaborating on whether or not this presence is one of citizenship or temporary residence. In spite of the declaration, the promise does not represent a prejudice against itself, as the nation that made it and the nations that supported it assert. The Balfour Declaration states that the only rights it possesses are religious and civil rights.

Since no capitalist state voiced opposition to the Declaration of Independence or any of its promises, we can infer that these states tacitly supported the document in accordance with the legal principle known as "silent in the face of necessity." The prevalent political ideology of the period was consistent with the demand for the right of people to self-determination, which Woodrow Wilson's campaign rhetoric helped to elevate. Therefore, it is evident that colonial states violated the democratic principles of self-determination and national sovereignty. Therefore, it is evident that colonial states violated the democratic principles of self-determination and national sovereignty.

The Balfour Declaration bestowed the character of a nation on the Jews, despite their varied lineage, culture, language, values, and customs. They were bonded only by religion, which is insufficient to be considered a nation according to European political thought and the definition of a modern state.[96] The declaration ignored the political and legal rights of the Arab people in Palestine, dismissed the character of the people, and ignored its Arab national identity. Also, the Palestinian citizen was not given rights and regarded only as a member of a non-Jewish sect. It is a blatant denial of the high degree of integration and homogeneity in terms of the history, language, culture, values, and customs of Palestinians, Muslim and Christian alike.

The declaration's contradictions are not due to the lack of knowledge or solely to the influence of Jewish pressure groups; they are deliberate, and a political and paradoxical outcome of the relationship between the global powers of exploitation and the Zionist movement to serve colonial interests.

The first dimension is to support every coercive Zionist attempt from the interaction, acculturation, and integration of the Jewish immigrants to Palestine and to dissolve the differences between them regarding their different origins, multiple languages, cultures, values, and customs. It aligns it within a homogeneous Zionist human structure distinguished qualitatively from the rest of the Jews in different parts of the world. It seeks to establish the only Jewish assembly that possesses unity of language and culture and a deep sense of destiny and common history. The second is to encourage social, religious, sectarian, and tribal division among Arab society in pursuit of the disruption of its social cohesion.

In 1917, the people of Palestine contained 650,000 Arab citizens, compared to 50,000 Jewish-Zionist settlers.[97] The Jews who were displaced from Russia and eastern Europe made up only 8.45 percent of the population. Their holdings were 481,000 dunums out of 8.76 million arable dunums, and the agricultural lands they acquired, which had been purchased in the majority of the fiefs, were only a small percentage of the arable land, equivalent to 1.83 percent or 26,323,023 dunums.[98] The area of the Palestinian territories, after excluding the area of the Dead Sea and Lake Tiberias and Hula from the total area of Palestine, amounted to 27,027,023 dunums.[99]

Lord Balfour wrote in 1919, "The great powers favored Zionism. Zionism, whether right or wrong, good or bad, is rooted in age-old traditions, and it is to be expected that in a world of competing claims, those claims will have to be submitted to the test of strength. The future is more important than the past, and the wishes of the 700,000 Arabs residing in the land today must be subordinated to the ultimate purpose of establishing a Jewish homeland."[100]

The British forces had not entered Palestine, and therefore the British government had no authority over the land of Palestine. No Arab social formation was covered by the British protection concession, such as those privileges that the Ottoman sultans used to grant to European countries. As a result, the Turkish government, not the British, had jurisdiction over Palestine, while Britain did not have a legal connection to the land of Palestine, which in no way qualified the British to be seen as the owners of Palestine or the legal inheritors of its land. Thus, the statement of the late Gamal Abdel Nasser of Egypt on the Balfour Declaration, that "it was issued by someone who does not possess the land to those who do not deserve it," seems completely true. Likewise, Jewish writer Arthur Koestler said, "It is a document, according to which another nation was formally promised the territory of a third nation, although this promised nation was not a nation but a religious sect, and the region in the time of promise belonged to a fourth nation."[101]

Sixth, Sharif Hussein, after his declaration of the revolution, was quick to declare the independence of the Arabs on June 27, 1916. On November 2, 1916, in the presence of a number of Arab leaders, he pledged to be king over the Arabs and formed a ministry headed by Prince 'Ali, in which Prince 'Abdullah assumed the position of minister of foreign affairs. However, Britain and France refused to recognize him as king of the Arabs, as they saw in it a serious violation of their colonial goals. After bargaining, they recognized him as king of Hijaz only.[102]

When he began preparing to start the attack on Palestine, he was acknowledged as the king in May by Sykes and Picot, with whom he had talks, during which they assured him of the Allies' promises to support the freedom and independence of the Arabs, which convinced him to continue his war efforts. In the aftermath of the October 1917 revolution in Russia, the revolutionary government headed by Vladimir Lenin revealed the colonial agreements, including the Sykes-Picot Agreement. When the nationalist elites involved in the revolt against the Turks learned that their alliance with the British was growing stronger, it multiplied their anxiety. Consequently, there was an increased call to cut ties with the Allies, and they eventually found a formula or approach for reaching an understanding with the Turks. Contacts began with Gamal Pasha, but he aborted their progress or potential benefits due to his intransigence.[103]

As for King Hussein, although he was only recognized as king of Hijaz, the elites and the masses of the Arab people viewed him as their king and historically responsible for their issues. Therefore, he felt infuriated upon learning of the Balfour Declaration, which he perceived to be in direct opposition to the agreements he had established with McMahon. He contacted the British consul in Egypt by writing a letter. On April 1, 1918, he received from the British Lieutenant Colonel Percy Cleghorn Hobart a telegram containing the statement regarding Palestine that a people should not submit to another people, while affirming the necessity of looking sympathetically toward the return of the Jews to Palestine and the British commitment to removing any obstacle that was inconsistent with doing so. The same telegram also stated that Jewish settlements would only be permitted when they were consistent with the economic and political freedom of the existing indigenous population.[104]

Hobart's telegram, woven along the lines of the Balfour Declaration, ignored both the social reality and the national affiliation of the Palestinian Arab people and only referred to "the existing indigenous people." He also noted that its reference to the return of the Jews to Palestine did not violate the commitment to the unhistorical claim that characterized the promise, because the statement of return included recognition of the historical connection of European Jews to Palestine, whose ancestors are not related to the Arab land.

In addition, the Jewish national home in Palestine was not mentioned in Hobart's telegram, as this required constructive ambiguity in answering King Hussein's questions; instead Hobart referred to the national homeland indirectly when he affirmed the commitment to remove any obstacle that conflicted with the return of the Jews to Palestine. In his memoirs, Hobart states that King Hussein did not give up on any of his Arab demands, and he would not have accepted an independent Jewish state in Palestine. Thus, Hobart did not receive instructions to inform him that Britain sought to establish the Jews in Palestine.[105]

On August 8, 1918, King Hussein received a letter from the British assistant undersecretary in Jeddah, Colonel John Retallack Bassett, stating, "His Majesty's government and its allies are more determined than ever to support the Arab peoples in their efforts to establish an Arab world in which the law replaces Ottoman arbitrariness. His Majesty's government affirms its previous promises related to the liberation of the Arab peoples."[106]

It seems that the king's fears were dispelled after getting reassurances from the British. King Abdullah I reportedly thought about moving Jews who lived on land owned by Arabs to a safer place. Rather, he wrote an article in the newspaper *al-Qibla*, issued in Makkah on March 23, 1918, in which he urged Arab citizens to undertake the duties of hospitality by receiving brotherly Jews and to behave in the same way in which they acted when the massacres of Armenians occurred in Anatolia in 1915. Sharif Hussein had written to the heads of Arab tribes urging them not to abuse the Armenian refugees, not to subject their women, and to receive them warmly, as also mentioned by the Armenian deputy patriarch in Jerusalem.[107]

The Arab world was shocked by the Sykes-Picot Agreement and the Balfour Declaration, despite the loyalty of Arab revolutionaries led by Sharif Hussein and some members of elite Arab allies under the English-French leadership. This was the case despite the fact that both documents were signed. It forced many powerful elites to reevaluate their standing in relation to the Allies as a result. Soon afterward, a national liberation and unitary movement began to emerge that rejected the agreements and promises of the Sykes-Picot Agreement and Balfour Declaration while committing to work toward achieving the unity of the Levant and rejecting the idea of a Jewish national homeland. The growth of this movement accelerated as soon as the war ended and the Allies' policies hostile to Arab ambitions emerged. As for Palestine, it witnessed noticeable tension between the Arabs and the Zionist settlers as soon as the British army, led by General Allenby, entered Jerusalem on December 11, 1917. This is because the British statements and Zionist practices provoked the Arab public, which was rudely awakened to the Zionist threat and the formidable challenge it presented.

A joint British-French statement issued on November 7, 1915, was hung in public places and published by newspapers in an effort to circumvent the popular position that rejected the Sykes-Picot Agreement and the Balfour Declaration.[108] The statement confirmed that France and Britain were driven to continue the war in the east in order to free the people who had long been persecuted by the Turks.[109] To them, the establishment of national governments and departments would enable the indigenous peoples to initiate and freely choose their national representatives. This statement achieved its aim and helped dispel the doubts of the Arabs concerning the British-French designs in the Levant and Iraq.[110]

NOTES

1. Laqueur 1976, pp. 114–119.
2. Schneer 2011.

3. Rogan 2009, pp. 197–198; Weinstock 1979, p. 106; Laqueur 1976, pp. 126–129.

4. Massad 2006, pp. 14–15; Shufani 2002, 1:171.

5. Weinstock 1979, p. 94; Zebel 1973, pp. 242–243; Egremont 1980, p. 292.

6. Stevens 1971, pp. 57–58; Gibbons 1919, 97:369–371; Stein 1961, p. 8.

7. Stevens 1971, p. 60.

8. Antonius 1961, p. 351; Sakhnini 1985, p. 68.

9. Tibawi 1969, p. 199; Shahabi 1961, p. 51.

10. Shufani 2003, p. 347.

11. Kayali 1985, p. 73.

12. The province of the Rashid family, of Jabal Shammar, or the province of Ha'il is a state established in 1834 in Najd in the city of Ha'il (north-central Arabia), by both 'Abdullah al-Rashid and his brother 'Ubaid al-'Ali al-Rashid, and they belonged to the second Saudi state. See Rashid 1991; Shufani 2003, p. 348.

13. Rashidat 1991, p. 59.

14. Kayali 1985, pp. 73–74.

15. Kayali 1985, p. 75.

16. Hassani 2013, pp. 2:49–50, 2:65–66.

17. Hassani 2013, pp. 2:324–325.

18. Hassani 2013, pp. 2:74–75, 2:327–329; Khadir 2003, p. 130.

19. Jeffries 2000, pp. 4:144–146.

20. Musa 1973, pp. 1:10–12, 1:25–32.

21. Rashidat 1991, pp. 61–62.

22. Zebel 1973, pp. 242–243; Egremont 1980, p. 292.

23. Ingrams 1972, p. 48; Sakhnini 1985, p. 42; Ovendale 1984, pp. 45–47.

24. Weinstock 1979, p. 94.

25. Heikal 1996, p. 1:99.

26. Nafi' 1999, p. 117; Darwazah 1971, p. 471; Sa'id 1997, pp. 46–48; Biru 1960, pp. 557–560; A'zami 1934, pp. 4:54–55; Saab 1956, pp. 141–142.

27. Heikal 1996, p. 1:112.

28. Heikal 1996, p. 1:112.

29. Rafiq 1974, p. 538.

30. Nafi' 1999, p. 117.

31. Hout 1981, p. 52.

32. Shufani 2003, p. 350.

33. Dawn 1960, pp. 11–34.

34. Dawn 1960, p. 350.

35. Hout 1981, p. 52.

36. Shufani 2003, p. 349.

37. Hout 1981, p. 53.

38. Harvey 1993, pp. 338–339.

39. Shufani 2003, p. 350.

40. Farsoun and Aruri 2018, pp. 184–186.

41. Hout 1981, pp. 56–57.

42. Allawi 2014, pp. 33–34.

43. Najjar 2005, p. 56.

44. Najjar 2005, pp. 57–58.
45. Hout 1981, p. 56.
46. Shufani 2003, p. 352.
47. Najjar 2005, pp. 57–58.
48. Erickson 2021, pp. 2–3.
49. Arna'ut 2020, pp. 81–84.
50. Allawi 2014, pp. 48–50; Fawaz 2014, pp. 248–249.
51. Shufani 2003, p. 352.
52. Rashidat 1991, p. 61.
53. Shufani 2003, pp. 349–350.
54. Polley 2022, p. 45.
55. See Shafir 2016, pp. 339–352.
56. Nafi 1997, pp. 1–24; Shindler 2011, p. 113.
57. Shindler 2011, p. 113.
58. Berlin 1970, pp. 37–68.
59. Tessler 2009, p. 192.
60. Heikal 1996, p. 1:153.
61. Shufani 2003, pp. 359–360.
62. Fawzi 2002, p. 121; Katz 2016, p. 166; Watts 2004, p. 110.
63. Heikal 1996, p. 1:114.
64. Shufani 2003, p. 360.
65. Hamdan 1985, p. 12.
66. Qasimiyyah 1973b, p. 306; Shufani 2003, p. 360; Talmi and Talmi 1988, p. 12.
67. Wallance 2018.
68. Fathi 2003, p. 186; Muharib 1981, p. 17.
69. Shufani 2003, p. 361.
70. Friesen 2020, pp. 39–40; Herremans 2013, pp. 77–94.
71. Khadir 2003, pp. 134–141.
72. Abu-Lughod 1971, p. 169.
73. Kolsky 1992, pp. 16–17; Weinstock 1979, p. 146.
74. Patai and Wing 1975, p. 116.
75. Shufani 2003, pp. 362–63.
76. Panayi 2020, p. 15.
77. Glick 2020, p. 63.
78. Sokolow 1919, p. 2:14; Hirst 2003, pp. 188–189; Rabinowicz 1960, p. 167.
79. Sykes 1965, p. 25.
80. Misiri 1997, p. 106, 398–405.
81. Rashidat 1991, pp. 44–48; Heikal 1996, p. 1:110.
82. Glick 2020, p. 63.
83. 'Ayid 1990, p. 6:550; Khalidi 1998, p. 31.
84. Hout 1991, p. 371.
85. Jiryis 1977, pp. 1:281–282; 'Uwaisi 1992, p. 182.
86. 'Ayid 1990, p. 6:550; Khalidi 1998, p. 31.
87. Hout 1991, p. 371.
88. Khadir 2003, pp. 141–143; Hirst 2003, p. 188.

89. 'Uwaisi 1992, p. 182.

90. Zaquq 2003, pp. 1:149–150.

91. Barghuthi and Tutah 2006, p. 234.

92. Sharif 1985, p. 122; Mahmud 2002, pp. 337–338; Kayali 1990, p. 1:482; Shufani 2003, p. 318.

93. Stevenson 2017, p. 340.

94. Sokolow 1919, pp. 2:329–331; Khadir 2003, pp. 144–145.

95. Khadir 2003, p. 145; Goldmann 1994, p. 187; Khalah 1982, p. 321; Bahjat 1982, pp. 249–253.

96. Masud 1993, pp. 191–192; Beckford and Demerath 2007, p. 215.

97. Bisisu 1990, p. 1:608; Tarbin 1990, pp. 2:1006–1007.

98. A unit of measurement of land area equal to one thousand square meters or about a quarter acre.

99. Zu'itir 1955; Rashidat 1991, p. 57; Salih 1985.

100. Khadir 2003, p. 147; Sokolow 1919, p. 2:14, pp. 2:329–331; Sa'dun 2010, p. 379; Khalidi 1987, pp. 201–211; Fisher 1988, pp. 129–170.

101. Koestler 1949, p. 97.

102. Shufani 2003, pp. 349–350.

103. Shufani 2003, pp. 351–352.

104. Khadir 2003, p. 153.

105. Khadir 2003, pp. 153–154.

106. Khadir 2003, p. 154.

107. Khadir 2003, p. 154.

108. Fitzgerald 1994, pp. 697–699.

109. See Rogan 2015.

110. Baron 1978, p. 40.

Chapter 2

Internationally Deciding Palestine's and Its Arab Inhabitants' Fate

Once World War I had ended, attention began to turn to the peace conference, in which the spoils of war were divided and the fate of the Ottoman Empire was decided. Therein, the future of Palestine and its Arab people became a major topic on the agendas of international conferences and committees and a subject of negotiation between Britain, France, and the World Zionist Organization.

Following the collapse of the Ottoman Empire, it became vital for the world's superpowers to split the Arab states among themselves and allocate the borders of the newly fragmented region according to their respective areas of concern. After an agreement had been reached to deny the Arab people their right to freedom and self-determination, which ran counter to the legitimate call for flags in the sky of the peace conference that was taking place at the time, the borders of Palestine were drawn, differentiating it from its Arab surroundings for the very first time in its history, which dates back to the fourth millennium BC.[1]

Due to the fact that Palestine was under British mandate at the time, Palestine's legal delegates were barred from attending the 1919 Paris Peace Conference. As a result, a territorial dispute arose in their absence.[2] In contrast, the leaders of the Zionist movement had an audible and influential voice behind the scenes.[3] Such was but one of a series of indications of the international powers' denial of the legitimate national rights of the Palestinian Arab people and indeed the human rights of the Palestinians to a free and secure life in the land of their fathers and forefathers.[4] In the following discussion, there is a comprehensive explanation of the international conspiracy against the future of Palestine and its Arab people in the aftermath of World War I.

DRAWING POLITICAL BORDERS FOR PALESTINE
FOR THE FIRST TIME IN HISTORY

Although Palestine is considered one of the first areas to witness human development, and despite the multiplicity of powers that ruled it, it did not witness, throughout its ancient history, a political entity independent from its Arab neighbors, distinguished by the borders of its geographical region and separated from its surroundings. Palestine was, until the beginning of the twentieth century, a geographic region, not a political entity. Since the rise of civilization in the region, Palestine had been either subordinate to the Egyptian Empire, to one of the Mesopotamian empires, or to the Persian Empire. In those cases, it did not have the prohibitive and separating borders from its geographical surroundings.[5] During the Byzantine Roman administration, Palestine was divided into three parts.

First, Palestine as an administrative unit was under the command of the governor-general of the Levant and included the region from south of Mount Carmel and Marj ibn 'Amir to a line that starts south of Rafah and extends east to the middle of the Dead Sea. Its eastern border starts from the south of Beit Shan/Bisan and crosses the Jordan River, so that it surrounds a part of present-day Jordan between Ajloun in the north and the northern Dead Sea. Second, Palestine included the mountains of Galilee, Marj ibn Ómir, and the highlands to the east of Lake Tiberias. Third, Palestine included the region from the south of the Rafah–Dead Sea line to the Gulf of Aqaba and the Sinai Desert.[6]

Palestine is a country with a long history that has embraced many ancient civilizations and with a unique geographical and strategic location, which attracted many people to settle and reside there. It is a country of religious importance that it is mentioned in the Qur'an in chapter 17, verse 1: "Glorified (and Exalted) be He (Allah) [above all that (evil) they associate with Him] [*Tafsir Qurtubi*, vol. 10, pp. 204] Who took His slave (Muhammad) for a journey by night from *Al-Masjid-al-Haram* (at Makkah) to the farthest mosque (in Jerusalem), the neighbourhood whereof We have blessed, in order that We might show him (Muhammad) of Our *Ayat* (proofs, evidences, lessons, signs, etc.). Verily, He is the All-Hearer, the All-Seer."

It was blessed by being the home of the birth of Christ. The Prophet Muhammad journeyed from Mecca to al-Masjid al-Aqsa (in Jerusalem). 'Umar ibn al-Khattab honored it with his conquest and humility, and Salah al-Dina al-Ayyubi restored its purification and dignity by liberating it from the Crusaders. Throughout its rich history, Palestine has come under the rule of many authorities and states, and every authority that ruled it has a story of beginning, development, and end. Control of Palestine fluctuated between differing political authorities until the chain of ruling powers reached the era of the Ottoman Empire. How did the story of the rule of the Ottoman state begin with Palestine? Historical documents narrate that the conquest of Palestine was carried out by the Ottoman Empire in 1516, after the conquest of the Levant through the Battle of Marj Dabiq. The leader of that fierce battle was the Ottoman sultan Selim I.

The Muslim Turk conquerors divided Palestine into two parts. The first is the *jund*/army of Palestine, which includes the first and third Palestine from the Byzantine division, with its capital at Lydda, until Suleiman ibn 'Abdul Malik 79/715 built Ramla and made it the administrative center of Palestine. The second division includes the second Palestine in the division of Byzantium, which was made part of the *jund*/army of Jordan, with Tiberias as its capital.[7] According to Suleiman al-Badur's *Palestine in the Umayyad Era*, studies that have touched on the economic life and social conditions during the Umayyad era have included the Levant in general and have not been exclusive to Palestine. The paucity of information about Palestine is due to the fact that after the Islamic conquest, Palestine remained a politically quiet region and was not the starting point for any ethnic groups or political or religious movements related to the struggle for power. It also goes back to the fact that historians who confronted the history of the Umayyad state directed most of their attention to political events in the regions of the Arab state and did not mention other economic or social aspects except in terms of their connection to these events.[8]

During the Ottoman era, the administrative divisions did not become permanent in the Arab states, as they were subject to change depending on the capabilities of the rulers and their relationship with the central authority in Istanbul. However, the last administrative division took place after the separation of Beirut from the state of Syria in the year 1887, at which time Palestine was divided into three brigades, the Acre brigade, which belonged to the province of Beirut and included the districts of Haifa, Tiberias, Safed, and Nazareth; the al-Balqa' province, also named for the district of Nablus, included the districts of Jenin, Bani Sa'ab, Juma'in, and Salt until 1905, when Salt was annexed to the Syrian state; and the Jerusalem metaphysical, which was directly affiliated with the Ottoman Sublime Porte and included the districts of Jaffa, Gaza, Beersheba, and Hebron. Between 1906 and 1909, the district of Nazareth was annexed and separated from the Acre district.[9]

The secret Sykes-Picot Agreement came with a new division, but this division was not taken into consideration, because Britain's goal of the agreement was evading it promises to give France Syria, including Palestine, France's share of the Ottoman legacy.[10] Once the British succeeded in thwarting the French and supporting Gen. Edmund Allenby's campaign against Palestine, even if only in a symbolic sense, they took control of the decision-making process for the foreseeable future of the region. The Sykes relationship was used to obtain a decision from the Zionists that Britain would be a trustee of Palestine without French participation and that the Zionist presence in Palestine would serve as a buffer state between the French sphere of influence in Syria and the British presence in Palestine.[11]

Once this was achieved, the new British-Zionist allies began the discussion of the borders of Palestine to be a British protectorate of a Zionist settlement project. While the British wanted to guarantee the borders had enough depth to defend the Suez Canal and communicate with Iraq, the Zionist party was looking forward to what was mentioned in biblical myths. Both scenarios clashed with French ambitions and interests and the will of the Arab people. At a time when Britain had little regard for the Arab side, France was experiencing a European Levant crisis that hindered French ambitions and interests in the Levant. In the meeting of David Lloyd George, the British prime minister, with Georges Clemenceau, the French prime minister, in London between December 1 and 4, 1918, the two prime ministers concluded an agreement whereby France waived Palestine and Mosul in exchange for Britain's support for France's obtaining Strasbourg and Metz, for the assignment to Syria of Damascus, Aleppo, Iskenderun, and Beirut, and for it to be given shares in the Turkish Oil Company in Mosul.[12]

In November 1918, the World Zionist Organization submitted a memo to the British government to present to the Paris Peace Conference in February 1919.[13] This outlined the borders of Palestine as follows: from the north, the northern and southern Litani River to latitude 33 and 45, and from there heading east-south to the border of Damascus, to the west of the Hijaz railway; in the east, a line parallel to the Hejaz railway, and in the south, a line extending from the point in the vicinity of Aqaba to Al-Arish, and in the west the Mediterranean.[14]

In accompanying Chaim Weizmann on his first visit to Palestine, William Ormsby Gore studied the reality on the ground and, based on this, submitted a memorandum to the British Foreign Office in August 1918, which stated,

Palestine at the moment is not a geographical expression, and the Peace Conference must define the borders of Palestine. . . . I believe that Palestine includes all of those areas where the Jewish national consciousness has been expressed in the colonies that exist now. It should not include any of Lebanon, Mount Druze and east of Jordan plateau, where Syrian and Arab consciousness prevail, so I propose that the northern borders be drawn from the mouth of the Litani River and then go east to the swamps, which lie directly to the north of Plain Hulah. As for the eastern borders, they should be in line with the western slopes that rise from the Jordan Valley, so that Jordan Valley headquarters within Palestine, and to stay Mount Druze in the north, Mount Ajloun in the centre, and the Moab Mountains in the east outside new Palestine. As for the south, it seems to me that there is much to say about keeping all the Bedouin region south of Beersheba in the Sinai region, so that the southern border of Palestine is a line drawn from Rafah and heading east to the Dead Sea.[15]

Despite Ormsby Gore's agreement with the Zionist proposals regarding the issue of borders, the recommendations that he made restricted interaction with the borders of Palestine. He proposed a national home for Jews in a region with a reasonably substantial population of Arabs and national emotions that were shared by both populations.[16] This is what Winston Churchill, minister of colonies, achieved in the Middle East conference that was held in Cairo on December 3, 1921, in agreement with Lloyd George.[17] They proposed East Jordan as an Arab province attached to Palestine and that its administration would be assigned to an Arab ruler responsible to the British high commissioner in Palestine.[18] The issue of the eastern borders was thus settled by adopting Ormsby Gore's recommendations.[19] As for the northern borders, there were numerous meetings between the representatives of Britain and France. The French were striving to push them south, while Britain was seeking to secure the water supplies needed by the Zionist project that it sponsored, especially the headwaters of the Jordan River.[20]

Following the signing of a border agreement between France and Britain on October 23, 1920, the Zionists made a demand for additional land to be added to Israel. Their demand included the Sea of Galilee, the Hulah Plain, and the Jordan River's headwaters.[21] After arduous negotiations, the borders were modified by the introduction of the Sea of Galilee and the village of al-Hamma located on the Yarmouk River in Palestine. The Hulah Plain was expanded, and the borders were extended in the north to include all the headwaters of the Jordan River, including the Dan Tal al-Qadi river.[22] The result of this was the extension of the borders of Palestine in what became known as the "finger of Galilee" with a length of 22 kilometers and a width of 14 kilometers and an area of about 352 square meters. These borders were implemented in 1926.[23]

WILSON'S FOURTEEN POINTS AND LEAGUE OF NATIONS MANDATE REGULATIONS

On May 27, 1916, President Woodrow Wilson announced that individuals possessed the freedom to choose the nation in which they wished to reside. As a result, he emphasized his support for the principle of self-determination and identified it as one of the goals of the conflict in which the United States was engaged alongside its allies.[24] He returned and confirmed this with his speech in the Senate titled "Peace without Victory" on January 22, 1917.[25] He said there is no peace that will or should continue if it does not recognize or embrace the idea that governments receive all their just powers from the governed.[26]

On January 8, 1918, in his speech before the Senate, he announced his fourteen points.[27] He outlined in his speech that, when the process of making peace gets started, we want it to be open to everybody without any exceptions, and we don't want it to include or permit any kind of secret agreement from that point on. This is both our aim and our goal. It is no longer possible to turn back the clock on the age of conquest and expansion.[28] With regard to colonial claims, the fifth point stated, "The interests of the population concerned must have the same weight with regard to the fair claims of the government whose legal right to adjudicate is considered."[29] On the twelfth point, he declared, "Full sovereignty should be guaranteed to the Turkish parts of the current Ottoman Empire. As for the other nationalities that are now living under Turkish rule, they should be guaranteed a life of unquestionable security, and an opportunity to develop along the path of self that no one can ever deny."[30]

The British prime minister Lloyd George welcomed the fourteen points of President Wilson with enthusiasm, as he found them identical to his statement on the goals of the war, which included, "The consent of the governed should be the basis of any regional settlement in this war." British aircrafts dropped leaflets containing the text of Wilson's twelfth point throughout the Ottoman Empire and other hostile countries. They became the principles of the peace conference and were a strong factor in fragmenting the enemy's resistance and in achieving victory.[31]

With the end of the war approaching, marking the victory of the Allies, Turkey, Austria, and then Germany aspired to establish peace on the conditions of Wilson's fourteen points, while a number of British thinkers and writers and their allies were discussing the formation of the League of Nations.[32] Marshal Jan Christian Smuts maintained close ties with the members of the Round Table Group in London.[33] This organization was responsible for much of the activity in this region. Also published on December 16, 1918, was a booklet titled "The League of Nations Is a Practical Suggestion," which was like an open constitution for the League.[34] It included twenty-one articles, the first nine of which revolved around the mandate.[35] Smuts's booklet received the most attention in what Lloyd George considered "the most efficient official document that people saw during the war period."[36]

Smuts recommended that the League of Nations be considered the reference to which the ultimate right to dispose of the affairs of the regions that belonged to Russia, Austria, Hungary, and Turkey were attached and that none of those areas should be attached to the territories of any of the victorious countries but rather should enjoy the right to self-determination and self-government under the supervision of a delegated state appointed by the League of Nations with the consent of their peoples. But Marshal Smuts distinguished between the areas that were to be given autonomy and those that had no scope for autonomy because the population was not homogeneous and not eligible for administrative cooperation.[37] Palestine and Armenia were the two cases that Smuts sad were not entitled to self-rule, saying, "There will in any case be cases like the case of Palestine and the case of Armenia, where the system of self-government cannot be introduced from the beginning for the reasons mentioned above, and where it is not possible to form accordingly, consulting the country regarding the question of the country delegated to it, and even in such cases, the League will follow, as far as possible, the direction of public opinion."[38]

Commenting on the recommendation of Marshal Smuts regarding Palestine, Joseph Mary Nagle Jeffries notes that he was involved deeply in the policy of the Balfour Declaration. He refutes his three allegations on which he based his claim to deny the people of Palestine the right to self-determination. In thinking and assuming positions of power, they did everything in their power to make Palestine a heterogeneous country. However, it was not a heterogeneous country, as 90 to 91 percent of the population of this country, according to Marshal Smuts himself, were Arabs. It was an Arab country with a small, recent Jewish colony.[39]

In refuting the claim of Marshal Smuts that the population of Palestine was ineligible for administrative cooperation, Jeffries writes,

> This [ineligibility of administrative cooperation] signifies that the Arab majority in Palestine cannot grant a small group of Zionists full authority over the entire indigenous population. They cannot and will not accept it. This ineligibility serves as a means of expressing the intended message desired by Marshal Smuts. The fundamental issue determining the future of the Charter lies in whether the Arab majority in Palestine will grant the members of this Jewish colony their complete rights as citizens or not.[40]

Jeffries answers his questions by stating,

> This thing was that the Arabs were ready to cooperate administratively with this Jewish minority, but the problem is that this Jewish minority was not ready to cooperate administratively. Or rather, this Jewish minority was unwilling to cooperate administratively with the Arabs, insofar as those Zionists cultivated and cultivated by Marshal Smuts and his friends in the Holy Land were unwilling to cooperate administratively. They are the non-collaborators, they wanted rights that their birth did not give them, and they wanted a political power that is

much greater than what their numerical ratio deserves from them, so this power that they demand was a form of dictatorship.[41]

President Wilson had written the first draft of the League of Nations charter in the light of its fourteen points, as it recommended not annexing to any country areas that belonged to Austria, Hungary, and Turkey, as well as the former German colonies, and that they enjoy the right of self-determination and the consent of their peoples to choose the shape of their governments. In addition, despite Zionist passions, the first three articles of this draft did not mention the exclusion of Palestine and its people from the right to self-determination. Before President Wilson traveled to Europe to attend the peace conference, he received a copy of Marshal Smuts's booklet. However, he wrote the second draft of the League of Nations charter without appearing influenced by the booklet that Lloyd George considered the most efficient document people saw during the war.[42]

It appeared as though Lord Robert Cecil, who was in charge of the section of the British delegation that represented the League of Nations at the peace conference, did not have much authority in the process of formulating the League's project.[43] His project was based on affirming the war alliance as an alliance of peace by having the League have a Governing Council composed of the heads of government of Britain, the United States, France, Italy, and Japan. The foreign ministers of the five countries (excluding the Soviet Union due to the existence of the communist regime) came together with the aim of supervising international relations and directing the foreign policies of all nations.[44] Their objective was to present a modern, democratic version of the Vienna Conference,[45] which symbolized the hegemony of colonial empires following Napoleon Bonaparte's defeat in 1815.[46]

Although Wilson and his foreign minister, Robert Lansing, did not initially agree to the Cecil project,[47] Wilson's second draft was subjected to a series of amendments that diminished its democratic dimension little by little. He had met Cecil, Henner, and David Hunter Miller, the legal advisor to the American delegation to research various texts. Then a meeting was attended by President Wilson and Colonel Frank J. Hazes, who was close to Marshal Smuts, Lord Cecil, Hatter, and Miller, in which it was agreed that Cecil and Miller would be tasked with drafting a new joint venture. They ended up with a compromise project that would satisfy the American and British parties.[48]

The peace conference discussions in Paris had started, and differences of views between the Americans and the Europeans were imposing themselves on the heated discussions on the mandate. On March 25, 1919, the British government gave its approval to a project that examined the League of Nations and the roles that Wilson, Cecil, and Marshal Smuts played in the organization's operations.[49] After numerous sessions, the contents of the charter were referred to a committee consisting of nineteen members. Ten of the committee's members represented the five major Allied countries, while nine of the committee's members represented the smallest states. The League of Nations charter was drafted after ten sessions of deliberation. Joseph Mary Nagle Jeffries notes that the final form taken by Article 22 of the charter, which concerned the mandate, was primarily the work of Marshal Smuts. Lansing regarded it as the carefully crafted solution embodied in Article 22. In this way, the American delegation carefully approved all four draft versions that President Wilson had written.[50]

Therefore, it is clear that the Charter of the League of Nations did not create the General Assembly of the League of Nations; nor did it create the five main states that composed it. In addition, it lacked objectivity and was not adequate for the task at hand, particularly in relation to Article 22, which Marshal Smuts and Lloyd George collaborated on creating in order to protect the interests of British colonial possessions. Article 22, which gave rise to the mandatory system, was said to have been created by a presumed person, or rather by the fabrication of two malicious men, and a government determined to draft it in such a way that it fit to the greatest extent possible its far ends.[51]

The eighth paragraph of Article 22 left the issue of final authority without a decision. Likewise, the question of who chooses the mandated countries, their selection, or the extent of supervision that the League could exercise were not determined. Similarly, there was no mention of grievance in Article 22 or whether the League of Nations or the state would determine when the people of the area in question would become able to manage their affairs alone. This solved the ambiguity that was formulated by Marshal Smuts, and as Lord Arthur Balfour stated, "There is no doubt that ambiguity was deposited in the Charter, and it was perhaps an intentional ambiguity."[52] Lloyd George admitted in 1938 that the Charter of the League of Nations owed its creation primarily to the efforts of a great British statesman, Marshal Smuts."[53] The British Imperial Ministry scrutinized all proposals before submitting them to the Allies Committee that drafted the charter.[54]

The Versailles Peace Conference issued on June 28, 1919, the Charter of the League of Nations without the colonized peoples, especially those who would fall under the mandate, having any opinion on the drafting of the charter. The position regarding Prince Faisal's participation in the peace conference made clear the extent of the Allies' retreat from the principles, promises, and covenants that they had proclaimed, preached, or concluded during the war. The delegates of the European colonial states, with the participation of the American delegation, came to an agreement that legalized colonialism and exploitation in their modern form. This agreement was made with the help of the American delegation through a system of mandates based on Article 22 of the League's charter and the following principles:

a. The colonies and countries that the results of the last war wiped out from the sovereignty of the states that were governing them, and those inhabited by people still unable to stand alone in the battlefield of the new life, must be applied to the principle that the good of these peoples and their sacred trust in the neck of civilization must be included in this charter guarantees to make this trust.

b. The ideal way to apply this principle is to entrust the training of these peoples to the elite/high-ranking nations whose resources or geographical location enable them to carry out this responsibility better than others, and are willing to accept this responsibility, and that the practice of such training as delegated by the League of Nations.

c. The characteristics of this mandate must differ according to the degree of the people in the level of advancement, the geographical location of the country, its economic conditions, and other such conditions.

d. That some groups that were previously subordinate to the Ottoman Empire had reached a level of sophistication with the degree to which they could be recognized as independent nations, provided that the administrative advice and assistance is provided to it by a mandated state, and that is until the time it becomes able to stand alone, provided that the wishes of these groups have a major consideration in choosing the mandated state.

We note that the Arab people in Palestine were among the groups that were subordinate to the Ottoman Empire, including what was included in item (d) above. But the Arab people in Palestine, Syria, Lebanon, and Iraq were not consulted on the choice of the state to which they were assigned. The League of Nations swapped what was unanimously agreed upon by the Arab people in Palestine and the Levant, independence,[55] or for the United States to be the mandated country if its independence was rejected, as stated in the report of the King-Crane Committee.[56]

After drafting the charter of the League of Nations, which included Article 22 and its intentionally ambiguous nature, Lord Miller proceeded to draft different categories of mandates. These mandates were formulated by a committee consisting of colonial experts from the five victorious major powers: Britain, France, Italy, Japan, and the United States." "The committee, which consisted of Lord Miller and other members, held its first meeting on June 28, 1919, predating the commencement of activities by the League of Nations. The League itself was established as part of the Treaty of Versailles, and therefore its official tasks could not be carried out until the conclusion of the treaty, which was ratified on January 10, 1920. Lord Miller, known as a prominent supporter of the Zionist movement, played a significant role in drafting the Balfour Declaration. He collaborated closely with the Zionists, working towards similar goals.[57]

In the spring of 1919, the experts of the British delegation to the peace conference had begun informal discussions with representatives of the Zionist Organization on the draft instrument of the mandate for Palestine.[58] To this end, the organization formed a political committee, whose most prominent members were Herbert Samuel and Jacobsen James de Rothschild, while Chaim Weizmann, Nahum Sokolov, and the American Zionist delegation undertook the preparation of the proposed projects to mandate Palestine.[59] The Zionists were keen on affirming the historical bond of the Jews with Palestine and their right to rebuild their national home and extend the homeland along its length and breadth. The Zionist leaders persevered in making contact with leading British political figures, pressing to include the mandate document.[60]

The British political departments witnessed a sharp debate about the Balfour Declaration's contradiction of the British pledges to the Arabs during the war and its neglect of justice and the right of the Arab people in Palestine to self-determination.[61] In Balfour's clarification of his government's policy, he sent a memo to Foreign Minister Lord Curzon on August 11, 1919, which stated, "The contrast between the Covenant and the Allies' policy is more striking in the case of an independent Palestine nation than in the case of an independent Syrian nation. In the case of Palestine, we do not intend to do the problems of investigating the desires of the current residents of the country, even though the American Committee is conducting problems inquiring about these desires."[62]

Ilyas Shufani, in his work, accused Balfour of hypocrisy for his statement in his memoir that Palestine was not yet an independent nation and was not on the path to becoming one, regardless of what the future of Palestine might hold. Regardless of how much weight one gives to the viewpoints of the people who lived there, the main countries, as far as Balfour was aware, did not intend to seek their input when selecting the countries that would be mandated. To summarize, the major countries did not issue a political declaration or a factual statement regarding Palestine, and the only political statement they issued was that they aimed to constantly, at the very least literally, violate it. This was the only political statement they issued. The statement made by Balfour is a clear indication of the desire of both his government and the governments of the Allies to deny the right of the Arab people living in Palestine to determine their own fate and to have national independence.[63]

When the Supreme Council of Allies approved the principle of the mandate, the secretary-general denounced the League of Nations in a note he submitted to the League on July 20, 1920, asserting that the distribution of the major powers of the mandate was not legal and could not be recognized.

This was supported by a Belgian delegate to the League of Nations, confirming that the Supreme Council of Allies violated the League of Nations charter when it distributed the mandates among its members. On the other hand, some specialists in international law came to the conclusion that the assignment of Palestine to its most important ally nation, Great Britain, was in violation of Article 22 of the League's charter text. As a result, it was invalid under the law and had no force.[64]

In the British cabinet, there was controversy over the drafting of the instrument before it was submitted to the League. This was because Foreign Minister Curzon opposed the inclusion of the Balfour Declaration, so that the mandate became the political, administrative, and economic creation of Palestine to create a Jewish national homeland. He said, "The Zionists are working to establish a Jewish state in Palestine in which the Arabs will be laborers and workers." He added, expressing his protest, "Nobody consulted me regarding this Mandate Instrument at an earlier stage, and I am unaware of any negotiations or commitments made in relation to it. . . I believe that the entire concept is flawed."[65] He continued denouncing a country that had 580,000 Arabs and 30,000 Jews. Judging from the noble principles of self-determination and the conclusion of a wonderful appeal to the League of Nations, we are now beginning to draft a document that represents a constitution for a Jewish state. Even poor Arabs are only allowed to view the keyhole as a non-Jewish sect.[66]

The majority in the British House of Lords was against the inclusion of the mandate instrument of the Balfour Declaration. In response to Lord Balfour's intervention defending the government's adoption, Lord Sydenham said, "It is possible that the damage that was produced by dumping a foreign people on an Arab continues, and by having Arabs everywhere in the background, can never be repaired. What we did in the Levant was not for the Jewish people, but rather for a Zionist extremist sector, and no one knows how long this ulcer will extend."[67] The House of Lords voted to cancel the inclusion of the mandate instrument and the Balfour Declaration.[68]

On November 9, 1920, the British Parliamentary Committee for Palestine Affairs headed by Lord Cecil issued the following decision: "Urging His Majesty's government to include specific provisions of the Palestinian Mandate in the specific recognition of the Historical Association of the Jewish People in Palestine, the status of the Zionist Organisation, and the policy of developing Palestine into a Palestinian Commonwealth that governs itself. The Times and the Manchester Guardian have also endorsed this view in editorials."[69]

In August, the draft mandates were on the agenda of the British House of Commons and were placed in the hands of members. It is established that the British Parliament did not study these texts and did not approve them as permitted by any legislation. The mandate was linked to a peace treaty with Turkey in order for the government to gain Parliament's approval. They had the support of the British Parliament and the people, who wanted the deal with Turkey to be finalized. As a result, the topic of the mandate was given the go-ahead by the Parliament without going through the usual review process.[70]

Joseph Mary Nagle Jeffries writes,

> Balfour has conducted the League's Concerning Palestine Affairs orchestra. After the French were calmed down about the boundaries of their mandated region, the Supreme Council in Palestine was simply an alias for Lloyd George, and Mr. Lloyd George in Palestine consorts Balfour. As a result, it is hardly exaggerated to say that when His Majesty the King's government announced that it would raise the mandatory drafts of Palestine and Mesopotamia to the League of Nations Council, this was little more than saying that Lord Balfour had drafted these two orders and sent them to Lord Balfour for approval.[71]

The League's General Assembly asked its Sixth Committee to study the draft mandates for Palestine and Iraq and referred the matter to a Special Committee headed by the Norwegian diplomat Dr. Fridtjof Nansen. However, the Supreme Council of the League declined to provide Nansen with a draft mandate. After urging, the council agreed to send it to him in his personal capacity, provided that it was not presented to the members of the committee in an official manner. Consequently, the members of the Special Committee did not have the possibility of thorough and careful review. It was thus unable to provide the Sixth Committee with an objective report that fulfilled the purpose for which it was tasked. Since Nansen's attempts to obtain the two drafts took a long time, the Sixth Committee did not have enough time to review and examine the Special Committee's report and submitted it only to the General Assembly without any change in content. Consequently, the General Assembly was unable to make any changes to the two drafts and was satisfied with recommendations that it submitted to the Supreme Council, two of which were most important. The first was that a basic law for the mandatory areas be developed and presented to the League of Nations before it became effective. The second was to announce to the public in future the drafts of the mandate in general before the League Council approved it.[72]

However, the issue of the basic law was not raised as a topic for discussion on any day of the League. When presenting the report of the Sixth Committee to the General Assembly of the League of Nations, the delegate of Canada expressed disappointment that the General Assembly was not given sufficient opportunity to study the subject of the mandate, and it showed its compatibility with what was announced to the world: that the regions that emerged from the grip of the defeated nations would not be treated as a spoil of the victor's sheep and that it would provide for its matriarchs. The Canadian delegate concluded his speech by saying, "With regard to all of these assignments, and from whatever category, the greatest and most important thing is that it should be shown in its natural credit texts in supervising the areas that the delegating countries trust."[73]

After Balfour's response to the Canadian delegate defending the major powers and the Supreme Council, the Australian delegate, a member of the Sixth Committee, said that sufficient time had not been given to that committee to study the recommendations that were presented to it with the necessary depth and insight. He announced that he would vote against all of them.[74]

In response to the request of the US State Department in February 1922 to provide it with drafts of the mandate to study for approval before the League approved it, the drafts of the mandate for Iraq and Palestine were sent. But the Americans did not send any comment, and it seemed as though they were not in a hurry, as they were concerned with securing opportunities for American companies in trade and oil concessions of increasing importance in economic life and the pursuit of tightening control over resources in the Levant. At the urging and insistence of British foreign secretary Curzon, the Americans responded at the end of August 1922, six months after the draft was published. It is noted that the Zionists were the ones who initiated their publication, as if they wanted to express their pride in the achievement they had achieved. It was published by the *Jewish Chronicle* in London, and from it the *Times* published the texts of the draft mandate project on February 5, 1922.[75]

In mid-May 1922, Balfour delivered a speech at the headquarters of the League of Nations in Geneva, saying,

> The mandates are not made by the League and the League cannot change its material. Our duties are of two types: Our duty in the first place is to take into account that the clear, detailed and explicit terms of reference are consistent with the decisions reached by the allied and cooperating countries in Article 22 of the Versailles Treaty. It is our duty in the second place to see that the mandated states, which are carrying out these mandates, are under the supervision of the League of Nations. And let them remember that the mandate was a restriction imposed by the conquerors themselves on their sovereignty, which they obtained in the areas they conquered. It is a limitation imposed by allied and cooperating nations on their behalf in favour of what they believe is the common good of mankind. They asked the League of Nations to assist them in seeking to make this policy clear. But the League of Nations was not the initiator of this policy, but its tool, and it is not it that invented this mandate system.[76]

In spite of Balfour's claim that the League of Nations was not responsible for creating the mandate system and that the League's task did not involve supervising countries with mandates, the League of Nations did establish the first system for the right of conquest. This is true even though the League of Nations' role was not to establish sovereignty over Palestine and Iraq at that time, and the peace treaty with Turkey had not yet been signed, thereby preventing the Allied countries from becoming officially sovereign.

It is clear, therefore, that both the Balfour Declaration and the instrument of the mandate it contained lacked international legitimacy, as they were contrary to the principles of the League of Nations, international law, and the right of the Arab people in Palestine to determine their patron. This was not a response to the pressures of extremist Zionists, as Lord Sydenham said; rather the British colonial strategy did not require diplomacy.[77] Their strategists saw in the Zionist movement the only functional tool appropriate to serve colonial interests in the Arab world. By virtue of the organic relationship between the colonial powers and the Zionist movement, it was natural that all the doors would be open to its representatives.

THE DEBATE ABOUT PALESTINE AT
THE PEACE CONFERENCE IN 1919

At the start of 1919, a peace conference was held in Paris to lay the foundations of international relations in the aftermath of World War I. The peoples of the colonies, the Arab people at the forefront, were optimistic that the principle of the right to self-determination, which had been preached by US President Wilson, would be implemented soon, while the Allied countries were seeking to share the legacy of the Ottoman and German empires. The Zionist movement had strong support at the conference, as the four major Allied countries had approved the Balfour Declaration as previously explained, and delegates of some other countries participating in the conference did not hide their sympathy for the Zionists,[78] led by South African president Marshal Jan Christian Smuts.

Because US President Woodrow Wilson and his administration were aware of the significance of the Zionist project in securing the interests of emerging American capitalism in the Levant, particularly its oil interests, the American delegation to the peace conference appeared to be evidently on the Zionist side. The American president's proposals for the future of Palestine were well received by the participants, in contrast to his view of the new scientific system contained in the fourteen discovered principles he presented regarding the self-determination of peoples living under foreign rule. Foreign Minister

Lansing, who was also Edward House's adviser, had been the link between the conference and the Zionist delegation.[79]

When considering the demands of President Wilson, his administration, and the US Congress in both chambers in the early 1920s, it became clear that the administration's first concern was to secure the rising interests of US capitalism. It did this by adopting the motto "open door policy" as its guiding principle. The markets in the colonies utilized the "Wilson Humanitarian Call" in an effort to put pressure on the European colonial states to respond to the American demand that they end their monopoly. This was the call that the president and his administration abandoned as soon as the European colonial countries decided not to monopolize the markets of the countries chosen to be included in the mandate in 1922. The markets in the colonies used this call in an attempt to get the European colonial states to respond to the American demand.[80]

President Wilson dealt with his call for the right to self-determination with a stark selection, if it served American interests. The charter, as previously explained, was devoid of a provision for the right to self-determination. In addition, some sources indicate that the formulation of the Balfour Declaration was prepared mainly by Zionist personalities in coordination with the United States and Britain. Balfour had asked Col. Edward House, who was close to Wilson, to give his opinion on his statement, and House had consulted Wilson regarding the matter. On October 16, 1917, before Balfour issued his statement, House wrote to President Wilson, saying, "I will inform the British government that the text/version they propose regarding the Zionist Movement has your approval."[81]

The Arabs had no official representation in the conference, despite their participation in the war alongside the Allies. They paid a heavy human and material cost to achieve their victory. King Hussein sent his son, Prince Faisal, to represent him at the conference, accompanied by a delegation that included Nuri al-Sa'id, Rustam Haider, and Maj. T. E. Lawrence, also known as "Lawrence of Arabia," a well-known intelligence officer. In Paris, Faisal joined the delegation, with 'Awni 'Abdel Hadi, one of the founders of al-Arabiya al-Shabab (the Young Arab Association), to take over what could be considered the prince's public relations affairs.[82]

The French president and members of his government did not engage in any political conversation with the Arab guest; nor did France recognize him as his father's official representative. France made the argument that the members of the conference did not recognize the Kingdom of Hijaz or Hussein as king, even if their true motivation was to oppose the demands that Faisal presented. Faisal was given a very ceremonial welcome in France, but the French president and members of his government did not hold any political conversations with the Arab guest. France, too, had reservations about the Anglo-Hashemite relationship; these reservations were reflected in the directive to Lawrence to leave French territory, which, as soon as it appeared in Marseille, was received by Faisal and his companions.[83]

Despite the official French hospitality and the honor of the French aristocracy bestowed on Faisal, the French government refused to include the Arab delegation among the delegations participating in the conference, arguing that the Hijaz administration was not an official party to the war. Also, the US State Department refused to include the Arab delegation among the participating delegations.[84] Accordingly, Faisal and the accompanying delegation went to London to remind the Lloyd George government that he had come to Europe at his invitation. In addition to that, his father had recommended two things: first, to demand the independence of the Arab countries; second, to comply with the orders of the English-friendly Arab government in order to secure the independence and unity of the Arab countries.[85]

In London, Lawrence tried to persuade Faisal to accept the Zionist policy of Britain, taking advantage of his feeling that he had no friend other than Britain and the assurances that his father had received about the Balfour Declaration. In addition, it would appear that Faisal was torn between the significance of going to the peace conference and the seriousness of the invitation extended by T. E. Lawrence. On January 13, 1919, he signed with Weizmann a note that was written in English by Lawrence and included the following information:[86]

Article 1: In everything related to mutual relations on the occasion of the negotiations that may take place, the Arab state and Palestine will be inspired by the desire for mutual understanding and readiness that drives them. To this end, Jewish and Arab representatives are duly named and are registered in the territories of both countries.

Article 2: The final borders between the Arab states and Palestine will be drawn, as soon as the Peace Conference deliberations end, by a committee appointed by mutual agreement between the two parties.

Article 3: In the constitution making and the administration of Palestine, all measures are taken to ensure the implementation of the British government declaration of 2nd of November 1917 (the Balfour Declaration).

Article 4: All necessary measures shall be taken to encourage the immigration of Jews to Palestine, and to stimulate them on a large scale, and for the stability of the Jews, in the shortest period of time, due to more intensive settlement and more abundant cultivation of the land. It is agreed that the protection of the rights of Arab peasants and farmers during the implementation of these measures will be secured, and these peasants and farmers will receive the assistance necessary for their economic development.

Article 5: Any law or regulation in any way should not conflict with or offend the freedom to practice religious rituals, and, in addition, take any discriminatory measure with regard to those in charge of worship or the practice of various faiths. No religious origin will be taken into account in the free exercise of civil or political rights.

Article 6: The Zionist Organisation shall send a committee of experts assigned to draw up a list of the total economic resources of the country and submit a report on the best means to secure its development. The Zionist Organisation will put the aforementioned committee at the disposal of the Arab state in order to carry out an in-depth investigation on the economic resources of the Arab state, and develop a report specifying the conditions that would secure its maximum development. The Zionist Organisation uses all its efforts to assist the Arab state in obtaining the means that are indispensable for the development of its natural resources and economic potential.

Article 7: The signatories below acknowledge that they have acted in agreement, with conformity and full harmony on all of the above issues, which will be discussed in the Peace Conference.

Article 8: Any dispute that may arise between the two contracting parties is subject to arbitration by the British government.

Because Faisal did not know a single word of English at the time, and despite his confidence that Lawrence was the author of the memo and his sense that signing it was his way to attend the peace conference, he wrote in its margin in Arabic, "If the foundations of the Arab government were established, as requested in my letter dated 4 June 1918 to the British Foreign Office, I pledge what was written in this agreement, and if changes are made, I am not responsible for implementing this agreement."[87]

According to American mediation and British support, Faisal was allowed to address the conference on June 2, 1919, when he demanded the independence of the Arab countries, excluding Palestine. He said in his speech, which did not exceed twenty minutes, "Palestine is left aside, considering its global character. Her case should be resolved by the stakeholders."[88]

He also presented to the peace conference a memorandum that included affirming his adherence to Arab unity and independence, from Iskenderun to the Indian Ocean. With regard to Palestine, he affirmed the kinship between the Arab and Jewish races and demanded the guardianship of a major country and an administration that would represent the will of the population and work to advance the country.[89] On the other hand, 'Awni 'Abdel-Hadi in his memoirs denies that Faisal presented such a memo.[90]

In *Trial and Error*,[91] Chaim Weizmann reported that on the sidelines of the peace conference, a meeting brought together Faisal Weizmann, Felix Frankfurter, an American Zionist jurist, and Lawrence and that Faisal sent a few days after the meeting a message to Felix Frankfurter on March 13, 1939, which stated,

> We feel Arabs and Jews are common children in race who suffer similar grievances at the hands of countries stronger than them. We Arabs, especially the intellectuals among us, look sympathetically at the Zionist Movement, we work together to reform and revive the Near East, and our two movements complement each other, the Jewish movement is a nationalist, not imperialist, as well as our nationalist and not imperialist movement, and there is a place in Syria for both of us, and I believe that no success can be achieved for any movement without the other.[92]

The Zionists produced a copy of this letter before the Shaw Commission in 1929. 'Awni 'Abdel-Hadi challenged the Zionist delegation to show the origin of the letter, denying that he had the slightest knowledge of the aforementioned meeting, even though he had served as the director of the Faisal office while he was in Paris on the occasion of the peace conference. After ten months, Faisal informed the Jewish Society of his involvement. In order to prevent himself from repeating the same mistake, he decided to use the *Jewish Chronicle*, the London newspaper published by the Jewish Society, to make the following statement on October 14, 1919:

> Palestine must remain a part of Syria, as they have no natural limit or separation. What affects one affects the other? The Arabs see Palestine as an Arab state and do not see it as a separate country. We are seeking to create an Arab empire consisting of at least Iraq, Syria and Palestine. I have been told that all Jews depend on the statement made by Lord Balfour, and they look forward to establishing a national homeland for them in Palestine, meaning that Palestine becomes a Jewish state. There is no doubt that these aspirations contradict the ideas of the Arabs and do not satisfy them. I appeal to the Jews, who are Semites before the Arabs, to help us in establishing the Kingdom of Arabia, even if there are many Jews in Palestine, it is easy to make a Jewish state one of the states of this Kingdom.[93]

In his statement, although he clarified the contradiction of the Balfour Declaration with the aspirations of the Arab people, he did not object to the Zionists' emigration to Palestine and its becoming a Jewish state within the Arab state monarchy. This is in sharp contrast to the position of the first

Palestinian conference and the consensus of the Arab people in Palestine to reject immigration and settlement.

In a message that Faisal sent to Allenby in Cairo, he made it clear that he accepted the invitation to the second peace conference on the condition that Palestine be considered part of Syria. He stated that he did not find in the Allenby letter sufficient clarity to suggest recognition that this country was an inseparable part of Syria. He also noted, "Given the question about my acceptance of the establishment of the national home for Jews in Palestine, I believe that there is a misunderstanding. All I accepted was that the rights of the Jews in that country be preserved, just as they did the natural rights of the Arab population, and that they be granted the same natural rights and privileges."[94]

Faisal attended the peace conference as a representative of the Kingdom of Hijaz, regardless of what he said in front of the peace conference or while in London and Paris at the time and whether it was attributed to him or not. This was true regardless of whether it was issued. The statements made about him and attributed to him are solely his responsibility, and they reflect poorly on the Kingdom of Hijaz. Furthermore, he had written in Lawrence's letter that if the foundations of the Arab government were not consolidated, as he had requested in his letter to the British Foreign Office, he would not be responsible for carrying out his agreement with Weizmann. Following that, he wrote a letter that he sent to the *Jewish Chronicle* newspaper in London, as well as another letter that he sent to General Allenby in Cairo. In these letters, he emphasized the Arabs' intense focus on their rights and stated that the Jews' rights in Palestine were limited to their enjoyment of the Arab population's natural rights. He also emphasized that the rights of Arabs were more important than the rights of Jews. Furthermore, he stated that Arabs were adamant about fighting for their rights. Furthermore, despite his popularity among Arabs, he was not a representative of the Arab people, particularly the Palestinian people, whose elected representatives had been barred from appearing before the conference. They were opposed to the Balfour Declaration, the Jewish national home, as well as Zionist immigration and settlement. He declared Palestine's independence within the Arab-Syrian unity, free of all dependence, in his telegram to the peace conference.

Therefore, it is not important to confirm or implement what was issued by Faisal or what was attributed to him while he was in London and Paris; what is important is to stress that he did not speak on behalf of Palestine and the Arab nation. What he said, his plan, and the historical value attributed to him are an example of the colonial-Zionist complicity in exploiting the colonial relations with their loyal Arab decision makers to weaken the Arab popular position of rejecting the colonial and Zionist settlement project. The Arab people in Palestine and throughout the Arab world have always affirmed this frank and categorical rejection of the Zionist project since the Balfour Declaration was issued in 1917. In addition, during his presence at the peace conference, Faisal did not mind making concessions that he did not see as essential. It is clear ignorance of the nature of the conflict, the location of the Zionist project in the colonial strategy of the region, and the lack of historical relevance of the majority of the Jews of the twentieth century to Palestine.

In exchange for the Arab presence represented by Prince Faisal and some consultants whose motives and goals are doubtful, the conference was attended by Zionist delegations from several countries, most notably the American delegation, and it included specialized political and legal advisers. By virtue of the relationship of the Zionist movement to the colonial powers of different countries, the official Zionist delegation and the supportive Jewish delegations whose members were permitted to attend as observers were given the opportunity to have influential presence in the conference. Due to the fact that Weizmann and the official delegation were not confronted with any challenges or pressures, they did not make even the slightest concession to any of the constants of the Zionist movement and, on the contrary, escalated their demands. The following requests were included in the memorandum that Zionists brought to the conference on March 2, 1919:[95]

> Recognition of the historical right of the Jewish people in Palestine.
> Drawing the borders of Palestine to the Litani River in the north, including the entire Jordan Basin, passing through line along the watershed divide in Jabal al-Sheikh, including Aqaba in the south.
> Handing sovereignty in Palestine to the League of Nations, and giving British a mandate for it.
> Adopting special political, administrative, and economic clauses in introducing this mandate, to secure the establishment of a Jewish national home, and to make the establishment of an independent state possible later.

In front of the League Council on February 27, 1919, Weizmann presented the memorandum, and in response to the American minister of foreign affairs, Lansing, he stressed the necessity of establishing in Palestine an administration that allowed immigration from seventy thousand to one hundred thousand Jews. He sought the building of Jewish schools to cultivate a nationalist agenda similar to French and British nationalism. Weizmann's memo and his speech before the peace conference brought about the qualitative shift that the Balfour Declaration was responsible for, and the Allied states endorsed it in response to the demand of the Zionist movement. Weizmann addressed the representatives of the colonial countries in his capacity as the representative of a movement that held significance and consideration in the eyes of the individuals he addressed.[96] This was contrary to the case of Faisal, in which he represented the movement that is viewed as embodying the greatest danger to global colonial interests. In light of what Prince Faisal felt about the bias of the League of Nations members toward the Zionists, he warned, in a statement to the Parisian newspaper Le Matin on March 19, 1999, of the consequences of this, saying, "If the Jews want to establish a state and claim sovereign rights in the country, I expect and fear that very new risks and conflicts will arise between them and other races."[97]

THE WILSON ADMINISTRATION'S RESPONSE TO THE KING-CRANE COMMITTEE'S REPORT AT THE VERSAILLES PEACE CONFERENCE

The debate took place over Prince Faisal's request to the Allied countries, particularly Britain, to fulfil its promises by establishing an Arab state. His claim was backed by documents including the pledges made by Britain and a reminder of the Arabs' participation in the war alongside the Allies.[98] While the French delegation was requesting the implementation of the Sykes-Picot Agreement, which stipulated France's mandate over Syria and Lebanon, Britain opposed this, protesting the Allies' promises to the Arabs.[99] France replied that it was not a party to the Hussein-McMahon talks and therefore was not obligated to honor them.[100]

To resolve the controversy, the American delegation proposed sending a committee to the Levant to explore the opinions of citizens and investigate the facts. Both Britain and France ended up opposing the dispatch of the committee after they had initially supported it, as their decision makers and the men of their various apparatuses were unaware that the Arab people had risen up against the attempt at Turkification, and they did not stand by the Allies except in the interest of the independence of their homeland and their right to self-determination and territorial integrity. They refused to acknowledge any limitation on their complete sovereignty over every square inch of it. They were unanimous in their decision to reject not only the demand made by the French government but also each and every demand made by the representatives of the World Zionist Congress.

However, US President Wilson formed an American fact-finding commission named for Henry King and Charles Crane, two members of the American delegation to the peace conference, in response to pressure from some delegation members and the advice of William Lynn Westerman and Henry White, his aides, and Howard Plus, president of the American University of Beirut, who warned about the consequences of responding to the Zion Declaration, as the American president was doing under the influence of the American

Zionist leaders and in particular his close friend, Supreme Court justice Louis Brandeis.[101]

The Arabs received the proposal of the US president enthusiastically, and Prince Faisal wrote to him on March 24, 1919, expressing his deep gratitude for announcing the dispatch of a committee that would allow the Arabs to make their voices heard.[102] On the other hand, despite the clear bias of the Wilson administration toward the Zionists and the awareness of Weizmann, Brandeis, and their companions of the extent of their influence on President Wilson and his administration, they expressed great indignation at forming the committee out of their belief that Arab opinion rejected the Zionists, Jews and non-Jews, and their conviction that the Arab people in Palestine would not accept a Jewish state in Palestine. Two months prior to the committee's arrival in Palestine, a meeting of prominent Arab figures took place in Jerusalem, where they reached a consensus to call for independence for all Arabs and to oppose Jewish immigration as well as the establishment of a Jewish national homeland. They were all in agreement that the Islamic Christian Society was the people's representative. During an expanded meeting, the Jerusalem Islamic Christian Society extended invitations to village dignitaries and notables, asking them to sign the text statement:[103]

> We, the signatories, our names below, have instructed the Christian Islamic Society in al-Quds al-Sharif/Jerusalem to fulfil our desires listed below to the ruling International Committee, and we all demonstrate to it in this way.

1. That Syria, which starts from the Taurus Mountains in the north to Rafah in the south, is completely independent.
2. Palestine (southern Syria), which is an integral part of Syria, is internally independent. All of its rulers are elected by the patriots, and its internal laws are enacted according to the wishes of its patriotic residents and the needs of the country.
3. Rejecting immigration of the Zionists, and we protest against their hopes in Palestine with all our strength. As for the original Jews who were in the country before the war, we consider them patriots, they have what we have and we have what they have.[104]

All the delegations that met the American committee adopted the three demands, whether they represented the municipalities, villages, societies, clubs, or sects, as those demands were mentioned in all the petitions submitted to the committee, which circled throughout Syria, internal and coastal, during the period from June 10 to August 18, 1919. The committee returned to Paris to submit a full report, which included, with regard to Palestine, the following:

> If the wishes of the population in Palestine were to be fulfilled, it must be recognised that the non-Jewish population, which is almost nine-tenths of the entire population,[105] totally rejects the Jewish programme. The streams prove that the people of Palestine did not agree on anything like their consensus on this rejection. It was also clear that the hostile feeling against Zionism is not confined to Palestine, but rather includes the population of Syria in general. For 72 percent of all petitions in Syria are against Zionism, and the demand for a higher percentage of these percentages is obtained only by Syrian unity and independence. The Syrian conference announced this general feeling in Articles 7, 8 and 12 of its statement.[106]

The American envoys, who were in support of the Zionist call, after learning the facts on the ground, ended up recording their reservations about the Balfour Declaration. Their report stated, "It is difficult to dispute that the Zionist ceiling programme must be addressed by important amendments, that the establishment of a national homeland for the Jewish people equals the transformation of Palestine into a Jewish state, and the establishment of a Jewish state cannot take place without inflicting severe abuses of the civil and religious rights of non-Jewish communities in Palestine."[107] In all of the conferences that the committee held with Jewish representatives, it had been abundantly clear that the Zionists had always envisioned the total expropriation of Jewish property through the use of a wide variety of land purchase schemes.[108]

On the committee's meetings in Palestine and the viewpoint of its citizens,[109] the report stated,

> The Muslims met, according to the last English census, about four-fifths of the population of Palestine, to claim the independence of occupied Syria, and the parties that met in Jaffa decided that Syria was the people of an independent government without a will, and if the Peace Conference insisted on appointing a state, they preferred the United States. People in Jerusalem and other cities of Palestine supported this decision, and they were referring the question of guardianship to the Syrian conference. The Christians in Palestine, who are 10 percent of the total population, all agreed with Muslims in rejecting Zionism, and were divided on the issue of guardianship. Latinos, Catholics, and the majority of Christians in the North and Nazareth agree with Muslims to seek independence, and leave the guardianship matter to the Syrian conference. The Roman Catholics and Maronites were asking for French tutelage, while the Orthodox agreed on English tutelage. The Jews, who constitute 10 percent of the population, support English Zionism, and demand that Palestine be made a

national home for the Jews, and that they differ on the details and the ways to achieve it.[110]

The committee did not fail to issue a warning against ignoring the sentiments of the Arab people, as its report included the following: "The Peace Conference should not ignore that the feeling against Zionism in Palestine and Syria is extremely severe, and it is not easy to underestimate it." All of the English employees who were questioned by the committee shared the view that the Zionist program could not be carried out by the armed forces, which also shared the view that the size of the armed forces needed to be at least fifty thousand soldiers.[111] This fact alone is sufficient evidence to demonstrate that the Zionist program is discriminatory toward the rights of people who are not Jewish. On the basis of the information presented above, the committee was of the opinion that it owed it to the peace conference to support only a moderate Zionist program, which must be implemented gradually; to put it another way, Jewish immigration to Palestine must be defined, and any plan to make Palestine a Jewish government must be abandoned entirely.[112]

It is clear that the report of the King-Crane Committee was objective in conveying the facts reached by its members, and therefore the optimism that spread among the Arab elites was justified, as it presented faithfully Arab views, even if it was not recommended to reject the Zionist project. Nor was it surprising that the committee report was not offered to the conference, as it contradicted Britain's strategy, which played the first role in formulating the League of Nations system in a way that preserves the colonial countries' interests in the colonies through the creation of the mandate system, which covers direct colonialism by claiming that the delegated country will consider the interests of the people who were delegated to them, until it became clear to those countries and the League that they had become able to govern themselves.[113]

The majority of the Arab people mistrusted Britain and France and considered them two colonial states, and because they had not yet tested the American administrations and apparatuses, it seemed logical that the vast majority of the people of Palestine favored American custody, in case the conference insisted that the country be put under foreign guardianship. This came as a result of the fact that the elites most influential in the Arab political-social movement at that time took President Wilson's words seriously about the right of peoples to self-determination. On the history of the Zionist settlement in Palestine, those who voiced an auspicious opinion about President Wilson and his administration to the American consul in Jerusalem, Warder Cresson, did not know who established the first Jewish settlement in Palestine in 1852[114]—that is, forty-four years preceding the publication of Theodor Herzl's 1896 pamphlet "Der Judenstaat" ("The State of the Jews").

Brandeis had traveled to Palestine while the King-Crane Committee was there and made trips to the Zionist settlements, then returned to continue his pressure on Wilson. The American president was not just sympathetic to Zionism but referred to himself as a Zionist in his talks with American Zionist leaders such as Louis Brandeis, Felix Frankfurter, Judge Julian Mac, and Rabbi Stephen Wise. As a result of this, Wilson did not take the report of the committee he ordered to form but rather adopted the report of the Intelligence Department in the American delegation to the Sabm Conference, which recommended that American interests required that the American delegation adopt at the peace conference the establishment of a Jewish state in Palestine, separate from its Arab neighbors, and that Britain be the mandated country under the supervision of the League of Nations.[115]

Henry Cabot Lodge, chairman of the Senate Foreign Affairs Committee, in April 1922 submitted a draft resolution confirming the statement in the Balfour Declaration. On May 31, the committee approved the project, including its belief that its conception of the concept of a national home meant the ultimate creation of a Jewish state. On June 30, the House of Representatives passed the recommendation, despite the testimony of Professor Edward Reid, professor of English literature at Yale University, before the House, which made clear that the Balfour Declaration was illegal and contrary to the right of the people of Palestine to self-determination. On September 21, 1922, both houses of Congress passed Resolution 322, expressing sympathy for the idea of creating a national home. After this decision, the League of Nations issued the Mandate Deed on July 24, 1922, and President Wilson allowed the publication of the King-Crane Report, which had been kept secret for nearly three years.[116]

Furthermore, the Wilson administration, which had declared the fourteen points and the call for the right of peoples to self-determination, also hit a brick wall with the will of the Syrian conference, which was held in Damascus in June 1919. The conference was attended by delegates from the Arab countries of Syria, Lebanon, Palestine, and Jordan. The delegates talked about the issues surrounding the Balfour Declaration, the future of the Levant after the war, the mission of the US investigation committee, and the conspiracies of colonial states. It came to a number of decisions, which were then given to the King-Crane Committee. Additionally, it sent pictures of those decisions to the peace conference as well as to the major powers. Among the most important was the statement "The Syrian people, spanning the coastal and interior regions, strongly upheld their desire for complete independence within a unified country. The people of the Levant rejected any form of protection or mandate, and they vehemently denounced both the Treaty of Sykes-Picot and the Balfour Declaration. They opposed any project that sought to divide Syria or establish a Jewish national home in Palestine."[117]

The Syrian conference was formed by the free, direct election of its delegates, according to the principles that were used in choosing the members of the Ottoman Envoys' Council. Thus, the conference would have possessed the characteristics of a parliament, and its decisions would be constitutional, expressing the will of the Arab people in all aspects of the Levant. Its decisions would represent the will of this people in its insistence on national liberation, Syrian unity, a rection of Sykes-Picot's partition, and Labour's promise to establish Zionist racial colonialism in a national home for Jews who were to be brought from their original homelands to Palestine.[118]

NOTES

1. Rogan 2009, pp. 197–198.
2. Kayali 1990, pp. 4:680–682; Zu'itir 1955, p. 50; 'Ayid 1990, p. 6:552.
3. Bahjat 1982, p. 276; Tarbin 1990, p. 1004.
4. Jeffries 2000, p. 2:140; Tarbin 1990, pp. 997–998; Bahjat 1982, pp. 249–253.
5. Zayadah 1990, pp. 144–145; Hamad 2004, pp. 45–50; Mu'awiyyah 1990, pt. 2, vol. 2, p. 117.
6. Hadi and Sayigh 1990, p. 3:457.
7. 'Aqil 1990, pp. 2:289–299.
8. Badur 2004, p. 7.
9. Sakhnini 1985, p. 32.
10. Rogan 2009, pp. 152–154; Sykes 2016; Berdine 2018, pp. 69–87.
11. Zebel 1973, p. 243.
12. Howard 1931, p. 202.
13. Darwazah 1971, p. 36; Khalah 1982, pp. 131–133; Kayali 1968, p. 3; Hout 1979, pp. 16–17.
14. Khalah 1982, p. 89.
15. Ingrams 1972, p. 38; Sakhnini 1985, pp. 64–65.
16. Galnoor 2012, pp. 49–50; Lieshout 2016, p. 389.
17. Darwazah 1984b, pp. 445–446; Sakhnini 1985, p. 64.
18. Sakhnini 1985, p. 64.
19. Khalah 1982, pp. 298–299; Hazmawi 1998, pp. 260–261; Hunidi 2003, pp. 223–227.
20. Luciani 2016, pp. 108–110.
21. Butenschøn, Stiansen, and Vollan 2016, p. 108.
22. Stein 1984, p. 201.
23. Shufani 2003, p. 374.
24. Jiryis 1977, pp. 1:288–298.
25. Knock 1992, p. 115.
26. Shufani 2003, p. 374.
27. Thompson 2018, pp. 19–20.
28. Roberts 2018, pp. 18–23.

29. Jeffries 2000, Vol. 1, p. 185.

30. Jeffries 2000, Vol. 1, p. 185; Ofuatey-Kodjoe 1977, p. 70; Thompson 2018, pp. 20–21.

31. Jeffries Vol. 1, 2000, p. 185.

32. Ambrosius 2002, p. 44.

33. Fromkin 2010, pp. 280–281.

34. Smuts 1918.

35. Jeffries 2000, Vol. 1., p. 187.

36. Stråth 2016; MacMillan 2007, p. 89.

37. MacMillan 2007, pp. 376–377.

38. MacMillan 2007, pp. 419–420; Jeffries 2000, Vol. 1, p. 190.

39. Jeffries 2000, Vol. 1, p. 190; MacMillan 2007, p. 88, and p. 420.

40. Jeffries 2000, Vol. 1, p. 192.

41. Jeffries 2000, p. 191.

42. Jeffries 2000, pp. 192–193.

43. Johnson 2016, p. 100.

44. Jeffries 2000, Vol. 1, pp. 195–196.

45. MacMillan 2007, pp. xxviii–xxix, p. 90.

46. MacMillan 2007, p. xxix.

47. MacMillan 2007, pp. 54–55.

48. MacMillan 2007, p. 198.

49. Johnson 2016, p. 102.

50. Jeffries 2000, Vol. 1, p. 207.

51. Jeffries 2000, p. 216.

52. Jeffries 2000, p. 213.

53. Jeffries 2000, p. 213.

54. Jeffries 2000, p. 214.

55. Keith 1922, 3rd series, p. 4:71.

56. Report of the King-Crane Commission 1947, p. 747; Muslih 1988, pp. 178–190.

57. Jeffries 2000, Vol. 1, pp. 223–224.

58. Mallison 1968, p. 556.

59. Weizmann 1945, p. 235.

60. Mallison and Mallison 1986, pp. 64–65.

61. Ovendale 1984, p. 47; Hunidi 2003, pp. 153–154.

62. Shufani 2003, p. 383.

63. Shufani 2003, p. 383.

64. Halderman 1968, p. 23:78; Keith 1922, p. 71; Essaid 2013, pp. 49–51; Kupferschmidt 1987, pp. 386–387; 'Uthman 1963.

65. Hunidi 2003, pp. 153–154.

66. Ovendale 1984, p. 47; Shufani 2003, p. 385.

67. Official Report Great Britain. *Parliamentary Debates* (House Lords), 5th series, vol. 50, col. `1021, 1922; Shufani 2003, p. 385.

68. Shufani 2003, p. 385; Jiryis 1977, p. 2:63; Kayali 1985, p. 162.

69. Jeffries 2000, Vol. 1, pp. 224–239.

70. Jeffries 2000, pp. 254–255.

71. Jeffries 2000, p. 243.

72. Jeffries 2000, pp. 250–252.

73. Jeffries 2000, pp. 250–252.

74. Jeffries 2000, pp. 250–252.

75. Jeffries 2000, pp. 240–243.

76. Jeffries 2000, pp. 260–261.

77. Henig 2001, p. 164.

78. Bahjat 1982, p. 276; Khalidi 2007, pp. 33–34.

79. Shufani 2003, p. 36.

80. Jiryis 1977, p. 1:288–289; Khalidi 2007, p. 185.

81. Manual 1949, pp. 167–169; Hodgson 2006, p. 126; Barr 2012, p. 89; Kamal 2000, p. 16.

82. Hadi 2002, p. 50; 'Umari 1969, pp. 239–238.

83. Hadi 2002, p. 52.

84. Shufani 2003, p. 364.

85. Hadi 2002, p. 55.

86. Stein 1961, pp. 641–643; Caplan 1983, pp. 561–614; Ahmed 1990, pp. 9–41.

87. Hout 1981, pp. 105–106.

88. Hout 1981, p. 102.

89. Kayali 1985, p. 112; Shufani 2003, p. 366.

90. Hadi 2002, p. 66.

91. Weizmann 1949.

92. Weizmann 1949, p. 317.

93. Hout 1981, p. 107.

94. Woodward and Butler 1946–1985, p. 13:250.

95. Khadir 2003, pp. 160–161.

96. Hyamson 1942, pp. 129–130.

97. Khadir 2003, p. 161.

98. Kayali 1985, p. 112.

99. Thompson 2022, pp. 54–57.

100. Khadir 2003, p. 161.

101. Ahmad 1996, p. 61.

102. Khadir 2003, p. 162.

103. Kayali 1985, p. 110; Muslih 1988, pp. 178–190; Tahat 2015, p. 72; Khilah 1974, p. 129; Pappe 2010, p. 175.

104. Khilah 1974, p. 528; Kayali 1985, p. 126; Tahat 2015, p. 72.

105. Patai 1986, p. 300; Scholoch 1985, p. 485.

106. Ahmad 1996, pp. 61–69.

107. Report of the King-Crane Commission 1947, p. 747.

108. Hyamson 1942, pp. 129–130.

109. Khalaf 2019; Qarqut 2006, pp. 17–18; Fromkin 1990, pp. 102–103; Zu'itir 1979; Qatan 1970; Khuli 1973.

110. Report of the King-Crane Commission 1947, p. 747; Kamil 1858, p. 285.

111. Report of the King-Crane Commission 1947, p. 747.

112. Report of the King-Crane Commission 1947, p. 747.

113. Hall 1948, p. 81.
114. Kobler 1956, p. 12; Sokolow 1919, p. 1:161.
115. Howard 1963, pp. 11–12; Bahjat 1982, pp. 249–253.
116. Shufani 2003, p. 367.
117. Hout 1981, pp. 114–118.
118. Fraser 2022, p. 6.

Chapter 3

The Arab Revolution and the First Partition Plan, 1936–1937

The Palestinian political entity did not emerge as a stand-alone unit until the political division of the Levant into areas of influence of the major countries according to the Sykes-Picot Agreement. This ended in the consolidating of the borders of the Arab homeland in the post–World War I treaties.[1] However, the Palestinian political movement, through its struggle within the framework of the Arab movement and its sensitivity to some of the issues that existed at the time, had preceded this date, and the methods of its struggle diversified. It is possible that the telegram that some leaders of Jerusalem sent to the grand vizier on June 24, 1891, represented the first official protest demanding the issuance of a security guard prohibiting Jews from entering Palestine and purchasing land there.[2]

The Zionist movement was only able to take possession of Palestinian lands in the Palestinian territories until 1918 (only 650,000 dunums during seventy years of attempts), and the population of Jews had only increased to fifty thousand people in 1897.[3] This was a significant increase, but it was not enough to make the Zionist movement successful. This campaign against immigration and the sale of land received support from the Arab press, such as the *al-Karmel* newspaper, which contributed to the campaign.[4]

The Palestinian political movement remained part of the Syrian movement, and it was called in all political circles "South Syria." In 1921, as the Zionist threat and settlement increased, Palestinian national groups emerged, advocating for the establishment of inclusive societies that transcended sectarian divisions. Initially, these societies were named Arab Societies, but the British authorities requested the founders use the designation Muslim-Christian Associations. This was done in the hope that these associations would appear as purely local entities, disconnected from the broader Arab National Movement.[5]

In addition, illiteracy was rampant throughout Palestinian society as a consequence of the myriad of factors that contributed to Ottoman attrition. The illiteracy rate among Muslims was 89 percent; among Christians, 52 percent; and among the general population, 85 percent.[6] This contributed to the low level of public awareness among the Palestinian people, as a natural reflection of the level of the socioeconomic and political development that the Palestinian people had reached at that stage. Spontaneity, not planning and organizing, was the main motivation for their uprising, which undertook to confront the Zionist and British occupations.[7] As a result, it was only natural that personal relationships would triumph over organizational relationships, marking the beginning of a national movement that was divided into regional allegiances and restricted groupings. The cities of Palestine were not very different from the countryside, because they were, for the most part and with the exception of sectors of expatriates, formed by family formations with families exerting significant political and social influence.[8]

In the midst of all of these internal and external factors, the Palestinian Executive Committee was formed, attempting to achieve its national goal of establishing a Palestinian state in addition to the British mandate and its pledges to establish a Zionist entity in Palestine, while dealing with the successors left by the Ottomans and the effects of the disintegration of the joint national work contract. At the beginning of the British mandate in Palestine, Palestinian society was divided into three social classes: peasants, urbanites, and Bedouins. However, it was mostly a rural community, in which the village formed the most prominent socioeconomic basis. Peasants formed the majority of the population, and the main work for most Palestinians was agriculture. In 1922, the number of residents in the Palestinian countryside reached 477,693 people, making up 70 percent of the total population.[9] Agriculture witnessed remarkable development during the period after the British mandate was imposed on Palestine. The cultivated areas expanded, the production of agricultural crops increased, the methods of cultivation of the land improved, and the multiple-cycle agricultural system appeared, in addition to the traditional bilateral cycle, as industrial development increased the need for wool, leather, flax, and other industrial crops.[10]

The growth of agriculture was accompanied by a development in the social structure. Some peasants were able to make a quick profit by opening workshops and consumer shops. This made them wealthy and able to use the farmworkers themselves; thus the wage-peasant segment emerged. In addition to that, the social arrangement in the countryside became more evident, especially among the families of notables who inherited the prominent religious and administrative positions, which placed them in social positions and qualified them for political leadership. Thus, social stratification began to take shape in the Palestinian countryside, strengthening the role of notables and owners, instead of the expansion of the destitute wage circle of peasants.[11] Another official report adds that the income of the peasant family, consisting of six people, was between £20 and £30 per month, but they needed £26 to buy necessities. If we know that the farmer paid about £6 of direct and indirect taxes and £8 of debt repayment, then what remained for them was not enough to survive.[12]

Within that atmosphere, a sector of land brokers emerged, whose work was to facilitate the sale of Arab lands to the Jews. A report in the *Palestine* newspaper on June 12, 1935, indicated the growth and strength of this sector. The newspaper article read, "Our land broker used to shy away from his misfortune, but now the shame of these dark faces has run out. These torturers hung their hard teeth, and the people saw them in their true form, stepping back and forth on the streets, their hands in the hands of their Zionist colleagues."[13]

As a result of the sale of lands to the Jews due to the bankruptcy of the peasants, John Hope Simpson estimated in his report in 1930, this group of farmers who did not obtain the minimum living standard numbered thirty-five thousand rural families, or 29.4 percent of the total, and were all rural Arab residents. Moreover, an important factor that led to a decrease in the number of nonowner farmers was rural migration to cities, which increased during the 1930s.[14]

In light of the social problems that the Palestinian countryside was suffering, the British measures centered around one goal, which was trying to preserve the traditional role of village elders as mediators between the population and the authorities. To demonstrate this, we can pause briefly to discuss local councils in the countryside. In 1920–1921, the mandate authorities issued the Law of Local Councils in Palestinian Cities and Villages, which aimed to place every large village, or group of small villages, under the administration of a local council. The task of this council was to provide financial aid to farmers, circulate laws issued by official departments, and supervise development projects. Although the authorities succeeded, in the first years after the passing of the law, in forming twenty local councils, Arab and Jewish, the effectiveness of the village councils remained limited. On the one hand, the hamlet's acute poverty precluded the local council from conducting any project apart from the central authorities, while on the other, the governor of the district was impeding the council's effort to bring forward particular initiatives to develop the village.[15]

Despite the enormous growth that Palestine witnessed toward capitalism and the clarity of social formations in light of this development, this did not imply a departure from the agrarian community. This development resulted in both of these developments. Throughout the era of the British mandate, Palestinian society remained essentially rural. The role of the village was not limited to economic aspects, and the ties that linked the Palestinian peasants were still based on the family. Despite the stability of the urban situation in Palestine, prior to the British mandate, and its confinement to some families and localities, the mandate accelerated the growth of Palestinian cities. Cities began to lose their old collective solidarity. Official statistics give a clear picture of this growth, as for the first time in the history of Palestine, a population census took place in 1922, followed by a second census in 1931. The population of Palestine in 1922 had reached about 757, 248 people, and their number increased to 1,035,831 people, in 1931.[16]

This was the stage of the great strike and the great revolution, because the demands of the National Movement to stop immigration were not fulfilled. Immigration, the movement to seize land, and Zionist challenges all increased, whether by the influx of weapons or by creating guards for the colonies and Zionist garrisons. The public oath went on to say that the performance of the national leadership was lagging and uncertain and that internal strife and the pursuit of gains were rendering it unable to move forward. Although they developed in a variety of directions beyond this point, the national lines of action remained the same throughout this stage as they were throughout the phases that came before.

On the level of the national leadership, attention remained focused on Arab and international political contacts and sending delegations. Contacts with the British high commissioner and representatives of the British government coming to Palestine and Egypt were high on the agenda, as was the task of sending delegations to Britain.

On the Palestinian level, on October 27, 1929, the Executive Committee called for a meeting of the General Assembly of the Palestinian Conference in Jerusalem, attended by members of the General Assembly, tribal leaders, a number of delegates from eastern Jordan, and Haj Amin al-Husseini, after the battle to drive Arabs from Zubeidat from their lands. A conference on January 25, 1935, for religious scholars was attended by about five hundred political, social, and religious leaders. On the subject of land, the meeting decided to prevent the sale of land.[17]

On January 12, 1931, Haj Amin al-Husseini, the head of the Supreme Islamic Council and one of the most prominent leaders of the National Movement, was invited to an Islamic conference in Jerusalem. The most influential personalities in Islamic history at that time were contacted by the committee that was preparing for the meeting, and the majority of them replied. Among them were 'Abd al-'Aziz al-Tha'alabi from Tunisia, who contributed to the idea of the conference. Lecturers at the conference included Muhammad Rashid Rida, Muhammad Hussein al-Kashif al-Ghita,' the great Pakistani poet Muhammad Iqbal, Shawkat 'Ali, a great figure from India, former prime minister of Iran Diya' al-Din Tabataba'i, Shukri al-Qutali, Riyadh al-Sulh, 'Umar al-Da'uq, and 'Abd al-Rahman 'Azzam.[18] The conference faced two of difficulties: the first due to the fear of the British administration and the Zionist movement; the second due to the difference between the leaders of Palestine regarding their respective roles.[19]

As Haj Amin al-Husseini was the initiator, his rivals tried to thwart the conference, and when they failed, they called for another conference. Despite such efforts to derail the conference, it proved successful and took important decisions, including

1.   Establishing a major Islamic university in Jerusalem called Al-Aqsa Mosque University and creating an Islamic Knowledge Department
2.   Defending Palestine because of its importance to the Islamic world, denouncing British-Zionist policy in it, and declaring the sanctity of al-Buraq
3.   Forming an Islamic company to save the lands of Palestine[20]

However, all these activities escaped the attention of the masses, who believed that the danger required different solutions. The Executive Committee tried to understand what people were worried about, so it took part in popular events like the Jerusalem demonstration on September 13, 1933. The British police attacked the demonstration, hurting one of the leaders and arresting others. Musa Qadhim al-Husseini was at the head of the demonstration despite his old age.[21]

On October 13, 1933, a demonstration quite similar to this one took place in Jaffa, and there was a conflict between the police and the demonstrators.[22] Musa Qadhim al-Husseini was injured, and the authorities arrested a number of other leaders. When Musa Qadhim al-Husseini died of his injury,[23] the Executive Committee could not agree on an alternative in light of personal and family rivalry and political conflict.

1. The popular participation in the demonstrations has expanded, and the demonstrations have turned to a more violent nature, and the demonstration at this stage has become a continuous and non-stop action despite the British repression. These demonstrations included the ones that took place in Jerusalem on September 13, 1933, the ones that took place in Jaffa on October 13, 1933, and the skirmishes that took place in other cities in Palestine on October 14, 1933. Without waiting for the position of the leadership or for the Sultan's authorization to enable a peaceful rally, the people vented their wrath by demonstrating their right to take revenge.

2. Popular initiatives by holding conferences and forming popular committees to express the popular position, including:

A. On July 31, 1931, a popular conference was organized in Nablus. It was called for by a committee that had been constituted specifically for this reason. The Executive Committee took action to prevent the conference from happening because it was held without their sanction. After agreeing to declare the strike as a form of protest against the policies of the British Government, which consented to equip the Zionist immigrants, the gathering reached a consensus to commit to taking the leadership position within the Executive Committee.

B. Holding popular celebrations to commemorate the Hittin battle.

C. A popular meeting in Beit Jibreen was attended by about 2,000 people, although none of the party leaders attended. The meeting called for: seeking understanding and unifying the word, seeking to stop the sale of lands, seeking to establish an Arab agricultural bank, working with possible means to stop the Zionist immigration.

D. Carrying out student, female, journalistic, and workers' movements resulted in the holding of a women's conference on October 26, 1929, which was attended by approximately one hundred delegates. On September 20, 1931, the journalists held a conference during which they discussed the issue of power outages for Arab newspapers and sent a telegram of protest to the government in order to protest against the disruption of newspapers. A telegram sent to the Executive Committee requested that it negotiate solely for independence within the context of Arab unity and denounced the policies that the Executive Committee had been pursuing.

E. Call for strikes, culminating in the six-month major strike.

3. On April 20, 1935, the National Committees were established in order to impose a strike and put an end to the complacency that had developed among the National Movement's leadership. On May 8, 1935, a general conference of the National Committees was called, and at that meeting, it was resolved to keep the strike going and to boycott the authorities in charge of the occupation.

4. Carrying out economic activities, one of which was the founding of the Arab Bank in 1934; following this, various types of financial institutions and banks were also founded.

5. The formation of armed cells, at the time when Sheikh 'Izz al-Din al-Qassam began developing its cells at the beginning of this stage; the Green Palm group appeared in late 1929, and there was frequent talk of forming armed cells and collecting donations for them.

On the other hand, the question of taking violent action did not arise until February 19, 1935, when al-Qassam traveled to the countryside in order to launch the revolution. He selected the Jenin region with the intention of getting in touch with the peasants and enlisting their participation in the armed revolution. He was unable to continue the march because British forces raided his hiding place and asked him to surrender. He fought until he and his companions were killed, except for a group that was separated from him before the battle led by Farhan al-Sa'di and other groups, under the leadership of Khalil 'Issa Abu Ibrahim al-Kabir,[24] that did not go out with him.

In spite of the fact that al-Qassam's death was the spark that started the fire in Palestine, the leaders of the National Movement did not take part in the burial services for him. A week before he passed away, he had a meeting with the high commissioner, during which he presented him with the national demands. These included halting the transfer of land to Zionists, putting an end to migration, and building a national government.

The anniversary of the conquest of Jerusalem holds great significance in the history of Palestine and its ongoing struggle for self-determination. On December 9th, during the celebration of the anniversary of the conquest of Jerusalem, Hamdi al-Husseini, a national leader dedicated to defending the interests of the people, expressed his criticism of the unsuccessful methods employed by the Palestinian national movement. He emphasized that these methods had inadvertently contributed to the strengthening of colonialism. Al-Husseini further elaborated on how the leadership's efforts to establish its own centers of power were merely exploited by the colonists as a facade of patriotism. Consequently, colonial forces took advantage of the sacrifices made by Palestinians in the years 1920, 1921, 1929, and 1933, leading to a waste of valuable lives and resources.[25]

There was a paradigm shift in public consciousness during those three years of the 1920s, which culminated in the martyrdom of al-Qassam. During this time, youth and some members of the Istiqlal Party formed a vanguard, calling for the overthrow of old leadership. On the occasion of the anniversary of the British occupation of Jerusalem, which was held in Jaffa on December 9, 1935, the conferees declared that the issue of the Arabs in Palestine was a matter of struggle and conflict between the Arabs and the British and that any aggression from the British that appeared against bodies, parties, or individuals was considered to be a crime against the homeland.[26]

They voiced their outrage at the loss of universal hope while at the same time paying honor to the memory of al-Qassam and his colleagues and calling on the *ummah* to commemorate them. In addition to this, they paid tribute to the anticolonial movement that was active in Egypt, Syria, and the other Arab countries.[27] Jerusalem witnessed a similar meeting, in which the Qassam photos were raised, and the speakers denounced the leaders and their policy that contributed to the consolidation of colonialism. Hamdi al-Husseini "accused the leadership of seeking to strengthen its positions only among the colonists by demonstrating patriotism, and took advantage of the colonialism with the fine blood that was shed in the years 20, 21, 29, and 33 until it lost in vain."[28]

The paradigm shift is represented not only by the emergence of youth, the strong tone of criticism of traditional leaders and their policy, and the growing role of the Qassamid League for adopting armed resistance but also in the consideration of the British as the primary enemy. This was the case despite the expanding powers and potential of the Zionists, who had a small population in comparison to the Arab residents of Palestine, owned 15 percent of the agricultural land, and were comparable to their Arab counterparts in terms of economic power and political efficacy.[29] They considered British colonialism responsible for the Zionist penetration and sought to neutralize British influence. Such a shift put the country on the threshold of the revolution in the face of the colonial alliance and Zionism.

THE PARADIGM SHIFT

The paradigm shift coincided with public awareness and the role of youth and the trend toward adopting armed struggle as a substitute for traditional political mobility with developments in the Arab and international environment. During the period, the Levant witnessed a national movement extending from Iraq to Egypt, in which youth played a remarkable role. Italian and German fascism was on the rise, and Italy's occupation of Ethiopia was a further reflection of the colonial agenda and lack of regard for Arab national demands. The Fascist and Nazi propaganda and counterdemocratic propaganda also had their effects on Arabs, especially in the Levant. However, the Arab National Movement was characterized by two phenomena that caused limited benefit both from the emerging popular movement and from the international circumstance that provided the opportunity to benefit from the contradictions of the colonial powers.

On the one hand, the movement continued to operate at the national level, despite the fact that it was taking place all at once in different parts of the Levant; on the other hand, the level of coordination among the leadership was extremely minimal, if not nonexistent. As a result of their social standing and worldview, they did not have the revolutionary drive or the holistic vision, and as a result they agreed to settlements under the deceptive name "take and seek." As for the 1936 treaties between Egypt and Britain and between Syria and France, which, although officially ending the mandate, added legitimacy to the British and French military presence on Arab lands and obligated the two countries to bear the burden of that presence, they did not weaken the political, economic, and cultural constraints.[30] As a result, the ruling group had aborted the popular movement on the altar of independence without any substance. They had gained no independence outside a name, lacked membership in international fora, and had no diplomatic representation abroad.

The Palestinian case was no better than the general Arab situation. Despite the qualitative shift achieved in public awareness, the increasing role of youth and some elements with a national orientation, and the sharpening criticism of leadership policies, the leaders continued to bet on British equity. The leaders of the party did not hesitate to respond to the high commissioner's call on April 2, 1936, to send a delegation to London to discuss with the British government the Legislative Council's matter, which the Houses of Lords and Commons had rejected in solidarity with the Zionist Agency, claiming that acceptance of it threatened the fate of German and Polish Jews. It was decided that the delegation, which would represent all parties, would take place on May 4, 1936.[31]

Despite this, the atmosphere could be described as fraught with anxiety.[32] On the same day, April 15, 1936, a band of armed robbers crossed the road that led to Anabta and were apprehended by authorities, along with two cars that belonged to Zionist settlers. In addition to the death of the driver and the wounding of two passengers, several Arab passengers were also among those who were killed or injured. The following day, members of the Haganah killed two Arab workers who were working in one of the orange groves on the Jaffa Road. At the same time, a group of Jews gathered and attacked Arab vegetable shops as well as Arab workers in Tel Aviv. They set fire to a number of Arab homes and businesses in the nearby city of Tel Aviv at the same time that Arabs demonstrated in Jaffa and attacked some Jews there. Nine people were killed in total, including Jews and Arabs; forty people were injured; and forty homes, the majority of which were Arab homes, were destroyed.[33] These unplanned clashes paved the way for an unnecessarily violent armed struggle.[34]

The peak year for the immigration of Zionists was 1933, when the number of new arrivals averaged tens of thousands. Along with it came a corresponding increase in the Zionist movement's and its institutions' appetite for the control of Palestinian land. The feudal lords continued to work together with the Zionist movement, and the government of the mandate forced the Palestinian peasants to leave the lands that they had been cultivating. As was the case with the Arabs of al-Hawarithiya, once the feudal lords sold the property, the people were forcibly evicted from Marj ibn 'Amir in 1933. This was due to the fact that the al-Tayyan family, from Lebanon, had sold the land to the Zionist movement in 1929.[35] Likewise, the Arabs of Zubeidat were evacuated from their lands in the village of al-Hawarithiya, after their feudal owners sold them to the Zionist movement. The British police used force to remove the Zabidat Arabs from their lands, resulting in the killing of a farmer and the injuring of others. These two incidents stripped more than twenty-five hundred farmers of their only means of livelihood.[36]

In the cities, the Jews robbed the Arab of his place of work, as the Zionists seized control of the economies of several major cities, which led to the organization of many labor strikes against the policy of oppression, discrimination, and denial of livelihood. Some thirty labor strikes took place in a period of three years prior to 1933.[37]

All of this led the Arab Executive Committee, which was leading the Arab National Movement in Palestine, to hold a meeting on October 8, 1933. The meeting was attended by twenty-two members, in the presence of its chairman, Mr. Musa Kadhim al-Husseini, the mayor of Jerusalem, and the vice president, Ya'qub al-Faraj. After examining the Zionist immigration order and its dangers, all attendees spoke about the sale of lands to Jews, the poor economic situation of the Arabs because of the huge influx of Jews to Palestine, and the Jews taking the lands and jobs of the Arabs; the meeting decided to declare a general strike by land and sea throughout Palestine. This took place on Friday, October 13.[38] The Arab Executive Committee issued a statement:

> To demonstrate the discontent of the Palestinian Arab nation—which has worked since it plagued British colonialism to deliver its voice to the conscience of the civilised world—from the British government's tampering with the rights of the landowners, and defying their national emotions. And its disregard for their national entity, and their social and economic interests, by opening the gates of the country to Jewish immigration, and facilitating the transfer of Arab lands to the Jews, and their tyranny by direct rule, the Executive Committee decided to invite the large nation to a general strike, by land and sea, on Friday, October 13, 1933, and held a major demonstration in Jerusalem that day, that the demonstration begins one pm, from the door of the Haram al-Sharif, known door Alqtanin, to the Church of the Resurrection to the door of Hebron.[39]

The Palestinian people supported the decision of the Executive Committee to call for a strike, which quickly spread across the country. It was comprehensive and fulfilled its intended purpose by covering both land and sea. As a result of the fact that everybody had attended the demonstration for Greater Jerusalem on October 13, 1933, there were some places where smaller local demonstrations were started.[40] The demonstration began early in the morning and lasted throughout the day as the masses gathered at the Noble Sanctuary. British soldiers and police officers heavily populated the area, with a significant presence at the Hebron Gate and Jaffa Street, where substantial forces were stationed. These two locations were particularly densely populated with these forces.[41]

The Executive Committee met in the morning in the house of the Supreme Islamic Council and decided to change the course of the demonstration to start from the Gate al-Silsila instead of Gate al-Qattanin and walk through the old town to the new gate, instead of the Hebron Gate, to prevent a clash with British soldiers.[42] The demonstration started immediately after noon prayer and was led by President Musa Kadhim al-Husseini. All members of the Executive Committee, notables of the city, and delegations of the country participated, and the number of demonstrators reached more than thirty thousand men and women. More than five hundred women participated in the demonstration, amid applause and cheering and the singing of patriotic songs, especially the song "We are the soldiers of God, the youth of the country. We hate humiliation and refuse persecution. So raise flags and walk for jihad, as our enemies have gone too far in vanity."[43]

The general populace voiced their disapproval of Zionism, immigration, and brokers while also expressing their desire for freedom and autonomy. When the protest reached the Hebron Gate, its leaders decided to change its route so that it would go by the soldiers stationed at the gate rather than through the Old City. It continued running until it reached the new gate, where a sizable police force was waiting for it to arrive. At this point, the director of the police force in Jerusalem, Major William F. Wainwright, gave the crowd the order to disperse and warned them not to proceed to the Bab al-'Umud; if they did, he would use force to subdue them. When the public refused his request, he ordered his men to attack, so the police officers used their sticks and clubs to disperse the demonstrators. To defend themselves the public threw stones at the police. Despite the brutal assault, irrespective of age or gender, the demonstrators regathered and continued to march until they reached Bab al-'Umud. They were preceded by a significant police force, and clashes occurred again and in the same way. The women tried to enter the place to protest the police assault, but they were prevented from doing so by force, resulting in some of them being slightly injured. After that, the clashes continued for another hour, and then the crowds broke up.[44]

Following the demonstration, the members of the Executive Committee met in the house of President Kadhim al-Husseini. The chairman and members of the Office of the Youth Conference Committee participated in the meeting, and the following decisions were taken: To hold demonstrations in the cities of Palestine, the first of which was to be in Jaffa on Friday, October 27, 1933, where a public demonstration would be held with a comprehensive strike. The members of the committee and its chairman were to meet on Thursday, October 26, in the house of the Christian Islamic Association in Jaffa, and another meeting would be held at 10 a.m. on the day of the demonstration. The course of the demonstration would be decided by both the Christian Islamic Society and the Executive Committee of the Youth

Conference. Following the demonstration, the Executive Committee would hold a meeting in Jaffa to approve the demonstration to follow. They would be sending telegrams to the League of Nations, the British government, the Ministry of Colonies, and the government of Palestine, stating the purpose of the demonstrations and denouncing the actions of the police, especially toward women. They were to express appreciation to Arab women for the sincere patriotism and sacrifice they had shown, while also acknowledging the Palestinian people who had demonstrated and those who had been injured.[45] The meeting ended at 7 p.m., but not before the president and the members started chanting for a life of independence and freedom.

Jaffa was ready for the big event of Friday, October 27, 1933.[46] During the day and night of Thursday, the crowd had been arriving in the city in preparation for the demonstration that would be launched from the Great Mosque of Jaffa. The Arab Executive Committee, the Christian Islamic Society, and the Youth Conference Committee held two meetings, one in the afternoon and the other at 7 p.m. On Friday, the strike was comprehensive, by land and sea, and the streets were filled with soldiers and policemen; military patrols circled the city, guarding the entrances and exits that reach the Jewish neighborhoods and Tel Aviv. Likewise, the police were searching passersby and those coming to Jaffa, after placing barriers on all the entrances to the city. At 10:30 a.m., all the roads leading to the Islamic Christian Association were full of enthusiastic masses chanting for the homeland, freedom, and independence. The masses were overflowing with optimism and hope for a future that would be better if the current revolutionary situation continued.[47]

At about 11 a.m., a group of Jerusalem women arrived to take part in the demonstration, and slogans, trills, and national anthems were performed at a beautiful Palestinian wedding ceremony. Since the morning, the British had been annoyed, tense, and afraid of the force of the event, and they intended to suppress the crowd by force, to break their strength and prevent them from continuing their demonstrations.[48] Therefore, before the demonstration began, the British cavalry assaulted the march by members of the Executive Committee. After this clash, Mr. H. W. D. Polak, Assistant District officer, and 'Azmi Effendi Nashashibi, the district commissioner of Jaffa, came to the assembly house and met with Ya'qub Bey al-Ghusin, a member of the Executive Committee. After the meeting, the assistant governor ordered the withdrawal of the soldiers from the demonstration route.[49]

The demonstrators were very angry, so they ripped wood from the shelves of the stores and shops and attacked the soldiers and policemen, and the battle became a fight between them and the horsemen, with the demonstrators having the upper hand. Then orders were issued to fire live bullets. The killed and the wounded fell, and this situation lasted for at least an hour and a half. Also in Mansheya, the police confronted the demonstrators, shot and killed several of them, and wounded dozens.[50] On the same day, the total number of killed reached nearly 30, and more than 250 were wounded. President Musa Kadhim al-Husseini was badly injured and bruised as a result of being beaten with batons. He remained in bed until he died two weeks after the demonstration.[51]

The British government announced martial law in Jaffa and prohibited being outside the house from 6 p.m. until 5 a.m. On the next day, demonstrations spread over a number of Arab cities and villages in Palestine. In Acre, a strike was declared for another day, and in Nablus, demonstrations took place the next day, as well as in Jenin, which struck another day, and Nazareth struck in response to the Jaffa call, where people demonstrated against the police attacks. After it continued striking for another two days, the authorities in Haifa declared martial law, and the police increased their level of security out of fear for the Jewish population. Over the course of the next two days, demonstrations were held in Tulkarm. In Bisan, demonstrations and strikes took place for an additional day, as was the case in Majdal and Jerusalem, in which bloody incidents occurred. Thus the uprising moved to other areas, while Jaffa continued its mass strike for a whole week and suffered from police repression.[52]

As for Britain, it tried the members of the Executive Committee and imposed heavy fines on them. The British colonial secretary set up a committee headed by Sir William Morrison to investigate the facts, but he was forced to investigate only the direct causes of the events and not to address Jewish immigration or theft of lands or Jewish colonies and the Balfour Declaration. The committee published its report in February 1934, stating that the Arabs had directed their anger at Britain, and not the Jews, as happened in the demonstrations of 1921 and 1929.[53]

Despite the steadfastness of the people, the burdens they bore, and their insistence on continuing the strike and the revolution, the leadership ordered a halt to the strike without obtaining any serious guarantee to achieve any of the national demands. Thus, the strike stopped without the people reaping direct political fruits, although the great strike had demonstrated the resilience of the Arab people in Palestine, a great willingness to give and sacrifice, and a stubborn insistence not to compromise their legitimate national rights.[54] Five factors interacted in a dialectical form so that the long strike did not achieve direct policy goals.

First, despite the development of events and the escalation of colonial violence, the Supreme Arab Committee's shortcomings and impotence, which achieved solidarity but did not go beyond being a merely oppositional alliance, prevented it from achieving its target goals. Quarrels took place among its members, which affected its activity,[55] as Naji 'Alush described: "When the strike started, and the revolution started, the masses were at the forefront and leadership at the rear and despite the vitality and effectiveness of Haj Amin, the leadership was unable to catch up with the masses."[56]

Second, the lack of participation of employees and the majority of the Arab police in the strike and the refusal of a number of mayors and members of municipalities to participate allowed the mandate government to continue its work without a hindrance. It is not denied that the memo the employees presented to the high commissioner had some effect,[57] except that the strike would have been more practical and more effective if all Arab officials and policemen had responded to it. The fact that the Haifa municipality and the workers in its Arab port did not participate in the strike allowed work in the first port in the country to continue.[58]

Pressure from stakeholders, such as members of the Supreme Committee and the National Committees, as well as other individuals whose interests had been jeopardized by the protracted strike, was the third factor. They saw Arab monarchs and princes using their influence to strengthen the Supreme Arab Committee's capabilities of negotiating with Britain, while others saw Arab mediation as an honorable way out of the impasse they faced. The Supreme Arab Committee responded to the call of the kings of Saudi Arabia, Iraq, and Yemen, as well as the prince of Jordan, in order to put an end to the strike and the revolution, which were contingent on the cooperation of the British government. This was accomplished through the combined influence of both parties.[59] Before the beginning of the citrus harvesting season, an announcement came out stating that the strike and the revolution would be put on hold. This suggests that the owners of the cisterns, who were prominent members of society and political institutions, had some influence on the prompt, unfulfilled, or unconditional response to the official request made by the Arabs.

Fourth, the military and the police protected Jewish and government communications, such as cars and trains, and imposed deterrent penalties for attempts to disrupt them.[60] This ensured that work in Haifa Port and official departments could continue without interruption. In addition, the government used the most severe forms of violence to break the strike and put an end to the revolution. The Zionist settlement bloc was able to limit the effects of the Arab strike on its economic activities in the country thanks to foreign capital. This prevented the country's various economic activities from being paralyzed and made it easier for the Mandate Authority to escalate acts of repression against Arabs without causing economic paralysis, forcing it to make political concessions to the Arab National Movement in anticipation of the negative effects that would paralyze the country's economic life.

Fifth, the Levant was living in the stage of political settlements with the British and French colonialists, and therefore, despite the popular support it provided to the strike and the revolution, it did not rise to the level of forming the leverage necessary for the Palestinian National Movement. It made a qualitative achievement for an appropriate national reality impossible.

1936 ARAB REVOLUTION

The Palestinian Arab National Movement had moved on since the 1929 al-Buraq uprising toward riots and public resistance to Zionist activities.[61] This was the result of a controversial interaction between the steady increase in Zionist immigration and the Zionists' seizure of large areas of the most fertile lands in the coastal plain, particular eastern Galilee. The consequent expansion of the principle of "Hebrew land and Hebrew labor" caused increasing expulsion of Arab peasants from the seized land and thus unemployment and the displacement of increasing numbers of peasants. As viewed by Theodor Herzl and other Zionist political figures, usurpation of the land and expulsion of Arabs by force was necessary to support Zionism.[62] It would be necessary, he thought, to get the Arabs out of Palestine. "We shall try to spirit the penniless population across the border by procuring employment for it in the transit countries, while denying it any employment in our own country. . . . Both the process of expropriation and the removal of the poor must be carried out discreetly and circumspectly."[63] Added to this were the negative effects of the global recession, where the most vulnerable economies, including the Arab economies, suffered most. The industrialized countries had succeeded in transferring a large part of their crisis to the countries of the third world, as well as maintaining a continuous support for the economy of the Zionist settlement.[64]

The Buraq uprising also served as a catalyst for a heightened sense of Arab nationalism and Islamic solidarity throughout the Levant, the rest of the Arab world, and Morocco.[65] The growth of the National Movement in Egypt, Syria, and Iraq, as well as the treaties signed between those three countries and Britain and France, served as a lever for the aspirations and demands of Palestinian national and opposition elites. Everyone agreed that they should strive for independence and attempt to negotiate a treaty with Britain, as Britain had previously done with Iraq and Egypt.[66] It has already been pointed out that the strike that Syria witnessed at the beginning of 1936 was one of the most prominent motives of the leaders of the Istiqlal Party for calling them to strike after the events in Jaffa.[67]

The rising powers descended on the field in a show of force, announcing a strike and protests with anticolonial and anti-Zionist chants, in response to traditional leadership's ineffectiveness in the face of the growing colonial-Zionist challenge as a result of the interplay between the worsening economic and social-political crises. Male and female students were the backbone of the demonstrations, led by al-Qassam's spiritual heir, Sheikh Farhan al-Sa'di, and had started armed resistance work with the first days of the strike.[68] Demonstrations and actions by the armed resistance, which were initially limited, escalated markedly, with the acceleration of events and the violence of the police officers' response to the demonstrators.[69]

On May 5, 1936, several bombs were dropped near government departments and police stations. On the same day, the high commissioner, Arthur Wauchoupe, sent a report to the Ministry of Colonies, which included the observation that "all the inhabitants of villages and cities are united, although more than 660 men have been arrested, and shootings, bombings and sabotage of railways are continuing and intensifying."[70] In his report, Wauchoupe stated that there would be a weekly development of the situation and that there would continue to be ongoing demonstrations of opposition to the Mandate Authority.[71]

After May 15 passed without a response from the Mandate Authority to the National Committees Conference addressing the three national demands, large crowds and more violent police officers took to the streets. As with all national liberation movements, violence on the part of the power structure contributed to an increase in the level of violence among the masses. On May 18, a conference was held in the village of Abu Ghosh, west of Jerusalem on the Jaffa Road, attended by thousands of neighboring villages, who declared support for the strike, their intention not to pay taxes, and their solidarity with the armed revolution. On the same day, the Mandate Authority announced permission for forty-five hundred Jews to emigrate within six months and stated that British military reinforcements would be brought in from Egypt and Malta. Wauchoupe went on to escalate the crisis by opening the port of Tel Aviv on May 19 as a substitute for the port of Jaffa, which was suspended due to the strike.[72]

On May 23, the secretary of the Supreme Arab Committee, 'Awni 'Abdel Hadi, was arrested for his "organizational talents and competency," as stated by the high commissioner. Another sixty activists of the National Committees were arrested. Once the news spread, the masses poured into the streets, to be faced with bullets. Four people were killed and seven wounded. Also, on the same day, three fighters and a woman who was carrying water for them were wounded near the village of Bala'a in the Tulkarm district, and the farmers of the area were called to take up arms for resistance. On that day, the strike transformed into an armed revolution, which initially began in Samaria's brigade and then spread throughout the rest of Palestine.[73]

From the first days of the strike, and before the actions of the individual armed resistance turned into a comprehensive popular revolution, the Palestinian countryside nurtured the inexhaustible revolution of the revolutionaries that guarded Palestinians from the escalating repression of the

British police and Haganah. It was the villages that protected the revolutionaries, and there they would meet and rest, especially in the mountainous regions. The peasants would provide the rebels with shelter, food, and care for the wounded. The female peasants carried water and food to the revolutionaries, whom they regarded as their brothers and children, while the peasants in their fields were the eyes of the revolutionaries, monitoring the police and army movements and alerting them to impending danger. In many cases, the peasantry formed a security cordon protecting the rebels with a human shield. The revolutionaries always took off their field clothes and wore a long, loose-sleeved outer garment, distinctive of the peasant's garb, to disappear into the village setting.[74]

Even though the Qassam League played a significant role in the beginning of the uprising, the public revolt that occurred was more of a coincidence than a planned act of the uprising. The uprising was more of a chain reaction than a coordinated act. The rural areas that participated in the uprising did so of their own accord, and the peasants frequently organized themselves and joined the rebellion on their own initiative. It was extremely unusual for the leaders of a faction to ask groups of people to join the rebellion or provide weapons.[75] They were passionate about their cause and visionaries.[76] Ted Swedenburg describes the prevailing situation: "The rebellion was considered the responsibility of the whole family, it is the family who collects money to buy his rifle, and the family was the one who decided who among its youth would go to fight and who would stay at home."[77]

Most historical Zionist writings describe the revolution as mere unrest, acts of banditry, murder, and theft, and a return to what Chaim Weizmann called the barbarism of the desert, in which primitive people stood with the encouragement of unscrupulous politicians, fanatical clerics, and international fascism against a higher civilization that they neither wanted nor understood.[78] British historian John Marlowe says, "Although it was the political leaders of Arab Palestine who instigated the Arab revolution and directed it to some extent and absolutely exploited it, this revolution was in fact a peasant revolution that derives its enthusiasm, heroism, organisation, and persistence from internal sources that were not properly understood, and were not known to be true."[79]

David Hirst says the reality is that the revolution in its origin was largely natural. Its primary motive was from the largest and lowest sectors of the people, from the peasants who were the ones who suffered most from the Zionist invasion. The revolution was a popular war and a new stage in the Arab resistance, which had begun more than fifty years ago in the 1930s with local and improvised incidents. This new phase was the use of armed violence in a continuous, organized, and targeted manner, not only against the Jews but against the British who brought them. After their politicians sought for twenty years to herald change through constitutional approaches, their efforts were in vain, as the British were either indifferent or hostile, leading the people "to speak with guns instead of lips."[80]

This revolution was the result of a mysterious but very natural development, and when the neighboring Arab countries sent money, weapons, and volunteers, the Palestinian struggle for the first time acquired a real comprehensive Arab dimension with no end in sight.[81] David Hirst highlights the facts of the revolution, saying,

> Fawzi al-Qawuqaji, like many Arabs at the time, saw Hitler's emergence as an event that could benefit the Arabs in their struggle against Britain. However, the pro-Arab outlook and propaganda that was launched from Italy and Germany did not mean what was echoed by the Zionists and the sympathetic Westerners that the revolution is only an arm of global fascism. It may be true that the revolution received foreign support, but its source was pure Palestine, especially from those peasants who sent Britain after the expansion of the revolution the planes showered them with leaflets urging them to abandon violence and place their trust in the Royal Commission. These were their local leaders, the most famous of whom was 'Abd al-Rahim al-Haj Muhammad, who was described by those who chased him as a straight Palestinian patriot.[82]

The initial actions of the resistance were carried out by small groups, each consisting of anywhere from five to seven revolutionary fighters. The situation then worsened, and the number of participants increased to somewhere between sixty and seventy. The Qassamids played a pioneering role at the beginning, and many members of the group of martyrs assumed leadership responsibilities, worked to spread the revolution in various parts of Palestine, and interacted positively with the various national elements that joined the revolution. These interactions made it possible for many of the martyrs to occupy the first roles in a number of regions. Akram Zu'aitir provides a history of the most prominent Qassam leaders who assumed leadership responsibilities during the revolution, such as Khalil Muhammad 'Issa (known as Abu Ibrahim al-Kabir), al-Shaiekh 'Atiyyah Ahmad 'Awad, Yusuf Sa'id Abu Durrah, Twfiq Ibrahim (known as Abu Ibrahim al-Saghir), Muhammad Salih al-Hamad, Nayif al-Muslih, Muhammad Mahmud al-Safuri, Ahmad al-Tubih, and Sulaiman 'Abd al-Jabar.[83]

From the beginning, the events in Palestine resonated across the Arab world. The operations of the revolutionaries were in the headlines of the Arab newspapers, which praised the heroism of the revolutionaries, noting the inability of thousands of British soldiers, with their modern military equipment, to eliminate hundreds of revolutionaries. It has often been remarked by Arab newspapers that if the entire Arab people had revolted with thousands of fighters, no European power could have suppressed them.[84] The widespread demonstrations spread to most of the cities and villages of Syria, Jordan, and Iraq, and popular festivals and public meetings were held in the cities of Egypt, Sudan, Morocco, Algeria, Tunisia, and Libya, where enthusiastic speeches in support of the Palestinian revolution, condemning British policy and the Zionist movement, and declaring commitment to the Arabism of Palestine were delivered.[85]

In the beginning of June 1936, dozens of Syrians, Lebanese, and Jordanians joined the revolution. Among them were many of the most prominent leaders of the previous Syrian revolutions, and among them were thirty fighters from the Syrian and Lebanese Druze led by Muhammad Sa'ab. Arab leaders once held key positions of authority in the land of Palestine, and local officials respected them for the leadership they displayed during that time. Sheikh Muhammad al-Ashmar, who was one of the most famous figures of the Syrian revolution, took over the leadership of the Nablus triangle and Tulkarm, and he chose Tulkarm as the location of his command structure. The Syrian leader Sa'id al-'Ass assumed the leadership of the Jerusalem triangle (Jerusalem, Bethlehem, and Hebron), assisted by 'Abd al-Qadir al-Husseini.[86]

In early August, the revolutionaries had taken control of the center of the country, especially the regions in the Galilee, the triangle of Nablus, Jenin, Tulkarm, and the mountains of Jerusalem and Hebron. This occurred at the same time as one hundred Iraqi fighters entered Palestine via Jordan. The Bedouins of the Baysan region assisted these individuals in crossing the border into Palestine. In the last week of the same month, Fawzi al-Qawuqaji arrived from Iraq, accompanied by eighty Arab fighters.[87] Immediately upon his arrival, he served as the commander in chief of the revolution, as all factions declared their loyalty to him, in recognition of his military experience, militant past, and reputation as a prominent national fighter. On the day after his arrival, he issued a pamphlet in the name of the general Arab revolution in southern Syria, confirming the national dimension of the Palestine revolution. Al-Qawuqaji, his rise to the position of general leadership, and the discourse in the new media have all generated a significant amount of resonance across all factors in Palestine. This can be seen in both the political and social spheres. The support of al-Qawuqaji and his companions, the enthusiasm shown by the people in Damascus led by Sheikh Muhammed al-Ashmar, and the vigor of the youth of Jabal al-Arab led by Mahmud Abu Yahya caused the people to feel that their revolution was supported by Arabs and now possessed military leadership and administrative efficiency.[88]

Al-Qawuqaji and the Nablus triangle, which included Jenin and Tulkarm, assumed the center of his leadership and immediately began organizing the revolutionary action.[89] Establishing the legal framework for the revolution and creating a tool to control behavior and prevent chaos from spreading in areas controlled by rebels and no longer subject to the mandate, on September

2, he made the announcement that the Revolutionary Court would be established to ensure justice, order, and security, as well as the abolition of treason and espionage.[90] He was accompanied by the Damascene journalist Munir al-Rayes, who took the lead in formulating leadership statements and what can be considered the media responsibility of the revolution. Munir al-Rayes succeeded in fanning feelings and inflaming enthusiasm.[91]

In his early days, al-Qawuqaji was successful in achieving a memorable victory when he fought with limited forces against an army detachment that was backed by aircraft in the Battle of Bal'a on September 9. In this engagement, al-Qawuqaji was able to force three planes to land, and one of them was burned, while its commander was killed. One British soldier was killed, and three others were injured.[92] Both the Battle of Tarshihaa (Acco District) and the Battle of al-Ja'una (Safad District) took place on September 9. The victory was viewed as supportive, which strengthened the position of al-Qawuqaji and the revolution and pushed the youth to join the revolutionaries. Despite the fact that the revolutionaries suffered losses as a result of the heavy losses sustained by the British forces, the victory was viewed as supportive. These new developments presented a significant obstacle, not only for the Mandatory Authority but also for the Zionist movement.[93]

In order to meet the risky challenges that lay ahead, Britain reinforced its forces in Palestine by transferring the first division of the British army from Britain to the region. This was in addition to the forces that it had transferred from Egypt and Malta. On September 22, Gen. John Dill, who had previously been appointed as commander in chief and would go on to become chief of staff of the British army, oversaw the arrival of the last of his forces.[94] Thus, the British forces in Palestine reached twenty-five thousand soldiers. Journalists noted that Britain had not witnessed such a major military movement since the end of World War I. Along with approximately twenty-five thousand additional police officers, the army was reinforced with additional planes, light tanks, armored cars, mortars, and heavy machine guns. The majority of the police officers were British and Jewish. The unreliable Arab policemen were demoted, and they were not given any duties involving direct combat.[95]

During the period beginning on September 24 and ending on October 11, a number of engagements took place between revolutionaries and the British army. These engagements made extensive use of an army's worth of aircraft. 'Abd al-Qadir al-Husseini was wounded and captured along with a number of militants during the battle that took place on September 9 near the village of Beit Ummreen, which is located to the northwest of Nablus. This was the battle that received the most attention because it involved four British battalions and seven aircraft, a large number of Palestinian fighters were killed, and the leader Sa'id al-'Ass was also killed.[96]

Responding to the call of the Arab kings and the statement of the Supreme Arab Committee to end the strike and stop the revolution, al-Qawuqaji announced the cessation of operations on October 11, and he asked the fighters to return to their homes and preserve their weapons until they were called to struggle. Thus, the first stage of the revolution was halted, at a time when it was growing in strength due to the vast popular response that was demonstrated by the successive battles between the revolutionaries and the British forces.

Although al-Qawuqaji announced the cessation of operations, and all factions responded to this, the British army continued its operations and saw the announcement of the end of the revolution and the response of the Supreme Arab Committee to the call of the Arab kings as an indicator of the weak will of the committee and the leadership of the revolution. On the pretext that al-Qawuqaji had established a group gathering in the mountains of Nablus, in which the fighters trained at the hands of his accompanying Arab officers, the British army warned the revolutionaries to dissolve their formations within twelve days. Before the deadline, on October 22, the army resumed its operations, shutting down the crossing points on the Jordan River and drawing closer to Qawuqaji and his associates in the Jenin region. Because the army did not cease its operations, the Higher Arab Committee took action and issued a warning that it would restart the strike on October 26.[97] A compromise was struck with the authority, and as part of that agreement, it was decided that al-Qawuqaji and all of the Arab guests would vacate the premises on October 25. They entered Jordan, where Prince Talal and the people of Jordan welcomed them with a warm reception upon their arrival.[98] However, al-Qawuqaji and his companions, except for Sheikh al-Ashmar,[99] were forced to return to Iraq and the rest to Syria after Prince Abdullah prohibited them from staying in Jordan. Al-Qawuqaji stated that the political leadership saw his stay in Palestine as impeding negotiations and threatening efforts to resolve the issue. Furthermore, he and his forces were now at increased risk of extermination.[100]

Despite the short period that al-Qawuqaji and the limited number of other Arab militants stayed in Palestine, which did not exceed two months, it had a positive impact on the Arab people in Palestine.[101] It inspired the Palestinian revolutionaries, who returned to their cities and villages, feeling they had fought honorable battles; they kept their weapons while awaiting the results of Britain's promises to the Arab kings.[102]

However, accounts differ about the role that al-Qawuqaji was entrusted to play in the revolution. Muhammad 'Izzat Darwazah states that Haj Amin al-Husseini was the one who sought the support of the government of Yassin al-Hashemi in Iraq to support the revolution in al-Qawuqaji.[103] Others raise doubts about the real motives of al-Qawuqaji's campaign, especially when considering his entry with such a large force from Iraq into Palestine without any objection and the withdrawal of his forces from the country once the Arab rulers intervened to stop the revolution and strike. This reinforced the suspicion that the goal of the al-Qawuqaji campaign was to contain the revolution.[104]

BRITISH-ZIONIST REPRESSION

On April 19, 1936, and then again on February 6, 1936, the mandate government declared a state of emergency and increased the penalties that were mandated. The government regarded the strike as an illegal act and instituted a policy that stipulated the death penalty or life imprisonment for anyone who fired a weapon at the military or the police, threw a bomb, or engaged in any other revolutionary act. Examples of arbitrary judgments include a prison sentence of six years for a pistol, a sentence of twelve years for a bomb, a sentence of five years for twelve bullets, a sentence of two years for carrying a gun, a sentence of five years for possession of gunpowder, and a sentence of five years for attempting to purchase ammunition from soldiers. All of these sentences range from five to twelve years in length.[105]

Under the guise of preparing the Zionist settlers for self-defense, the mandate government facilitated the acquisition of firearms and ammunition by Zionists, armed Zionist settlements, and trained Zionist settlers. At the end of 1936, the Zionist community of Yishov contained three thousand individuals who were legally permitted to possess a firearm. The British were well aware of the fact that the Haganah gained legal status due to their guarding duties. The guardianship marked the beginning of a new era of collaboration with the governing bodies, which lasted for almost ten years. This cooperation was of great value because it came at a crucial time for Haganah, which was dealing with a challenging situation.[106]

Successive arrests of political leaders and activists, as well as anyone suspected of supporting the revolutionaries, were extensive until the number of detainees exceeded ten thousand, none of whom were brought to trial. The detention extended to both old and young people from different groups, including sheikhs and priests, so that a national unity was achieved in detention that had not been achieved outside it. In this way, the arbitrary policy of sanctions adopted by the army and the police achieved the exact opposite of its intended purpose. The arrest warrants were printed and ready and only needed the name of the detainee and the signature of the district commander. Also, house arrest was imposed on some leaders, as well as on Nabih al-'Azamih and Sami al-Sarraj, the Syrian fighters who were residing in Palestine.[107]

The strike continued, and the revolution increased in intensity, despite the expansion of arrests, the imposition of house arrest, and the imposition of curfews on cities and most villages at night.[108] In many cases, the curfew reached twenty-two hours a day.[109] Collective penalties were adopted, with fines imposed on the cities. Nablus was fined £5,000, and when the people refused to pay, the authority confiscated their belongings.[110] It was therefore not possible to sell them at the auction, and they were returned to their owners. A fine of £1,000 was imposed on Hebron but could not be collected, so the British mandate army decided to blow up some of the houses to undermine the disobedience of the people.[111] The matter ended in a settlement by mutual consent, so that the house of one of the vineyards was blown up. Of 250 villages that received fines, every village that refused to pay was subject to the expropriation of its lands, forcing farmers to pay.[112]

The villages faced the greatest part of the sanctions, as a result of the large role that the peasants played in embracing the revolution and supporting the revolutionaries.[113] The British military leaders sought to kill the revolution by tightening sanctions on the peasants.[114] On this, Percy Cox, a senior army officer, wrote,

> It is clear that the only way to recover the initiative from the rebels is to take measures against the villages from which the rebels originate. Then I began to cooperate with police inspectors in searching the villages. On the pretext, searches were taking place, on the pretext of searching for weapons on wanted persons. But the fact is that the procedures that the police were following, and that were going along the same lines as the old Turkish procedures, are severe disciplinary measures.[115]

The British army committed the crime of blowing up houses, and the blasting operations were carried out in the cities of Nablus, Hebron, Lydda, Safed, Majdal, Bethlehem, Khan Yunis, and Qalqilya.[116] In addition to this, many large houses and clan houses across thirty-five villages were destroyed when the bomb went off.[117] This inhumanity, which had been present throughout, reached its zenith on the morning of June 18, when the Mandate Authority blew up the old neighborhoods of Jaffa under the pretext of opening two new streets.[118] In reality, the blasting operation, which affected 220 homes, was a form of retaliation for the resistance shown by the old neighborhoods and for harboring the rebels. In the outskirts of Jaffa 850 wooden houses were also blown up for alleged violations of the law regulating cities, thus displacing more than six thousand people.[119] When one of the Arab citizens whose home was demolished filed a lawsuit against the high commissioner, Judge Michael MacDonald condemned the decision and accused the high commissioner of lying when he claimed that the demolition intended to beautify the city, even though it was for military purposes.[120] Some activists printed thousands of copies of this ruling and distributed it to the British soldiers, aiming to influence their anti-Arab stance.[121] However, this did not help, as the soldiers were implementing instructions of an administration very hostile to the Arabs, with a commitment to the official British position based on imposing Zionist settlement colonialism on Arab soil in Palestine.[122]

The entire apparatus of power in the country was thrown into disarray as a result of an internal crisis that broke out among the senior officials in England. The staff members were split up into two teams, each of which was led by one of the highest-ranking officials in the department. High Commissioner Arthur Wauchoupe was in charge of one of the teams, and Judge Michael MacDonald was in charge of the other team. It was decided that Wauchoupe was a senior Zionist delegate and that, during his tenure, more than two hundred thousand Jews immigrated to Palestine, while MacDonald was accused of representing those who hated the Zionist group (the Yashub) and sympathized with the Arabs.[123] Because of the liberal traditions that were prevalent in Britain at the time, the judicial system used by the Mandate Administration was autonomous and not under the authority of the high commissioner. Despite this, the chief justice and the judges have been accused of not adhering to the teachings outlined in the directives and of meting out punishments to Arabs that were less severe than those outlined in the directives.[124]

There was no major contradiction between the authority of the administration and the army and that of the judiciary during the mandate era, because the two authorities were subject to national legislative authority, while the British Colonial Ministry was committed to implementing the provisions of the mandatory instrument and establishing the Jewish national home. Consequently, the differentiation in the positions complained of did not go beyond being a functional division in the performance of the task to which both parties were obligated. The administration and the army, for example, were able to keep the revolution in check, and it was up to the judiciary to try to keep the Palestinian political leadership in a moderate position by presenting it with a moderate view. The proof of this became clear after William Ormsby Gore, considered a pro-Zionist British politician,[125] assumed the colonial office and forced Chief Judge Michael MacDonald to resign and retire.[126]

THE REPERCUSSIONS OF THE REVOLUTION ON THE ZIONIST SETTLEMENT BLOC

The Jewish Agency, taking advantage of the British forces' inability to suppress the revolution and protect settlements, demanded more measures to suppress Arab citizens and to emphasize the importance of strengthening the Zionist military capabilities to confront the dangers faced by settlers. A memorandum submitted by the agency's Executive Committee to the high commissioner at the beginning of the revolution accused the mandate government of complacency. This resulted in widespread unrest and criminal acts, while the Jews demonstrated a superior ability to deter ongoing neglect in the countryside and urban areas. This was repeated in more than one memo.[127]

The high commissioner held several meetings with David Ben-Gurion, the head of the Jewish Agency's Executive Committee, the agency's security official, and the commander of the Haganah to discuss the Haganah's involvement in repressing the revolution. These meetings took place despite the pressure of a series of escalating stress reactions. These meetings ended in giving the Haganah legal status, allowing Capt. Lord Charles Wingate to informally collaborate with the Haganah, expanding its base, establishing a Jewish police force for the Jewish colonies, providing the government with weapons, and paying the salaries of its associates.[128]

Wingate formed special teams for the night squads, from selected members of the Haganah, under the supervision of British officers, who took over the protection of the Iraqi oil pipeline to the port of Haifa.[129] The Haganah members found in Wingate, a British officer, an irregular Jewish adventurer and viewed him as a hero.[130] Wingate became one of the most prominent officers of Israel who inspired several students, including Yigal Allon and Moshe Dayan.[131] Isaac Sadia collaborated with him. Yigal Allon considered Sadia a military genius, one of the greatest leaders in Jewish history, and the teacher of most of the Jewish leaders.[132] On the repercussions of the revolution on the Haganah, Shabtai Teveth wrote, "In the aftermath of the events of 1936, the Haganah Organisation became a tool to help achieve the goals of Zionism, first and foremost, a tool for implementing the settlement policy in Palestine. And its role was highlighted in sponsoring the establishment of settlements (wall and tower) and organising illegal Jewish immigration. In other words, the Zionist Movement had become a fighting movement."[133]

The strike and the revolution had a severe impact on Jewish immigration. This is despite the fact that its incentives in 1936 were more than in the previous year, after the Nazi regime issued the first Nuremberg Laws in 1935. After the number of immigrants to Palestine reached 61,854 in 1935, it fell to 29,727, while the reverse immigration leaving Israel reached its highest number since the beginning of the settlements. To meet the challenges on this level, the Zionist movement raised the slogan "Immigration is ahead of peace" as a war cry.[134] It saw immigration not only as a way to save the Jews of Germany and central Europe but also as a tool to strengthen settlement in Palestine.

The high commissioner, senior British officials in Palestine, and the minister of colonies in London had asked the Zionist leaders to declare a moratorium on immigration for a period of six months to calm the Arabs and to provide an appropriate climate for the royal commission to investigate the facts in Palestine. Weizmann and Ben-Gurion refused to respond to the request, arguing that it touched the foundations of the mandate and the national homeland and contradicted the White Book of 1922 and Ramsey MacDonald's letter to Weizmann in 1931. In addition to the security dimension, the Zionists dealt with immigration in light of their prospects for the future. It would have been easy for them to reach a compromise if the research had been restricted to the present, but their aspiration was to achieve a Jewish majority that would change Palestine's Arab identity, and so they rejected all efforts to limit or stop immigration.[135]

The Jewish Agency also took advantage of the strike and the boycott to promote and develop the Zionist economy. The Jaffa port workers' strike led to increased efforts to build a dump dock in Tel Aviv. It was completed a month after the start of the Jaffa port workers' strike. To compensate for the decline in the Jewish market's supply of Arab vegetables, work was intensified on Zionist farms to secure needed vegetables and fruits. When the Arab workers refused to work in Jewish reservoirs, they were replaced by Jewish workers. In this way, thousands of Jewish workers found employment in Jewish projects and farms that Arab workers had boycotted. The Jewish Agency found this justification for requesting increased quotas for immigration.[136]

The Zionist leadership worked to generalize and deepen the feeling among the Zionist Yishuv assembly that destroying the Arab strike was a condition for the national survival of the Zionist settlement. Since it was impossible to compel the Arabs to stop the strike without achieving some of their demands, which contradicted the Zionist project and its strategic plan, it was necessary to work with all possible means to limit the negative effects of the Arab strike on the Zionist economy.[137] Many of the Zionist projects were damaged initially, but with external financial support, British protection, and intensifying efforts in various sectors, the Zionists succeeded not only in preventing the paralysis of their economy but also in developing it and achieving significant progress in applying the principle of "Hebrew work."[138]

Even though Shabtai Teveth says, based on British sources, that eight hundred Arabs were killed by the security forces on October 15, 1936,[139] the British colonial minister submitted a contradictory report to the House of Commons on the injuries up to October 15, 1936. It stated that up to October 19, 1936, there were 187 Arab-Muslims killed and 768 wounded; 10 Arab Christians dead and 55 wounded; 21 dead and 104 wounded from the army; 7 dead and 40 wounded British policemen; and 9 killed and 115 wounded Arab policemen.[140] Contradicting the two accounts is evidence that the minister of colonies submitted a false report to the House of Commons in an attempt to conceal the truth.[141] Muhammad 'Izzat Darwazah's *Lessons of*

Arab History: From Antiquity to Present Times claims there was an issue of authenticity in regard to the report's numbers in connection with injuries of British soldiers and makes a comparison between it and the statement issued by the Publications Department of the mandate government on September 30, including higher figures for the injuries of British officers and soldiers. In addition, concerning the major battles that took place after September 30, it was reported that three hospital ships docked in the port of Alexandria during the first week of October. A total of 410 injured English officers and soldiers were aboard these ships. The injuries of the Arabs were much greater than indicated in the report, as the rebels withdrew their dead and wounded from the field whenever possible.[142]

In the end, Ben-Gurion presented his analysis of the events to the core of the Mapai Party on April 16, 1936. He stated that there was no chance of reaching an agreement with the Arabs unless this agreement was imposed by a great Jewish force and this force used Britain and its warships. Based on his analysis of the events, Ben-Gurion came to this conclusion.[143] On another occasion, he said, "We are facing national contradictions, a national war is against us, and we now have no way to resist this war other than immigration and fortifying Jewish settlements in Palestine."[144]

In clarifying the Arab response to the Zionist challenge, Ben-Gurion said that the Arabs' resistance to the Zionist movement was the element that helped in establishing the Arab National Movement. He stated, "We ourselves, in the fact of our return to Palestine, and in the reality of our project, we created the movement of Arab patriotism. . . . This does not mean that such a movement would not have taken place without the Zionist Movement, but Zionism was the catalyst for it. As the whole world is boiling, and the Arabs are no less than other peoples."[145]

ARAB MONARCHS INTERVENED TO END
THE STRIKE AND REVOLUTION

The Zionist leadership has been trying to stop the growth of the unrest from the very beginning because they are concerned about the effect it will have on their colonial settlement project. This responsibility was given to an organization known as the Group of Five, which consisted of Judge Gad Frumkin, President of the Hebrew University, Judah L. Magnes, Pinhas Rottenberg, Moshe Smilansky, and Moshes Novumaysky. A plan to settle the conflict was presented to these individuals, and it called for the legalization of three hundred thousand Jewish immigrants over the course of the next ten years and the establishment of a Legislative Council in which Arabs and Jews would each hold an equal number of seats.[146] Both of these proposals were accepted. Through Judge Fromkin, the proposal was brought to the attention of Musa al-'Alami.[147] However, the talks ran into a snag when it came to the immigration obstacle, as the Arab side envisioned its suspension, even if temporarily for a period of six months. This was rejected by Moshe Sharett (Shartok) in his talks with Musa al-'Alami, as he saw the stopping of immigration as an act symbolizing peace, and no Jew could agree to this. Moshe Sharett (Shartok) was negotiating with Musa al-'Alami.[148] The British government and the administration of the mandate for Palestine made an effort to sway the position of the Arabs by announcing a moratorium on immigration for a period of six months and engaging in dialogue with the leaders of Zionism in an effort to convince them to agree with the moratorium. This was done in the hopes of swaying the position of the Arabs. In a letter that he wrote to Weizmann and Ben-Gurion, Colonial Minister Ormsby Gore informed them that his government was considering establishing a maximum immigration limit in order to calm the Arabs. Weizmann's response was that such a policy violated the foundations of both the mandate and the national homeland, as well as contradicted the interpretations provided in the White Book of 1922 and the clear statements contained in the letter written by the British prime minister on February 14, 1931.[149]

In the face of the revolution's escalation and the army's inability to suppress it, despite increasing punitive measures, and in anticipation of the revolution in Palestine turning into an Arab national revolution striking many British interests and threatening the present and future of the Zionist project, Britain found itself looking for a way out by mediating with Arab kings. Prince Abdullah attempted mediation twice but received no response from the committee. On August 26, 1936, the Iraqi minister of foreign affairs at the time, Nuri al-Sa'id, made a visit to the Arab Higher Committee and proposed that the strike and revolution be called off in exchange for the Iraqi government mediating with the British government to meet Arab demands.[150]

Nuri al-Sa'id was appointed by the British Foreign Office to serve as a mediator, although Zionist leaders perceived him as a representative of the administrative apparatus and a figure aligned with British colonial interests.[151] Within the Higher Arab Committee, discussions intensified regarding whether to accept Sa'id's mediation. The majority of committee members considered his role through the lens of his position as the foreign minister of Iraq, a country seen as a key supporter of Arab unity and liberation, akin to Russia's role for the Arabs. Additionally, King Ghazi was regarded by many committee members as a pivotal figure, comparable to Bismarck, responsible for unifying and liberating the Arab world.[152] In addition Nuri al-Sa'id represented a member state of the League of Nations and an ally of Britain, which had oil and nonoil interests. Consequently, the majority of the committee members estimated that the mediation of Nuri al-Sa'id was more beneficial than that of Prince Abdullah.[153]

Likewise, the admiration of the majority of the members of the Supreme Arab Committee was an indication that none of them took into account the restrictions imposed by the 1930 treaty on the independence of the will of the Iraqi government; nor was Nuri al-Sa'id the first Englishman in Iraq, if not in the Arab East. It is sufficient to note that when Nuri al-Sa'id came as an intermediary, a guest of the high commissioner came to his house. The fact that the image of Iraq and Nuri al-Sa'id's regime became outdated with the passage of time was sufficient on its own to make people realize the official role that Iraq played in the conflict. However, the fact that the majority of members of the Arab Higher Committee wanted to arrive at a decision kept them from allowing the dilemma to consume them as the revolution continued to make progress. They were able to overcome the influence that their perceptions of the past had on them, allowing them to read current events objectively at the time.[154]

On the first day of Nuri al-Sa'id's mediation, work began on the tenth amendment to the 1936 Emergency Law.[155] This was an amendment that doubled the punitive measures. It was as if the mandate government wanted to terrorize political prisoners, most of whom were among the most militant elements in favor of continuing the strike and the revolution until Britain formally committed to stopping immigration and pledging to seriously consider their national demands.[156]

The British promised Nuri al-Sa'id an opportunity for Iraq to have an influential role in the fate of the land of Israel and to appear before the Royal Committee to find a link between Arabs and Israel, hinting in their conversations with the Arab Higher Committee that its mediation would be in solidarity with Riyadh, Sana'a, and Muscat.[157] The following statement was also sent to the Arab Committee: "The Iraqi government, which feels a strong feeling of the National League that links the Iraqi people to the Arab people in Palestine, believes that it is imperative that they advance successful mediation between the Arab people and the British government, with which they have strong ties of friendship and alliance, in order to end the current situation in Palestine."[158]

In light of the foregoing, the Iraqi government believed that it was appropriate to present the great responsibilities that this mediation placed on itself toward Arabs in general and the Arabs of Palestine in particular.[159] The Iraqi government felt it should submit to the committee the following proposal: (1) The Arab Higher Committee should take all effective measures to end the current strike and unrest. (2) The Iraqi government should mediate with the British government to fulfil all the legitimate demands of the Arabs of Palestine. It would therefore use all possible means to achieve the mentioned requirements, whether these demands were caused by the movement present in Palestine or in relation to its general policy.[160]

Nuri al-Sa'id's initiative, while specified in the "first" item, was not specified in the "second," and because of that, the views of the committee members differed regarding what was offered by the Iraqi foreign minister. While the mufti and some members advocated for the strike, revolution, and civil disobedience to continue until the British government stopped all immigration and declared its willingness to accept the principles of preventing the sale of lands to Jews and the formation of a government accountable to an elected parliament, Raghib al-Nashashibi and the majority of the members considered accepting Nuri al-Sa'id's offer to end the strike and revolution.[161]

Nuri al-Sa'id visited the detainees, where he met 'Awni 'Abdel Hadi and Nabih al-'Azmih. He told them that his government was keen to find a way out of the crisis, preserving the country's dignity and guaranteeing its rights. They assured him that the condition of the detainees to stop the strike and the revolution was to stop the Jewish immigration first and that Britain announced its commitment to meet the demands of stopping the sale of land and establishing an elected parliamentary system. 'Awni 'Abdel Hadi was then temporarily removed from detention for medical treatment, where he met some members of the committee. When he returned, he told his "independent" comrades that the committee had two views: The first was to continue the present movement until the British government completely stopped Jewish immigration and declared its readiness to accept the principles of preventing the sale of lands to Jews and the formation of a national government responsible to an elected parliament. The second was to end the present situation if the government of Iraq guaranteed a complete cessation of Jewish immigration, that is, to stop all types of immigration, and pledged to fulfil the legitimate demands of the Arabs in preventing the sale of lands and the formation of a national government responsible to an elected parliament.

After deliberating with the rest of the detainees, most of them supported the position of the mufti and his companions and demanded that the revolution escalate to put pressure on Britain. They were left to the decision-making committee in light of its ability to develop the strike, with the participation of employees and other municipalities. In the event that this was not feasible, it would be preferable to end the situation through the mediation of the Arab kings, who would benefit from their relationship with the British government. This would be the case in the event that the governments of Iraq, Saudi Arabia, and Yemen declared that they bore the responsibility for a failure to fulfill the Palestinian demands. Commentary should be left on the charges and crimes that have arisen as a direct result of the ongoing strike and unrest, as well as on the freeing of those who had been arrested as a direct result of it, the elimination of any fines that had been imposed, and the granting of amnesty to prisoners who had been sentenced as a direct result of the revolution.[162]

After extensive deliberations among the members of the committee, and between them and Nuri al-Sa'id, the committee issued on the August 30, 1936, the following statement:

> The negotiations between the Supreme Arab Committee and His Excellency Nuri al-Sa'id Pasha, Iraq's Minister of Foreign Affairs, lasted a few days and covered all aspects of the Arab-Palestinian conflict. A complete understanding and approval of the mediation of the Iraqi government, their majesties and high-nesses, the Arab kings and their princes, resulted in complete relief and reassurance in an atmosphere of trust and frankness, and accordingly, the Minister will carry out the necessary official intelligence in this regard, and the Higher Arab Committee will present the matter to the nation through its National Committees in a general conference to obtain its opinion. And, God willing, the nation will continue its comprehensive strike with the same firmness and certainty with which it was known that the leadership was firmly rooted in faith until these negotiations achieve the desired result that preserves this valiant nation, gives it its rights, and helps it achieve its aspirations.[163]

The statement largely adopted the viewpoint of the mufti and the minority of members, which indicates the strength of the influence of the resistance movement in Palestine. This explains how the high commissioner did not hide his disappointment with the statement of the committee, which he called miserable.[164] Commenting on the mediation of Nuri al-Sa'id, in a letter to the Ministry of Colonies, he noted that Haj Amin did not abide by the truce but rather urged his followers and pushed them to continue the resistance until the Arab demands were fulfilled.[165] As for Raghib al-Nashashibi, who was known for his moderation and cooperation, he took the opposite path since following his participation in the committee.[166] He showed more enthusiasm and extremism than the mufti. The high commissioner believed that this was merely a ruse to implicate the mufti in situations that led to his disagreement with the mandate government.[167]

Despite Arthur Wauchoupe's disappointment with the statement of the Higher Arab Committee, Nuri al-Sa'id carried a copy of it signed by all members of the committee and went to London, where he met Chaim Weizmann, whom he had known since 1918. However, their talks were stalled because Weizmann refused to halt immigration, even if only temporarily. At that point, Nuri al-Sa'id thought that he would be more influential with the Jewish Agency in Palestine, so he returned to Jerusalem, where he met the representative of the agency, Moshe Sharett (Shartok), who in turn refused to stop immigration and reiterated that he considered this to be a surrender to violence.[168]

Although the British government had charged Nuri al-Sa'id with media-tion, the Jewish Agency had not opposed it, and the two sides were looking for Arab mediation that would put an end to the strike and revolution and their dangerous repercussions, the parties' commitment to establishing the Jewish national homeland made them reject Nuri al-Sa'id's mediation. Nor would express any serious commitment to any of the Arab demands. Ben-Gurion did not hide his fear of Nuri al-Sa'id's efforts, especially his offer to stop the strike and revolution in exchange for stopping Jewish immigration. He also did not hide his dissatisfaction with the role of British Foreign Office envoys with the Iraqi minister, despite the fact that he believed "migration is progressing towards peace."[169] Wauchoupe tried to deal with Nuri al-Sa'id through personal mediation and not in the name of his government. However, Nuri al-Sa'id explained to him that this would weaken mediation. The British government disagreed and sent a telegram to the high commissioner stating that they did not accept Nuri al-Sa'id's position as an official in mediation. This was done because the British government saw it as foreign government interference. Furthermore, the letter demanded that the Arabs provide uncon-ditional acceptance of the Royal Commission sent to investigate the facts in Palestine.[170]

Just as the Zionists were affected by the paralysis of economic life caused by the strike, the revolution, and civil disobedience, so were the major mer-chants and Arab landowners, including key participants in the Arab Higher Committee and the National Committees. From the start, they were pushing for the strike to be limited, and the citrus season soon doubled the pressure to accept Arab mediation. At the same time, after Britain and the Jewish Agency thwarted the mediation of Nuri al-Sa'id, the escalation proceeded, as martial law was announced at the end of September. The army was given command in an attempt to prevent the revolution from spreading, which would have ramifications for Britain's position in the Levant, especially as the cold war between Britain, Germany, and Italy deteriorated.[171]

The general political situation, especially British-Italian relations, and the restrictions imposed by the 1936 agreement with Egypt on the size of the British garrison there gave rise to new considerations that necessitated the presence of a large British force on land, near the Suez Canal. Because of this, the army initially tended to support calming the country by making con-cessions to the Arabs, mainly of course by closing the doors of immigration. However, after the mobilization of forces equal to the size of the entire parti-tion plan, the army changed its position. The army's position, which had been lured by untrained gangs due to civilian authority, was in jeopardy, and the army at that time became a temporary political ally of the Jewish Agency.[172] Nuri al-Sa'id's position was that the most important thing was to demonstrate Britain's strong grip on putting down the revolution and eliminating gangs and that, after that was accomplished, politicians could come in and do whatever they pleased.[173]

On September 2, the British Council of Ministers decided to keep the doors of immigration open and transferred authority to the army commander if necessary. This was done at the end of the same month. The mandate government exploited the fear of military rule and the escalation of its repression against the Arab people in Palestine. This increased the pressure of those demanding the acceptance of Arab mediation from the members of the Higher Arab Committee and the National Committees. As a result of the pressure brought on by the possibility of a military escalation, some Arab capitals responded to the British intervention by issuing statements urging the strikers and protesters to stop their actions. On October 8, 1936, King 'Abd al-'Aziz communicated with the leader of the Higher Arab Committee through the medium of a telegram. It stated, "We have suffered a lot from the situation prevailing in Palestine, so we, in agreement with our brothers the Arab kings and Prince 'Abdullah, invite you to immortalisation to avoid bloodshed, counting on the goodwill of our friend, the British government, and her stated desire to do justice. Rest assured that we will continue to strive for your help."[174]

A similar appeal was issued from both King Ghazi of Iraq, and Prince 'Abdullah of Jordan. The fact that the telegram of the king of Saudi Arabia, the appeal of the king of Iraq, and the letter of the prince of Jordan all have similar formulation lends credence to the theory that they were all written by the same person or people. They unanimously supported the notion that one should rely on "the goodwill of the British government" rather than on a clearly defined agreement with the British government. They failed to make any mention of the Palestinian demand to put an end to immigration and the sale of land or the establishment of a government accountable to an elected parliament.

It is noted that the intervention of the two kings and the prince came without any of them obtaining a British commitment to respond to any of the demands of the Palestinian National Movement, even though Britain was in urgent need of Arab intervention because of the embarrassment of its position internationally and in Palestine. Those with a firm grasp of the realities of the global community found it relatively simple to make a profit off the internal contradictions of colonial states. In addition, the capabilities that were readily available from the Arab world were not taken into account. In particular, the Arab people of Palestine and the surrounding areas, despite having a very small number of revolutionaries, were able to benefit from the prestige of the British Empire's army and enjoy its benefits. In addition to the British mandate to mediate, the revolution in Palestine and its repercussions across Arabia constituted a major contradiction to the fragmentation of the ruling regimes. This contradiction led to the calls of the kings and the prince on behalf of the British to contain the revolution. This intervention would not have been accepted if it had not provided the Arab Higher Committee with the appropriate opportunity to get out of what it was suffering due to its class nature and its lack of unity in the face of the colonial alliance and Zionism.

As a consequence of this, the telegram as well as the two appeals received a warm reception from the Supreme Arab Committee. On the morning of November 11, 1936, the committee issued a statement to this effect, which it then sent to the people. The statement included the following information:

> The Supreme Arab Committee decided unanimously, after consulting the delegates of the National Committees and obtaining their approval by consensus, to fulfil the call of their Majesties the Kings of the Arabs and His Highness the Prince with the statement published above. And to invite the honourable Arab nation in Palestine to calm down and end the strike and unrest, beginning on the morning of the blessed Monday on Rajab 26 in 1355 according to October 12 in 1936.[175]

The acceptance of mediation without any guarantees other than reliance on the good-will of the British government and the lack of a statement by the Arab Higher Committee to emphasize the national demands indicate the primacy of the self-interests of the elites who were supposed to champion the national interest. Despite the primacy of their role in ending the revolution, they were not solely responsible for the historical abortion of the Palestinian National Movement. The Palestinian leadership, especially its top people, didn't make the best use of the resources they had. Their inefficiency and mistakes had negative effects that can't be denied. For example, by focusing on Arab leadership, which sometimes leaned toward colonialism and sometimes toward Arab unity, they didn't have a clear and unified position.

The Arab Workers' Association expressed the sentiments of the Palestinian masses in a statement issued on December 12, 1936, averring that responding to the call to end the strike did not imply submission to mighty power and unjust tyranny or acceptance of brutal colonialism in the face of the Judaization of the country. It did not indicate that they preferred to end the strike and raise the flag of peace for fear of their lives, property, and money. The statement addressed the workers, saying,

> Today, we are offering the British government an opportunity to rectify its misguided policies that have resulted in repeated revolutions and widespread unrest. These policies have turned our land into a continuous cycle of turmoil and suffering. We are granting them another chance to acknowledge our legitimate rights and aspirations for a free and independent life. We expect them to show appreciation for our desires and work towards eradicating the remnants of the past and its detrimental effects. . . . And the government, after having

found our return and found it unbroken, will make sure that making the country a battlefield does not restore stability and peace to it, but one thing that can do that is that we obtain our full rights and recognise the impossibility of judaising the country. They called the workers to be vigilant, sacrifice and patience. And to always mention that they are responsible for saving Palestine and keeping it Arab forever, and that the righteous martyrs did not present themselves on the altar of the holy homeland except to pay the price of Palestine's independence and as a token of its salvation from the grip of colonialism and the restrictions of the offender Balfour Declaration.[176]

The contrast between the statement of the Arab Workers' Association and the statement of the Higher Arab Committee is significant; both were indications of the reality of the day after the strike was stopped. The workers, in their statement, expressed the feeling of confidence that the strike and revolt gave to the Arab people in Palestine after learning they had confronted the greatest state of their time, forcing the Zionist movement supported by the various colonial powers to mediate with the Arab kings. The workers' statement demonstrated the willingness of the Palestinian people to resist and withstand, while at the same time revealing the deficiencies of the political and social elites and their appalling failure to advocate for the will of the people. It is true that the cessation of the strike and the first stage of the revolution that accompanied it came in response to the call of the two kings and the prince, but that response was only an expression of the palaces and the inability of the Palestinian leadership to make the shift that was required to confront the escalation of British repression. In other words, the palaces couldn't make the change that was needed to deal with the increase in British repression.[177]

The cessation of the strike and the revolution led to the easing of military measures. It was announced by the chief executive officer that the inspection campaigns would be discontinued, that they would be less strict with drivers and car owners, that the curfew hours would be reduced, and that detainees would begin to be released.[178] Following the departure of the Royal Commission from London on May 11, 1936, there was a brief period of calm throughout the country before its arrival in the country. The following day, Colonial Secretary Ramsey Gore stated that the British government had not mandated Arab kings or other individuals to intervene to stop the strike and that some of them had called on their own people to remain silent and did not oppose the British government.[179] This was the British answer to the dependence of the Arab kings on the good-will of their friend, the British government, and its stated desire to achieve justice. As for the Jewish Agency, Ben-Gurion was reported to have said at the center of the Mapai Party, "We may succeed in expelling the interference of the Arab kings, just as we have previously succeeded in driving out Satan with the image of Nuri Pasha."[180]

It should be noted that neither the government of Egypt, the most populous Arab state with political weight and a historical role, nor the Syrian national leaders, with historical ties to the Palestinian leadership, had a role in advising or appealing to end the strike and stop the revolution. The British government was not losing influence in both Cairo and Damascus at the time. Despite this, Britain chose not to involve Egypt, with all of its historical weight and national presence, in a conflict that was initially intended to find a foreign human separation that separates Arab Asia from Arab Arabs and constitutes a weakening of Egypt's national effectiveness. The original goal of the conflict was to find a foreign human barrier that would separate Arab Asia from Arab Arabs. Since the 1930s, Egypt had begun to witness Arab national awareness and elite and public interest in the Arab-Zionist conflict due to the impact of what was happening in the land of Palestine. This led the colonial-Zionist alliance to exclude Egypt.

At the same time, Syria had, since the beginning of the revolution, shaped the strategy of the Palestine revolution. Moreover, the success of the Syrian strike forced France to agree to enter into negotiations that ended in the 1936 agreement.[181] A similar agreement with Britain was the subject of the Palestinian National Movement's ambition. The great Palestine strike started following the example of the Syrian strike.[182] This led Britain to exclude Syria from its maneuvering with the Palestinians. Consequently, the British endeavor was limited to those Arab capitals that the colonial-Zionist decision makers did not regard as a threat to their agenda.[183]

The British government was also keen on preventing Arab leaders known for nationalist positions from having a role in the course of affairs. The Ministry of Colonies refused to grant entry visas to Palestine to Shukri al-Quwatli, Rashid 'Ali al-Kilani, and Yassin al-Hashimi.[184] Nor did the high commissioner give a visa to Sa'id Thabit, fearing that he would have to give the other three the required visas. However, Nuri al-Sa'id was given a visa and allowed to stay for a few days in Jerusalem to make contact with leaders of the Palestinian National Movement and opposition leaders.[185]

THE ROYAL COMMISSION AND THE
PARTITION PLAN DECISION OF 1937

The Royal Committee, which was led by Lord Peel, the former prime minister of Britain, embarked on a trip to Palestine on November 5, 1936. The British government, which was in charge of the committee, had the objective of giving the Arabs the impression that the commission was impartial.[186] However, the disclosure of the British documents in 1966 clearly showed that the lord and the members of the committee spent about two months in

London before heading to Palestine in intensive and secret meetings with senior Zionist leaders and British experts who supported Zionism.[187] They met Chaim Weizmann, Vladimir Jabotinsky, David Lloyd George, and James Malcolm. Nahum Goldmann states that Professor Reginald Coupland, the most intellectually distinguished member of the committee, expressed his conviction that partition was the best solution to the Palestinian problem.[188]

On August 17, 1936, nine days before Nuri al-Sa'id went to Jerusalem, Malcolm sent a lengthy letter to Lord Peel explaining his position on Zionism, the Jewish national homeland, and the importance of Jewish immigration to Transjordan. The letter was deeply contemptuous of the Arabs and hostile to their demands and the claim that their civil and political rights were protected under the mandate.[189] He did not hesitate to say, "When the Jews become the majority in Palestine, this should not lead to any national catastrophe for the Arabs, because the wealthy of them who still reside there will sell their possessions with pleasure and leave, while middle-class children can find work. But if it is an Arab who does not like civilized living conditions, he can either migrate or simply return to the neighboring Arab countries."[190]

Thus, the Royal Commission, described as neutral, had traveled to Palestine after it had fully conceived the British-Zionist view in its most extreme form. On the day the Royal Commission left London, the minister of colonies stated in the House of Commons that the reasons for halting immigration while the Royal Commission conducted its inquiry were not economically justified. This was done so that the Arabs would have to face the truth and stop believing their own lies.[191] He issued a decision not to stop immigration in addition to issuing new certificates for the immigration of eighteen hundred Jewish workers.[192]

The Supreme Arab Committee saw in the minister's statement a contradiction of the assertions of Nuri al-Sa'id that immigration would be stopped, if only temporarily. Despite the shock, the Arab Committee faced a difficult situation, as the views of its members differed regarding the statement and the decision of the minister of colonies. After a futile interview with the high commissioner, who adopted the minister's position, the Supreme Arab Committee issued a strongly worded statement of condemnation declaring its boycott of the British committee and calling on the people to also boycott it. The decision to boycott was accepted by various Arab bodies, figures, and newspapers, while some called for a strike on the day the Royal Commission arrived. When the high commissioner held a reception in its honor, only two Arab employees attended the ceremony. As a result, the Peel Commission began its work by interviewing British officials and Zionist leaders in hostile Arab environments.[193]

While the boycott decision shocked the high commissioner, the Peel Commission, and the British government, it also revealed the weaknesses of the Palestinian National Movement and the lack of Arab support. In Palestine, the National Committees expressed a favorable stance toward the boycott, while the Defense Party expressed its criticism of extremism and questioned the viability of the boycott. The *Palestine* newspaper, which had become a spokesperson for the Defense Party, criticized the boycott decision.[194] Meanwhile, Hassan Sidqi al-Dajani, one of the leaders of the Defense Party, announced his intention to meet the Peel Commission, in violation of the boycott decision.[195]

Prince 'Abdullah and King 'Abd al-'Aziz put a lot of pressure on the Supreme Arab Committee. The pressure came in the form of telegrams from the two monarchs demanding that the committee meet with the Royal Committee, present the Arab point of view, and accept what was offered. The official Arab pressure demanding to meet the Royal Commission, as well as the feeling of its members that the national tide of pressure had ebbed after the strike ended, meant that the revolution had stopped.[196]

The Supreme Arab Committee made the decision to dispatch 'Awni 'Abdel Hadi, Muhammad 'Izzat Darwazah, Mu'in al-Madi, and Sheikh Kamel al-Qassab to Baghdad and Riyadh. Their mission was to serve as mediators and engage in negotiations with the Iraqi and Saudi kings. The delegation did not succeed in dissuading the two royals, who insisted on the necessity of meeting the Peel Commission, keeping pace with the British, and not embarrassing and angering them. This is despite the fact that they had no reliable British promises, just a reliance on British traditions. To save the face of the delegation, it was decided that the two monarchs would write to the Higher Arab Committee explaining their position.[197] Naji 'Alush states that the opinion of the Syrian government was not contrary to the views of the rulers of Amman, Riyadh, and Baghdad, and they too advised meeting the Royal Committee.[198]

The Saudi king's letter of Shawwal 18, 1355 (January 1, 1937), stated, "Given the confidence we have in the goodwill of the British government in fairing the Arabs, we have seen that the interest requires contacting the Royal Commission and giving it to your just demands because that guarantees your rights and is called to help your friends in good defence of you."[199]

The letter sent by King Ghazi dated 20 Shawwal 1355 (January 3, 1937) contained similar content to the letter from King 'Abd al-'Aziz. In the compatibility of the two letters, it is assumed that the two kings, although they differed in origin, culture, and consciousness, had a single position regarding the Arab-Zionist conflict. Also, the two letters indicate that the two kings dealt with the people of Palestine as friends, which does not assume an ideological commitment to what was happening in Palestine. However, King Ghazi, who was considered a leader of the wider traditional trend, did not express any national feelings regarding the issue that threatened the core of the Arab world. In a similar vein, King 'Abd al-'Aziz, who led the Wahhabi group, did not reflect an Islamic attitude toward the threats that were made against al-Quds/Jerusalem (the first of the two *Kiblah*/direction to which Muslims turn in prayers), the third of the Two Holy Mosques, and the land of Isra' and Mi'raj (the night of Prophet Muhammed's ascension to the seven heavens). It can be said that neither of these kings displayed an Islamic attitude toward the threats that were directed at al-Quds in particular and at Palestine in general.

The Higher Arab Committee issued the following statement on June 1, 1937, as a result of a set of phenomena in the composition of the committee and its class nature, the departure of the Defense Party from its consensus in response to the invitation of the two kings, and the pressure from advocates of realism:

> The Supreme Arab Committee held its presentations in the presence of the delegation that had returned from its trip to Baghdad and Riyadh, and after hearing its statements, I read the books of His Majesties the King of Iraq and the King of the Kingdom of Saudi Arabia, the two men who carried the delegation and whose texts were published above, and they could not help but respond to the supreme request, so they decided to contact the Royal Committee and extend the Arab I Because of the interest, good harmony, and avoidance of confusion and repetition, the Higher Arab Committee will contact the Royal Committee on behalf of the Arab people and extend the case, and it requests that all who have information or data that inform the case send it in writing to the committee to see its opinion on it, and that no one submit a unilateral testimony without the approval of the Arab Committee. God is the guardian of success.[200]

At a time when the Supreme Arab Committee was dedicated to the decision to boycott, the Royal Committee continued its work without paying any attention to the boycott that was being carried out by the Arabs.[201] During the first three weeks, it heard what the heads of government departments had to say about different Palestinian issues.[202] The governor of the Galilee Brigade, Lewis Yelland Andrews, was the most enthusiastic in defending the Zionist view, claiming that the Zionist settlement had no negative impact on the Arab peasants,[203] whereas the Zionists were carrying out a wide publicity campaign whose content included their right to establish a kingdom in their historic homeland. After the Peel Commission heard the heads of departments, it began to hear the testimonies of the Zionist leaders. Moshe Sharett (Shartok), representative of the Jewish Agency, stated that the agency could not help the government in preventing immigration, which it called illegal, because all immigration was legal in the eyes of the agency.[204] The leader of the "Correctors," Jabotinsky, made the issue of security his primary concern. He asserted that the Zionists had the ability to defend themselves and did not need the assistance of the British army, which had dispatched twenty-three Palestine brigades at the time, which was roughly equivalent to one-sixth of the entire British army.[205] He also demanded that eastern Jordan be considered a complement of Palestine and stated that the Zionists did not accept the division of Palestine or the equality of the two peoples. He was not interested in the consent of the Arabs and did not see the necessity of persuading them because they would give in to the status quo. Addressing the committee, he added, "Tell the Arabs frankly, there must be a Jewish state in which you will be a minority."[206]

Weizmann began his speech by talking about the suffering of Jews in central Europe and the danger that threatened them; he said that the Jews only had Palestine, while the Arabs had vast countries. Furthermore, every Jewish man, woman, and child was ready to fight for survival in the land of Israel, and there was nobody stronger than someone fighting with his back to the wall. He claimed that the purpose of the Balfour Declaration was to revive the land of Judah and return it to the Jews, so that it was Jewish just as England was English. He stressed that the Jews would not accept minority status and would fight until the last and that the most important difficulties they faced were the growth of Arab nationalism and the exit of the Arabs from the war, because the Arabs viewed Palestine as an Arab country and regarded Jews as invaders and aggressors.[207]

Ben-Gurion's testimony was the strongest:

> The Torah and not the Balfour Declaration and the Mandate Instrument gave us the right to the national homeland, which is a goal in itself. We come to the country because this is our right, whether it is beneficial to others or not useful. . . . If The concept of the national homeland is much broader than the state, the state's men can close its doors to new immigrants. But Britain and all the peoples of the world have recognised the right of all people to enter this homeland. And as long as the world is a forced Jew or wants to immigrate to the Land of Israel, and it has a place for it Even the Jews of the Land of Israel cannot prevent him from entering the country.[208]

The Jewish National Council also submitted a memorandum to the Peel Commission, which included the announcement of standing with the Jewish Agency on all matters relating to political issues. It stressed the security problem and stated that the settlement group Al-Yashov was attacked not only by the Palestinian Arab revolutionaries but also by regular forces brought in from neighboring countries, especially from Syria and Iraq. It demanded the expansion of the country's public security forces, its radical reorganization, and special attention to arming what it called defense units in the Jewish population centers under the supervision of the government.[209]

Zionist parties and figures had been active in holding conferences and issuing statements that disclosed the reality of the Zionist position. As a means of providing a response, Theodor Herzl penned an article in which he stated that granting political rights to Arabs would be in direct opposition to the Zionist principle. At its conference, the Mizrahi Party made the demand that restrictions on immigration should not be imposed and that political rights should only be granted to Jews living on the banks of the Jordan River. Concerning the Reformist Party, its demands included the simultaneous formation of a Jewish army and the establishment of a Jewish kingdom on both sides of the Jordan River.[210]

Ben-Gurion, the "leftist," did not differ from right-wing Jabotinsky in the explicit adoption of racist concepts. Both denied the legitimacy of the right of the Arab people of Palestine to their historical homeland and did not hesitate to announce that the Zionist settler colonial grouping had exclusive rights to Palestine. And while Ben-Gurion did not hesitate to state that he did not care whether Jewish immigration was beneficial to non-Jews or not useful in the sense that he was not interested in causing harm to the legitimate owners of the land,[211] we find Jabotinsky refusing to equate the Arab people with the Zionist community and being indifferent to the Arabs' refusal to prejudice their rights, and he did not see the need to convince them of anything.[212] As for Chaim Weizmann, he claimed that the purpose of the Balfour Declaration was to displace the Palestinian Arabs from their homes for Palestine to be the land of Judea for Judaism as England was for the English.[213] The testimony of the three leaders did not recognize any legitimate right of the Arab people in Palestine.[214]

The Arab leaders who decided to meet the Peel Commission did not prepare their testimonies sufficiently, as some of them came at short notice. This was due not only to the limited time for them to prepare but also because the two months that passed between the arrival of the committee in Palestine and the decision to appear before it were used to debate whether or not to attend. In spite of the deficiencies in the Arab leadership and its underdeveloped political performance, they met with the committee with seventeen Arab political and trade union figures testifying, most notably Mufti Haj Amin al-Husseini, Bishop Gregory Hajjar, 'Awni 'Abdel Hadi, Muhammad 'Izzat Darwazah, Dr. Hussein Fakhri al-Khaldi, and George Antonius.[215] Due to the importance of what took place between the mufti and the chairman of the committee, Lord Peel, the following section from the dialogue has been highlighted in many studies concerning the performance of the Palestinian leadership:

Lord Bell: Your Eminence is asking you to establish a national government in the country, so what do you do with the 400,000 Jews here?

Mufti: This is not the first time that the Jews have been in the protection of an Arab country, as the Arab countries were the most merciful in the world to them.

History always tells that the Jews did not rest in all ages except under Arab rule, and the East was always a refuge for Jews fleeing European pressure.

Lord Peel: You said that the number of Jews began to increase greatly because the Arabs were, at the time of occupation, about ninety percent, and now they are about seventy percent of the population.

Mufti: Yes.

Lord Peel: However, if you made a treaty with the British, would you be Arabs ready to keep Jews in the country?

Mufti: This is the matter of the government that will be formed at that time, whose principle will be justice and consideration of the country's interests and benefits above all.

Lord Peel: Do you think that the Jews accept this statement without having anything fixed because such a statement does not convince them.

Mufti: Jews in all Arab countries today enjoy their rights and freedom.

Lord Peel: I think I can say what the Jews say about this.[216]

It is clear from this previous text that the mufti did not go beyond the historical truth and the facts of the reality in the Arab environment. In addition, he affirmed the commitment of any future Arab government to the rules of justice and consideration of the country's interest, without committing himself and the National Movement to what the colonial-Zionist alliance might exploit. In the text, there is no suspicion of racism; yet it was the object of Lord Peel's condemnation, as evidenced by the last sentence. On the other hand, there are no historical sources that mention the meetings of the Royal Commission with the Zionist leaders or any reservation by the head of the committee or one of its members to the blatant racist statements issued by Jabotinsky, Ben-Gurion, and Weizmann, among others. Also, there is no evidence that a member of the investigation committee drew the attention of any of the Zionist leaders that denying the Arabs' legitimate right to their historical homeland contradicted the right of internationally recognized self-determination, which the League of Nations adopted when issuing the instrument of the mandate.

Lord Peel's denunciation of the grand mufti's testimony, whose passion and silence, as well as that of members of his committee, did not approve of the Zionist leaders' racist attitudes, showed his and his committee's commitment to facilitating the Zionist settlement project.[217] Whereas the Zionist leaders' consensus was to deny all the legitimate rights of the Arab people in Palestine, the main factor in the mufti's concern was not to commit himself and the National Movement to a position that could be exploited by the colonial-Zionist alliance. Nevertheless, the mufti's initial position was—and still is—a subject of criticism from those who claim that by not giving him firm guarantees to keep Jews under the next Arab state, he caused the Peel Commission's recommendation to divide Palestine. The authors of this claim drop from their account Britain's commitment to establishing the Zionist project and that the purpose of the committees that it was sending was only to accommodate the resistance of the Arabs whenever the Arab National Movement constituted a threat to the project, which is at the heart of the colonial strategy of the region.

In addition, the critics completely ignored the testimony of 'Awni 'Abdel Hadi, the secretary of the Higher Arab Committee and its political spokesman. Even though he had been against the concept of a national homeland as well as the continuation of immigration, he testified in front of the committee and announced that Jews who had previously entered the country would not be expelled, even though he was against both of those ideas.[218] He also explained that the Arab peasant in the Ottoman era was better off, as foreigners did not have the right to own farmland, and Jews had not been permitted to do so except in recent years. When he was told that Sultan Abdulhamid had vast areas, he replied that the sultan had not expelled one farmer from his land, contrary to what happened when the Zionists seized the land, causing the unemployment of thousands of farmers. In response to the president's question about not migrating to the Arab countries, where there were many fields to work, he answered that the Arab, like every human being, is tied to the land on which he was born, and he prefers to die on it rather than forcibly migrate from it.[219] He added, "Anyone who thinks that the Arabs are monsters, or who have moved their tents from one place to another, has made a great mistake. The Arabs believe that they have their ancient civilisation, and they carry the strongest national feeling carried by the finest people of the world."[220]

He also made clear that peace in Palestine was a matter of justice, that hostility against the Jews was caused by Zionism, and that Arabism and Zionism were incompatible. In response to the statement of the committee member Sir Laurie Hammond that Britain pledged to fifty-three countries to support the Jewish national home, he replied, "It is an invalid commitment." The people of Palestine were not consulted when the mandate was imposed on them. He rejected the mandate, and the alternative, in his view, was the independence of Palestine and the conclusion of a treaty with Britain that guaranteed the interests of all.[221]

In his testimony, Muhammad 'Izzat Darwazah stated that during the Ottoman era the Arabs enjoyed their full rights and that their clash with the Turks was motivated by their ambition for independence. Palestinian Arabs joined the Arab army, which allied itself with the British, in response to the pamphlets signed by King Hussein that were received by British aircrafts. He also commented on the testimony of Chaim Weizmann regarding King Faisal, explaining that the General Syrian Congress, which represented all parts of Syria, including Palestine, declared Syria's independence in July 1920, calling for Faisal to be king on the foundations of Arab unity and rejecting the nation's national policy and Zionist politics. On this basis, King Faisal and his government accepted the decision. All Zionist allegations that King Faisal was sympathetic to Zionism must be considered false.[222]

In his testimony, Dr. Hussein Fakhri al-Khaldi, the mayor of Jerusalem, explained that the proposed Legislative Council in 1935 was less powerful than the 1922 assembly.[223] He said that the establishment of an Arab agency would not have achieved Arab national aspirations, because the agency's members were not elected but appointed by the high commissioner, while the Arabs had an elected Executive Committee representing them, which could be entrusted with the tasks entrusted to the proposed agency. In response to a question asked by the member of the investigation committee, Sir Horace George Montagu Rumbold, about what the Executive Committee had been doing in previous years, al-Khaldi replied, "It used to submit complaints and protests after the protests, notes and letters." He added sarcastically that they got "very great results."[224]

As for George Antonius, author of *Yaqzat al-'Arab* (Arab Awakening), he presented an objective testimony in fine English, which attracted the attention of the audience as if they were listening to a symphony. He made it clear that the Arab movement was not territorial and was not characterized by a regional character until after the war, and the settlements that followed resulted in fragmentation. Accordingly, the owners who were staying in Beirut and other cities of the Levant were considered foreigners. They faced passport problems and problems of every kind that would make their lands waste an important part of their value in terms of their ability to care for and cultivate them. This was a Zionist strategy to undervalue the sale and seize the lands.[225]

In his testimony, Bishop Hajjar emphasized the unity of the position of Arab Muslims and Christians toward the Zionist project, which he saw as a moral and social danger and a serious threat to the holy places and their sanctity. He also made it clear that the Allies, by supporting the establishment of a national home for the Jews, contradicted the foundations that depended on nationalism, as they meant nationalism only for the Jewish religion.[226]

Despite the limited time, insufficient preparation, and lack of awareness of most of the personalities who met the committee, the National Movement had reached the masses. The Royal Commission heard an Arab position clearly expressing national demands. In addition, the Arab Higher Committee had submitted a memorandum reviewing Arab-British relations and noting that Britain was breaking its promises to the Arabs. It also demanded the abandonment of the Jewish National Home Project, which in its opinion was proven to be failing, a complete and immediate cessation of Jewish immigration, a total and immediate transfer of land ownership from the Jews, and a solution to the question of Palestine on the basis of which the issues of Iraq, Syria, and Lebanon were resolved. They demanded ending the mandate and concluding a treaty between Britain and Palestine, in which a national government with constitutional rule would be established, in which all elements would be represented and justice and freedom would be guaranteed to all. More than one witness indicated that the Balfour Declaration and the decision of the League of Nations to assign Britain to Palestine contradicted the right to self-determination adopted by the League of Nations.[227]

In this way, the Arab Higher Committee would have recognized the right of citizenship for Palestinians residing in Palestine and recognized their political and civil rights on an equal basis with the legitimate Arab landowners. The committee stated unequivocally that the mandate era was marked by severe prejudice against Arabs as well as favoritism in mandate management practices toward Zionists, particularly the burden on the public budget of protecting and empowering Zionists and their occupation of a percentage of management jobs that more than doubled their numerical number. It enacted laws to protect Jewish industry while neglecting and displacing Arab farmers. The mandate administration and Jewish employees governed Arab education, while Jewish education enjoyed freedom and independence.[228]

On January 13, 1937, the Royal Committee embarked on a journey from Palestine to London. Because of this, the window of opportunity provided to Arab leaders to testify in front of the Bell Committee was limited to no more than one week. It spent the first two months of its presence in Palestine listening to British officials and Zionist leaders after spending the first two months of its presence in London listening to Zionist leaders. The Supreme Arab Committee listened to the testimonies of Arab spokesmen after the strike was over and the revolution had come to a halt. The fact that the Supreme Arab Committee had a fight shows that its members were united not only by class or goal. When people from Syria, Iraq, Lebanon, and Jordan came to Palestine to join the revolution, it showed that Arab solidarity on a popular level was supportive. The kings of Iraq, Saudi Arabia, Yemen, and Transjordan turned it into an official press release stating their solidarity. This was shown by the fact that people who wanted to change things came to Palestine from Syria, Iraq, Lebanon, and Jordan. Because of this, the chairman and other members of the Higher Arab Committee felt much less powerful and influential when meeting with the Peel Commission.[229]

Accordingly, it seems clear that the Arab leadership, in its response to the prince and the Arab kings, neglected the most important achievements of the strike and revolution, despite the high economic price that the people had borne, the blood of their children, and their suffering. And given that the Arab people in Palestine received no official Arab financial support during the six months of the strike and revolution, that Arab popular support was very limited, and that the revolutionary opposition factors in most of them did not go beyond the issuance of statements and telegrams, it is clear that the response to the kings' and Arab princes' calls did not stem from a desire to continue financial support. Moreover, the peasants of Palestine, who were the source of revolutionary support, did not show any evidence of weakness; on the contrary the farmers were racing until they were selling their wives' jewelry or their sumpters, on which they relied to cultivate the field, in order to buy guns to fight with and earn the honor of martyrdom.[230] Despite this, the national leadership did not seek to utilize and develop the anger of its people, to reinforce the revolutionary aggression in the face of the threat of escalation of the violence of the colonial state.

However, despite being aware of the British government's influence in the capitals of Arab nations, the leadership decided to seek advice from Arab heads of state and comply with their requests. This was due to three interconnected factors: the reality of class leadership and the membership of elements allied with British colonialism; the absence of any role for field revolution leaders and the peasant masses bearing the burden of the revolution in political decision making; and the lack of Palestinian national thought and action toward a comprehensive and permanent strategy for dealing with the colonial-Zionist alliance. All of this was the product of the backward Arab social reality inherited from the period of Ottoman domination and organized colonial efforts to deepen conflicts between local sectarian leaders and city elders.

On the other hand, circumstances favored the Zionist movement. The Zionist settlement bloc seemed to have withstood the strongest Arab attack aimed at uprooting it, and propaganda had inflated what it had accomplished economically. In addition, the racism and persecution of the Nazis in Europe had produced the greatest European and American support since the beginning of the rise of the Zionist movement on the stage of international politics. It is sufficient to refer to the consensus of the members of the British House of Commons in their support of the overly ambitious Zionist demands. Only three deputies, one of whom was the communist deputy William Gallacher, accused the Zionists of being the tool of British imperialism.[231]

Between the departure of the Peel Commission and the issuance of its decision on July 7, 1937, life in Palestine was marked by a number of phenomena, the most prominent of which was the anxious coexistence between the high commissioner and the Mandate Administration and between the mufti and the Arab Higher Committee. This was because the British bias toward the Zionist movement and the highest levels of violence against Arab citizens during the months of the strike and revolution deepened feelings of hostility against the British, the mandate administration, and the army, as well as the growing feeling that the British were responsible for all problems followed by the Zionists. While the British concluded at the end of the strike that the mufti was primarily responsible for supporting the revolution with money and arms, donations he collected from Palestine and Arab countries, and extended relations in the Arab world, the high commissioner and the minister of colonies thought about displacing the mufti and the committee, but they did not do so in anticipation that this would lead to renewed unrest and because of the conviction that the mufti and the commission were the weakest link compared to the peasant masses, which had shown commitment during the months of the revolution.[232]

Wauchoupe, in his quest to restore calm and stability, tried to persuade the mufti and the Arab Higher Committee to be moderate, and although the majority of the members of the committee were inclined toward that, the prevailing political climate prevented the restoration of reconciliation with the mandate administration, which was reflected in the refusal to attend any Arab ceremonies crowning the king of Britain. In a meeting with the high commissioner, the mufti and 'Awni 'Abdel Hadi expressed their conviction that the sooner the friendly relations between Britain and the Arabs could return, the better for the Arabs. In a letter from the high commissioner to the minister of colonies, he attributed the moderation of the mufti to the influence of Ibn Saud and moderate Arab leaders outside Palestine and expressed his fear of the pressure from Palestinian Arab youth and members of the Independence Party. While there were three factors that impeded the moderation that Wauchoupe wanted, it pushed the mufti to take a radical position that was unknown before 1936.

The first factor was the objective reality of farmers and workers: 29 percent of the Arab peasants did not own land, while the workers were suffering from unemployment and discrimination in employment and wages for the benefit of Jewish workers. In building many public roads, the Arabs were paid a little more than half of what the Jewish workers were receiving for similar production. The Arab workers' anxiety and discontent was increased by the declaration allowing the immigration of new Jewish workers. The mufti protested against the new immigration regulations, albeit "in a friendly manner," and he offered cooperation in the housing of workers residing in Haifa huts in the Waqf lands. The second factor was the issue of detainees, as the mufti was urging the government to release all political detainees. This issue made things worse and forced the two sides to agree that 180 political prisoners from the Galilee strike and the solidarity prisoners in Acre and Haifa should be set free. The third was the frequency of rumors and leaks about the recommendations of the Peel Commission and its adoption of the division of Palestine, which included the section intended to be allocated to Arabs in eastern Jordan, which meant placing the High Arab Committee under the rule of Prince Abdullah. Palestine had witnessed a sharp division regarding this possibility. At a time when the mufti and two councils had reservations about him, the opponents led by Raghib al-Nashashibi and the Defense Party were enthusiastic. While they gave a warm farewell to Prince Abdullah when he passed through Palestine traveling to London to attend the coronation ceremony of the king of England, and they congratulated him on his safe arrival to Amman on his return, the mufti and the two councils refrained from participating in the farewell and reception parties.[233]

It is important to point out that the desire for independence in the Palestinian national decision did not in any way cause the sharp divergence in opinions regarding the nature of the relationship with Jordan and Prince Abdullah. It was well known that this was a national position, and the Arab people were also aware of their strong ties to Palestine and its Arab nation. In addition, they were well aware of the fact that Palestine was a nation in its own right. Since it was first published in 1927, the Palestinian *Arab League* newspaper, which represented the Arab Party and was founded by Munif al-Husseini, one of the leaders of the national and literary movement, had consistently advocated for Arab unity.[234] It was closer to adopting the point of view of reform advocates in the last quarter of the nineteenth century, such as Imam Muhammad 'Abdu, Jamal al-Din al-Afghani, and others, in its analysis of the reasons for Arab society's weakness.[235]

In addition, the Palestinian political elites' divergent perspectives on the matter are not something new; rather, they date back to the early 1920s, when the issue was first brought up. In 1923, the Cairo newspaper al-Ahram reported that the British were considering placing Palestine and eastern Jordan under the crown of Prince 'Abdullah.[236] This news was based on information obtained from British officials. This idea was not well received by the Palestine newspaper because the publication did not have faith in the prince's administration. On the other hand, Darwish Abu al-'Afiyah, 'Issa al-Bandak, and Ibrahim Salim al-Najjar criticized the prince's policy in newspapers: *al-Jazeera*, *Sawt al-'Arab*, and *Lisan al-'Arab* supported and criticized the attack on the prince's policy.[237] In 1929, the topic became controversial as a result of statements made by the British Labour Party regarding its adoption of the idea of the unity of Palestine and eastern Jordan. At that time, the idea was met with opposition from the al-Karmel newspaper, which believed that it was a Zionist plot to open the doors of eastern Jordan to Jewish immigration. Supporters of the idea saw that the unification of the two countries would bring together a million Arabs. This would make sure that the majority was stronger than the Zionist minority and give the Arab people more power as they took part in the war. Those who advocated for the idea saw this as an opportunity to advance their cause.[238]

In 1934, it was rumored that Prince 'Abdullah's purpose in visiting London was to search for the unity of Palestine and Transjordan and to appoint him as their king.[239] On that day, the *Arab League* newspaper, speaking for the Arab Party and the mufti, saw that the project was fictitious and that the aim of the Zionist movement was to welcome it to colonize eastern Jordan. The newspaper concluded its comment by saying,

> We write what we write sincerely, whole-heartedly, and agonising over all pain. We are among the people most interested in the prince's dignity and his name and prestige, and in the unity of the two countries and the sovereignty of the Arabs in them. But in our circumstances, the conditions of eastern Jordan, the conditions of the prince himself, and the conditions of Palestine, the Jews and the English, which makes us pessimistic about all the pessimism about this game, and we consider it a serious illusion that is not based on anything from the truth.[240]

In addition to the Arab League, al-Karmel was responding to the regional call and its advocates, defending the idea of the Arab League, explaining that it was necessary for the following reasons: "The Arabs won't be able to reach their goals of regaining their independence, improving their political status, keeping their homes, and protecting their rights if they can't agree on their language and culture, give it a single voice, and start their own educational system."[241]

In response to the regional skeptics of unity, who saw in the call to unity a threat to the interests of their countries, *al-Karmel* wrote, "We hope the originators of this idea, who are keen on the interests of their general provinces, to think a little about what remains for us to fear from losing, are our commercial and legal interests, or our rights? Politics, our customs, traditions and dignity? Or our rights and freedom in our homelands?"[242]

Al-Karmel answered its previous questions:

> Some argue that working for the Arab League distracts us from pursuing our interests as individuals from different provinces. However, the truth is quite the opposite. Just as working to protect the interests of local districts preserves individual private interests, the Arab League's overarching work safeguards the interests of each province separately. It acts as a protective barrier for individuals within their own nations. Just like individuals from English, French, German, Italian, and American backgrounds do not inherently excel over others, their respect is derived from the strength of their respective nations. If these nations were fragmented into small and weak provinces, governments, and

sects, we would not have a unified and influential presence among international entities.[243]

Al-Karmel concluded by saying,

> The work of the Arab League is the only remedy to heal our social diseases and to enlarge our souls. It is the only remedy that saves us from the divisions of Shiite, Sunni, Druze, Christian, Orthodox, Catholic and Maronite. Measured that from the divisions that we exaggerated in their support and exaggerated us, so that our souls became small and we no longer sing except for them. We also judge ourselves and our future generations by the eternal slavery of colonialism.[244]

Al-Karmel suggested the establishment of a general Arab Party operating for Arab nationalism.

Haj Amin al-Husseini took advantage of the calm period and traveled to Damascus, accompanied by a delegation, to congratulate the leaders of the Syrian National Movement on assuming power under the provisions of the 1936 treaty. Here, all the leaders of the Syrian National Movement, a number of Syrian and Lebanese politicians and journalists, and some Iraqis met and discussed the possibilities of partition and agreed to hold an Arab conference to discuss the future of Palestine. Haj Amin al-Husseini also held meetings with some Syrian revolutionaries known for their militant activity, such as Sheikh Muhammad al-Ashmar. However, he shortened his visit when he was informed of the arrest of a number of the National Movement activists. The Defense Party found the absence of the mufti from the country at that difficult time, without the permission of the Arab Higher Committee, an argument for his removal from its membership.[245] This took place four days before the Peel Commission issued its report. Haj Amin al-Husseini explained the removal of the mufti as a protest against the assassination attempt on the prominent party member Fakhri al-Nashashibi.[246] Raghib al-Nashashibi is accused of having hoped that, with the assistance of the British government, he could take over the political leadership after the British government decided to exclude Haj Amin al-Husseini from the political scene. This accusation was made while Raghib al-Nashashibi was explaining the desire of the party leaders to break free from their association with the Arab Higher Committee and to work alone to achieve their goals.[247] Although the withdrawal of the Defense Party was met with intense criticism, and it was viewed as weakening the Arab position vis-à-vis the British, it did not much affect the National Movement or national unity.[248]

On July 7, 1937, the report of the Royal Commission was issued in four hundred pages in English, including full details of the Arab-Zionist conflict.

In its first section, it dealt with the problem historically, especially the history of the Zionist movement. It also discussed the flow of immigration and the Arab reaction that rejected it, the al-Qassam movement, martyrdom, and the funeral associated with it. It detailed the British Parliament's opposition to establishing a Legislative Council and self-rule in Palestine. It talked about how the deals that Egypt and Syria made in 1936 affected the Palestinian Arabs in Palestine. Even though it denied that Italy's invasion of Abyssinia had any effect, it did say that the situation in Palestine was already bad before Italy's invasion in September 1935, so the start of unrest in April 1936 was not a surprise.[249]

The report went on to talk about the revolution, noting that the 1936 revolution had overshadowed all previous revolutions. It lasted for a longer time, included the entire country, and was more elaborate in organization.[250] The turmoil in Palestine was arousing the interest and sympathy of the neighboring Arab peoples, but this time it not only showed hostile popular sentiments against the British government and the Jews but also saw many volunteering to fight, including "al-Qawuqji" from Syria and Iraq, and it was difficult to prevent the Arabs in eastern Jordan from participating in the fighting.[251] On the reasons for the revolution, it mentioned that the Arab complaint was against not the application of the mandate instrument but rather the existence of the mandate itself, which they saw as contradicting the Charter of the League of Nations and the right to self-determination.[252] It stressed that the Arab claim to independence and fear of the establishment of the Jewish national homeland were the causes of the unrest.[253]

As for the situation of the Arab National Movement, it stipulated,

> Every city has a national committee, which has its branches in the neighbouring villages, and the movement's strength has been informed that when the Arab Higher Committee declared our province, no Arab has ever approached us. When the district was cancelled, the witnesses who were allowed to make their statements in front of us—except for four—were members or delegates. On behalf of the Arab Higher Committee, and these four supported the Supreme Committee and supported its demands.[254]

The discussion continued on to more in-depth subjects after that, including the Arab newspapers, the students, their activities, and their participation in the ongoing strike; the role of inflammatory scouting; the national spirit of the youth; the national consensus; the solidarity of Muslims and Arab Christians; and the unity and its destiny. The report made sure to include a reference to the "terrorism" that was associated with the Arab National Movement. However, it ignored the Jews and instead concentrated on the striking Arabs as well as those who financed the movement.

According to the report, the costs associated with "public security" bal-looned from £250,000 in 1933 to £2,230,000 in 1936 and 1937. This increase was mentioned (revolutionary year). It was observed that there were not many people sentenced to death during the revolutions of 1929 and 1936 and that imposing the appropriate punishment on the criminal in a timely manner was an essential component in ensuring the continued existence of law and order. The report suggested that a stringent collection of fines should be imposed and that disciplinary police should be established in villages or cities at the expense of the people living there until the fines were paid. In addition to this recommendation, it was suggested that the Publications Law be amended to allow for the seizure of both supplies and the press. In terms of land availabil-ity, it was stated that there was a scarcity of land due to the increase in Arab population rather than the acquisition of land by Jews. It blamed the increase in immigration on the US government's tightening of immigration restric-tions, the actions of the Nazi regime in Germany, and increased economic pressure on Jews in Bologna.[255]

The report also examined in detail the development of the Zionist settle-ment grouping: "In 1936 the Jewish national homeland grew and made it more like what is in a state within a state. The Jewish community in Palestine has 400,000 people, the capital is Tel Aviv, a national flag, and a national anthem, a cultural system, its social services, its agricultural and industrial economy, and is linked to global Judaism by the Jewish Agency, while its internal affairs are managed by a National Assembly and a Rabbinical Council."[256]

On the issues of immigration and land, the report recommended what it considered "painkillers," as it called for the restriction of immigration of all types to twelve thousand per year and to prevent the transfer of lands to Jews in some areas. While rejecting the idea of establishing a legislative coun-cil, which the Arabs were demanding, it replaced it by recommending the expansion of the consultative council by adding nonstaff members to it but specifying its powers so that such members were not involved in accepting or rejecting the budget or any other legislative measures. The report concluded that, as long as the mandate remained in place, it was impossible to reconcile Arab and Jewish aspirations given the contradiction of obligations and that any government established, if led by a Jew, would represent a Jewish major-ity, while an Arab would represent an Arab majority. In conclusion, it was decided that the contradictory national problems of Arabs and Jews could only be solved by dividing Palestine into three parts.[257]

The first was to be Arabic; it included the Gaza area, Beersheba, the Negev, Hebron, and Nablus, and the eastern part of the Tulkarm, Jenin, Baysan, and Jaffa cities, so that it joined eastern Jordan to form an Arab kingdom bound by Britain in a treaty.

The second was to be Jewish and included all the coast from the borders of Lebanon to Majdal, the plains of Saron, Marj Ibn Amir, Baysan, and eastern and western Galilee. This was a sovereign Jewish state linked to Britain by a treaty.

The third was to be subject to the British mandate, which included the areas of the cities of Jerusalem, Bethlehem, and Nazareth and a passageway from Jerusalem to Jaffa that included the villages of this road and the cities of Lydda and Ramla. The report also recommended that the cities of Haifa, Acre, Safed, Tiberias, and Aqaba be kept under the administration of the mandate government for a period.

Each country was to be independent in its decision on matters of immigration, land purchase, public works, education, health, and choosing its official language. Meanwhile, the British mandate's central government would maintain foreign affairs, defense, communications, and customs matters.

It is noted that the Arab section included only 1,250 Jews who owned about 100,000 dunums; the Jewish section included about 325,000 Arabs owning 3.25 million dunums. The Arabs were about half of the population of this section and owned three-quarters of its land. The report recommended a gradual and forced exchange of the population if necessary and the purchase by each department of the lands belonging to the other nationality in its department. It recalled that in the settlement between Turkey and Greece in 1923 there was an exchange of 1.3 million Turks with 400,000 Greeks. But the commission admitted that the conditions were not the same. The report did not miss noting that it stripped the Arab part of fertile land and economic potential.

The Peel Commission gave a full account of the facts of the Arab-Zionist conflict and the development of both the Zionist movement and the Arab-Palestinian National Movement. It also included accurate analyses of the sociopolitical reality that gave rise to the Arab revolution. In addition, it ended with an objective conclusion, as it decided that the question of Palestine was not merely a political issue and that it was a national issue in that the Arab national ambition was organically linked to the struggle against Zionist settler colonialism. It specified that in Palestine a request for national independence applied to a request to stop immigration and the sale of lands, and defining the national homeland would not remove the root cause of the Arabs' complaint.

There were three distinguishing features that characterized the report. First, there is a lack of objectivity in the claim that the primary cause of the shortage of land, as well as the resulting displacement and unemployment of Arab peasants, was not the sale of land but rather the growth of the Arab population. The second negative feature included its working against human rights and opposing public freedoms, despite the fact that there were relatively few executions; demanding harsher penalties on villages and cities in order to collect fines; calling for the suppression of freedom of the press and for stricter publication laws, going so far as to demand the confiscation of presses; and so on.

Concerning the report's third negative feature, it adopted the Zionist viewpoint, singing the national anthem, and the fact that it was a refuge for Jews fleeing persecution, which supported thousands of trained and armed fighters and forty thousand reserves. "We must also take into account the Jewish resistance, and we believe that Jews armed themselves somewhat secretly, realizing that an Arab government could put an end to all their efforts and aspirations, turning the national homeland into a narrower and more dangerous ghetto. They are likely to fight and refuse to submit to Arab rule."[258]

Completely ignoring the role of the Mandate Authority in enabling the Zionists and providing requirements for their progress in various fields, the Royal Commission reached a sound and realistic appreciation of the power of the Yishuv and did not ignore this force in its political project. It declared that it would have resisted with all its energy any solution that favored the Arabs, and it was also able to guarantee the security of the Jewish state when it was established.

Moreover, we note that the report of the Peel Commission completely ignored the Arab historical experience, which the mufti referred to in his testimony before the committee, where the Jews lived in safety and freedom in the shadow of the Arab countries and that wherever they were found in the Arab world, they enjoyed all the rights of citizenship and did not suffer from forced or optional isolation. Furthermore, the British report failed to mention the Arab settlement offers that had followed since the mediation of St. John Bridger Philby (Abdullah Philby) in 1930 and the outbreak of the 1936 spring unrest.[259] It was not difficult for Lord Peel and his committee, who elaborated on the details, to know the generous offer carried by Dr. Magnes to Ben-Gurion in 1934, as Arabs were prepared to allow immigration until the Jews reached 44 percent of the citizens of Palestine and to establish a democratic state in which Jews enjoyed all their constitutional rights.[260]

Not only did the report ignore, on purpose and with a purposeful attitude, the right of the Palestinian people to self-determination, which is a right that belongs to all peoples on earth, but it also ignored the report's recommendation that a democratic government be established. It also ignored the serious research into the possibility of Jews living as citizens in a country with an Arab majority, as was the case for the Jews of Egypt, Iraq, Morocco, and other Arab countries. As a result, when deciding on racial partition, the committee issuing the report indicated its commitment to the colonial strategy of establishing a foreign colony as an instrument of colonial powers in disrupting Arab unity and impeding Arab progress.

There are those who confirm that the partition plans were prepared prior to the Royal Commission's leaving London for Palestine. The Cairo-based *al-Muqttam* newspaper wrote on October 7, 1937, three days after the report was issued, that the division project was not postponed, but the committee carried it with it when it came.[261] This confirms that Reginald Coupland, professor of colonial history at Oxford University and one of the committee's members, worked tirelessly throughout the process.[262] The committee in Palestine studied the project, collected information about it, and elaborated its details. It did not refrain from approaching the Arabs and consulting them concerning its findings. Dr. James Henry Thomas, secretary of state for the colonies, asserted that Raghib al-Nashashibi was one of those who saw the decision and blessed it before it was published.[263]

THE ARAB AND ZIONIST POSITIONS ON THE DECISION OF THE FIRST PARTITION

The high commissioner summoned members of the Arab Higher Committee and advised them to be careful before issuing an opinion on the report, in what was considered an ultimatum against any national movement. The Arab Higher Committee met on August 7, 1937, and decided to appeal to the Arab kings and heads of government to draw their attention to the disaster. The Arab Higher Committee's appeal mentioned that Palestine belonged not only to the Arabs of Palestine but to the Arab and Islamic worlds and that it was going through crises and needed the guidance and support of Arab kings and princes.[264] It stated, "The Arab people living in Palestine have made an appeal to your majesty, pleading with you to assist and direct them through this challenging period in history. They also ask you to use the sanctity of these countries, as well as Arab gallantry and religious duties, in your efforts to rescue them from the harms of colonialism, threats, and the process of tearing them apart."[265]

On July 23, 1937, the Arab Higher Committee issued a statement to the high commissioner, the British minister of colonies, and the head of the League of Nations Mandate Committee, expressing Arab dissatisfaction with the report. The report not only equated the Arab majority with a historical presence in Palestine and the emerging Jewish minority but also considered the Jewish issue to be the original and core issue and the Arab issue to revolve around it. It demonstrated that the political ties of the Jews to the country had been severed approximately two thousand years before and that the desire to establish a national homeland did not have the justified rights of nations and was based only on the Balfour Declaration and the British armed force. This was a promise that the Arabs had rejected and resisted since it was issued.

The statement expressed as a regret that the investigation committee had not carried out an investigation that was objective into the series of protests that had been staged by Arabs against the anti-Zionist policies of the government of the mandate. It also condemned the committee's negligence and questioned the mandate's authority to reject the Arabs' demand for independence and to put down their peaceful demonstrations with force. In addition, it criticized the committee for its lack of attention to detail. The statement argued that the issue could be resolved by embracing the foundation for justice, the rights of individual nations, and the established principles all over the world. On the other hand, the Royal Committee came up with some peculiar suggestions, which only served to make the situation worse by supporting and bolstering the Zionist viewpoint.

The statement considered the Peel Commission's proposal of a national homeland as a solution to the problem of the persecution of Jews in Europe, arguing that the world was able to find a way to protect the Jews and their interests in their present countries of residence and that the provinces excluded them from the rights to their property and their vast lands. The statement warned that the best agricultural lands and the most fertile plains, as well as the majority of the Palestinian coast, belonged to the Jewish state. In addition to the fact that Arabs owned 75 percent of the total land designated by Jews, this region was also home to 87.5 percent of the orange groves that Arabs had in their possession.[266] It was also pointed out that the report's recommended exchange of population between the Jewish state and the section of the report devoted to Arabs was intended to forcibly evict Arabs from their homes and take over their property and lands.

The statement addressed what was considered a mandatory region and explained that it included fertile land and that all of it, with the exception of the Jerusalem area, was inhabited by Arabs. Additionally, the statement mentioned that the region included fertile land. It was a difficult decision for the Arabs to abandon the holy sites of their religions, Christianity and Islam. In addition, the Jerusalem area divided the land that had been allotted to the Arabs into two parts: the north and the south. It warned that increasing Jewish immigration to the mandate region, particularly to Jerusalem, would not be difficult for the Jews and that this trend would continue until the Arabs had been assimilated by the Jews and the holy places had been taken away from them for good. In addition to this, the Arab citizens who lived in this region of the country were subjected to the perversion of their culture as well as the obscuring of their national identity. It was brought to the reader's attention that the proposals to allocate the mandatory area focused on military, influence, and resource considerations more than on religious ones.

In light of the statement's commitment to the concept of Arab unity, the idea of annexing the Arab section of eastern Jordan was greeted with general approval.[267] After that, it discussed the harm that the report had caused to societal unity as well as the economies of Arab countries as a direct result of the division caused by the report. In addition, it cast doubt on the issue of the British and Jewish grant to the Arab section in order for it to be attached to Jordan and considered this to be an insult to the dignity of the Arab people. Following confirmation that the report of the Royal Commission would be rejected, the statement went on to identify four foundations for a solution that could be adopted by providing justice and consolidating peace. The following are the foundations:

1. Recognizing the Arabs' right to complete independence in their country
2. Refraining from establishing the Jewish national home
3. Terminating the mandate and replacing it with a treaty similar to the British-Iraqi, British-Egyptian, and Syrian-French treaties
4. Stopping Jewish immigration and sale of land to the Jews pending the conclusion of the treaty

At the conclusion of its statement, the Supreme Arab Committee expressed the Arabs' willingness to negotiate with the British government on acceptable grounds, preserving reasonable British interests and agreeing on the necessary guarantees to preserve the holy places and their visiting rights and to protect all the legitimate rights of the Jewish population and other minorities in Palestine.[268]

It was a consensus among all Arab parties and personalities, including the Defense Party, to oppose the partition of Palestine. The Defense Party's statement, which was issued on November 7, 1937, included the party's unanimous decision to oppose the proposed partition of Palestine on the grounds that it ran counter to national interests and unity and posed a threat to peace in the Holy Land. The party issued a call to the nation, urging its people to keep their emotions in check and maintain their level of maturity so that the country's workers could continue on the path toward success.[269] Despite the fact that the party had prior knowledge of the decision to split and despite the revolutionary climate that was prevalent at the time in Palestine and the Arab world, Emile Touma was not on board with the decision.[270] Muhammad 'Izzat Darwazah was confident in his response to Raghib al-Nashashibi's statement, in which he refuted the claim that the Defense Party was consulted over the decision to partition the country and gave its approval prior to the document's publication. The members of the opposition were not taken aback by the fact that there was a partition; however, they were taken aback by the large number of Jews received,[271] which affected the property of a great number of people, particularly in the Galilee region.[272]

In rejecting the partition resolution, the Communist Party believed that the decision fell within the framework of the policy of Neville Chamberlain, the prime minister of Britain, who, in the midst of his war preparations, needed a strong strategic base in one of the most essential locations in the British Empire.[273] But this was not in the interest of the Arab and Jewish populations in Palestine and in eastern Jordan. In its statement, the party added, there will be no peace in a Palestine divided between Jews and Arabs; rather, partition would spread hatred, repression, and the desire for revenge.[274] It warned that Ben-Gurion, a supporter of partition, had promised that his supporters could occupy the Arab part of Palestine after strengthening the Jewish section.[275] Touma also warned that Britain would use a "divide and rule" strategy between the two parties, pitting one against the other.[276] In the conclusion of his statement, Touma called on the Communist Party to cancel the Balfour Declaration, to grant democratic rights to all the inhabitants of Palestine, and to achieve independence.[277]

The Arab world was filled with anger and disapproval. Protests against the decision were held in Cairo, Baghdad, Damascus, Beirut, Amman, Taif, Makkah, and Madinah. This wave of anger and condemnation swept across the Arab world from east to west. There was not a single center-left political party in Tunisia, Algeria, or Morocco that did not protest the project of partitioning the country.[278] Cairo emerged as the epicenter of negotiations between Arab delegates and the Egyptian government for the purpose of formulating a cooperative strategy. During its presentation of the matter to the League of Nations in Geneva, the Egyptian government committed to providing assistance and said it would do so immediately.[279]

On May 15, 1937, or approximately three months before the Royal Commission issued a decision, the Iraqi government sent a secret note to the British government stating that King Ghazi and his government felt historical responsibility for their request to the people of Palestine to stop the strike and revolution.[280] As a result, the memorandum called for a review of the document known as the mandate and considered that the British government had implemented the Balfour Declaration in its entirety, given that the number of Jews in the country had reached a quarter of the population by the year 1936. In addition, the memorandum considered that the British government had called for a review of the mandate document. Hebrew was now recognized as an official language, or a par with Arabic, despite the fact that each had its own political, administrative, and social institutions.[281] The memorandum called for the establishment of a maximum limit for Jewish immigration that would not exceed a certain percentage of the population. In addition, the memorandum called for the definition of the sale of land and the events that were required by the autonomy.[282]

The Iraqi Foreign Ministry issued a secret memo to its commissions abroad on November 7, 1937, requesting that they clarify that the request to the Arab kings from the Arabs of Palestine to stop the revolution was based on the good-will of the British government. This memo came in the wake of the issuance of the partition resolution and was addressed to its commissions abroad. It was not in anyone's best interest to split up an Arab nation, which is why the Iraqi government was holding out high hopes that the Royal Commission would go along with its suggestions. In the final part of its memorandum, it requested that its commissions protest against the concept of partition and appeal to the British government to reconsider the destiny of Palestine.[283]

The Syrian government headed by Jamil Mardam rejected the partition, and it was also denounced by Yemen. King 'Abd al-'Aziz replied to the call of the Supreme Arab Committee that he would spare no effort to help the people of Palestine and preserve their rights. The Egyptian government, headed by Mustapha al-Nahas, remained silent, leaving the field for political figures and popular organizations to condemn the project.[284] This was led by Muhammed Mahmud, leader of the opposition, along with scholars of al-Azhar, as well as Muslim leaders in India, Iran, and Afghanistan. Some of the messages and telegrams urged the Palestinian Arabs to stand firm and to continue the struggle along with a promise to help them.[285] In the meantime, Prince 'Abdullah and those who support him in Palestine seemed ready to agree to the partition plan. This would put the prince in charge of an Arab nation that included land on both sides of the Jordan River.[286]

In spite of the fact that the Peel Commission's report was clearly biased in favor of the Zionist view and favored the proposed division project at the expense of the Arabs, both the report and the project were met with a variety of responses from Zionist leaders and their supporters among English politicians.[287] The report and the project were viewed with a degree of ambivalence by the Arabs.[288] Although the resolution to partition Palestine represented recognition of the Zionists' right to an independent state, it also suggested putting a stop to their achievements by freezing their number in a limited part of Palestine.[289] Herbert Samuel, the first high commissioner, attacked the project vigorously in the British House of Lords by saying, "The partition will not bring peace, because the Jewish state that will be established will include 225 thousand Jews compared to 325 thousand Arabs. It will be necessary to conduct an exchange of population that the Arab population will not be satisfied with, and it will be impossible to defend the borders proposed by the committee/commission."[290]

Regarding the findings of the Peel Commission report, Zionist parties and leaders held contrasting viewpoints, which resulted in a heated discussion at the twentieth conference, which took place in Zurich from August 3 to 16,

1937. Weizmann and Ben-Gurion viewed the establishment of a Jewish state, even if it was only on a portion of the land of Israel, as a significant political achievement whose benefits outweighed its drawbacks. They believed that this was the case despite the fact that the land was not entirely Jewish. They issued a warning that, in light of the growth of the Arab movement, it would be impossible to carry on the Zionist work in the absence of an independent Jewish state. They made it abundantly clear that restricting the state to a portion of the land of Israel was not a permanent solution, and they emphasized that the political situation of millions of Jews living in exile necessitated the establishment of a Jewish state as soon as possible. They demanded that negotiations take place with Britain in order to modify its proposals in a way that would make it possible for the Zionists to found an independent state and ease the burden placed on Jews living in other countries. As for the opponents, who were led by Menachem Ovechkin, Berel Katznelson, Yad Yitzhak Tabenkin, and Zeev Jabotenksy, they revolted against the partition, and they asserted that the fight for settlement and the construction of the national homeland could continue while the territory was still under mandate control. Some people were under the impression that the project of partition would not be carried out by Britain and that the Jews would be the only ones to give up a portion of their historical homeland.[291] This trend had the support of the "Correctors" led by Jabotinsky, who were not represented at the conference.[292]

A third team was led by Dr. Judah L. Magnes and included a number of non-Zionist American Jews. This team opposed the idea of partition, said that the establishment of a Jewish state posed a threat to the Jews in Palestine and the world, and called for understanding with the Arabs on the basis of establishing a constitutional rule in which Jews participated on a relative basis. This team threatened to withdraw from the conference in the event of an insistence on partition and the establishment of a Jewish state. Weizmann responded to this invitation on the pretext that the Arabs only accepted participation on the condition that the Jews would always remain a minority. After some controversy, it was agreed to discuss the Arabs on the basis of the Balfour Declaration and the mandate, and this made it possible to persuade the non-Zionists to remain within the conference and participate in the membership of the Jewish Agency, which included seven Zionists and five non-Zionists.[293]

To resolve the dispute and preserve the unity of the Zionist movement, the twentieth conference ended by denouncing the decision of the Peel Commission that the mandate was not applicable, opposing every proposal to reduce the rights of Jews in the transitional period, and mandating that the Jewish Agency hold discussions with the British government to clarify the exact conditions for the establishment of the Jewish state. The conference reserved its report that the Executive Committee, while carrying out these negotiations, had no right to commit to anything. It would be the right of the next conference to decide on the matter if the negotiations resulted in a specific project to establish a Jewish state.[294] The debate between supporters and opponents continued for a year and a half. The difference of opinion also extended to the Haganah ranks, as a number of its members joined the opponents, while the majority, led by Eliyahu Golomb, supported the partition resolution, with requests for amendments in the borders in the Baysan valley and the annexation of Jerusalem and the Negev, as well as asking that the Jewish Agency assume immigration affairs and establish a Jewish force once the project was accepted.[295]

Through the use of Dr. Judah L. Magnes's request and the company he brought, an effort was made to break up the ranks of the Arabs. He and some of his supporters reached out to some Arab personalities known for their positions on the truce, and they invited them to cooperate with the appropriate solution.[296] A number of them accepted the invitation, and as a result the Palestine newspaper published an article advocating for an alternative approach. In order to discuss the matter, the organization held a number of meetings with Arab leaders, including the mufti in some of those meetings. And when it became clear that the authors of the Jewish call for understanding did not represent an influential force in the Zionist milieu and that some of them asked the Arabs to recognize the national homeland and the continuation of immigration as a condition for negotiations, it became clear to all that all Jews were equal and that the purpose of the contacts was to create confusion in the ranks of the Arabs and to obtain consent for the national homeland and freedom of immigration.[297]

Ben-Gurion, while announcing his acceptance of the partition, did not hide his belief in the imperative of future expansion. In January 1937, at a symposium of working Zionist youth, he said, "The state will not shrink, but rather expand, if our work now in this country is to gather Jewish power for broader actions in the future."[298]

In his meeting with the leaders of the Jewish workers in New York who opposed the partition, he said in October 1937, "The proposed Jewish state won't be able to take in Jews just because it's big and has big borders. Instead, it will depend on what the Jewish people can do. Furthermore, the proposed Jewish state's borders will not be permanent for all eternity."[299]

During the mandate era, the British were fond of forming commissions of inquiry whenever the Palestinians took up arms in the face of British colonial rule and Zionist settlement. The task of these committees was to investigate the causes of what the British called "unrest" and to make recommendations for developing policies that would improve the situation. Often the commissioners would spend several weeks in Palestine, during which they would interview hundreds of people, including British officials living and working in Palestine and leading figures in the Palestinian and Jewish communities. Four British committees visited Palestine in the 1920s and 1930s—namely, the Haycraft Commission (1921), the Shaw Commission (1929), the Peel Commission (1936–1937), and the Woodhead Commission (1938). The Peel Commission was the most prominent of these because it recommended in its final report, issued in July 1937, that Palestine be divided into two states, one Jewish and the other Arab. This was the first time that a British political body formally endorsed the idea of a Jewish "state" in Palestine instead of the more limited idea of a Jewish national home. The report also recommended the deportation of more than two hundred thousand Palestinians from their homes to make way for the establishment of the new Jewish state.[300]

On July 7, 1937, the final report was published, and the recommendation for partition was briefly printed at the end, with an attached map. The Jewish Agency and the Zionist Organization were consulted about the borders drawn in the map before the report was issued, which enabled them to persuade the British to include specific areas of great importance within the borders of the Jewish state, including the Hula Valley. When the report was published, the Zionist leadership was divided on how to respond; the principle of division was approved, but without an acceptance of the details of the map recommended by the Peel Commission. As for the Palestinian leadership, it was angered, condemned the partition recommendation, affirmed its firm commitment to establishing an independent Palestinian state on the entire land of Palestine, and was not prepared to cede the most fertile areas to European colonists.

The recommendations of the Peel report were not implemented at the time. The Woodhead Commission, which visited Palestine in 1938, studied the logistics of the partition closely and decided it was not enforceable. But for the Zionist leadership, the Peel report was a clear indication of British willingness (at the official level) to support the principle of a Jewish state in Palestine. The partition map included in the Peel report was subsequently used as the basis for the partition map approved by the United Nations in 1947.[301] In other words, although it took another ten years to partition Palestine, through the 1948 war and the ethnic cleansing that killed 750,000 Palestinians, the recommendations of the Peel Commission could be considered a turning point, when the catastrophe (*nakba*) became the most likely end to the British occupation of Palestine.[302]

NOTES

1. Rizq 1968, p. 201.

2. 'Alush 1967, p. 28.

3. Kayali 1985, p. 41.

4. Qasimiyyah 1973a, pp. 101–123.

5. Porath 1974, p. 33.

6. 'Alush 1967, p. 22; Report on Illiteracy in Palestine (1935). Submitted to Member of the British Parliament by the Palestine Arab Party, Jerusalem: Beyt-ul-Makdes Press, 10 June, p. 1.

7. Shahin 1985, p. 5.

8. 'Alush 1967, p. 22.

9. Regan 2018, pp. 168–170.

10. Jana 1938, p. 55; 'Awad 1983, p. 107.

11. Hamadih 1937, p. 73.

12. Yassin 1980, p. 32; Kayali 1968, pp. 566–567.

13. Sa'd 1985, p. 86.

14. Simpson 1932, p. 96.

15. Simpson 1932, p. 42; Jadir 1976, p. 371.

16. 'Alush 1967, p. 163; *Palestine Conference Reports*, Jaffa, October 12, 1935.

17. 'Alush 1967, p. 129.

18. For the conference membership and decisions, see Hout 1981, pp. 243–249; 'Alush 1967, pp. 80–83.

19. Hout 1981, p. 249.

20. Kayali 1985, pp. 249–263; Hout 1981, pp. 243–249.

21. Zu'itir 1979, p. 322; Gharib 2014, pp. 65–74.

22. Za'im 2019, pp. 176–178.

23. Gharib 2014, p. 169.

24. Zu'itir 1979, pp. 404–405; 'Alush 1967, p. 129; Safari 1937, pp. 124–129; Khilah 1974, pp. 451–460; Sadaqah 1946, pp. 107–122.

25. 'Alush 1967, p. 163.

26. Lachman 2015, pp. 73–74.

27. Zu'itir 1979, p. 406.

28. 'Alush 1967, p. 120.

29. See Stein 1984; Jabareen 2017, pp. 238–265.

30. Fawcett 2013, p. 345; Fieldhouse 2006, pp. 95–96.

31. Jiryis 1995, pp. 53–54; Khilah 1974, p. 39.

32. Jiryis 1995., pp. 51–53.

33. Darwazah 1984b, pp. 132–133; Shufani 2003, p. 460.

34. Jiryis 1995, pp. 53–54.

35. Cohen 2008, pp. 31–32.

36. Jiryis 1977, p. 2:412; 'Abd al-Ra'uf 1979, pp. 62063; Zu'itir 1955, pp. 75–76.

37. Darwazah 1971, pp. 3:112–113.

38. *Falastin*, Jaffa, October 13, 1933, p. 2; Ghuri 1972, p. 159.

39. Kayali 1968, p. 337; Ghuri 1972, pp. 159–160; Ghunaym 1980, pp. 137–139; Safari 1937, pp. 210–211.

40. Ghuri 1972, p. 159.

41. Kayali 1968, p. 337.

42. Safari 1937, pp. 209–210; Kayali 1985, p. 278; Ghuri 1972, p. 165.

43. *Mir'at al-Sharq*, Jerusalem, November 7, 1933.

44. Safari 1937, p. 210; Kayali 1985, p. 337; Ghuri 1972, p. 160.

45. Kayali 1968, p. 340.

46. Kolinsky 1993, p. 170.

47. Kayali 1968, p. 256; Darwazah 1984b, pp. 123–124.

48. Hout 1981, p. 342.

49. Safari 1937, pp. 2:38–39.

50. Muhafazah 1989, p. 109.

51. Safari 1937, p. 2:210.

52. 'Alush 1967, p. 99; Kayali 1985, p. 277.

53. Muhafazah 1989, p. 110.

54. Darwazah 1984b, p. 125.

55. Zu'itir 1979, pp. 430–431.

56. 'Alush 1967, p. 127.

57. Hout 1981, p. 345.

58. A good example is Hassan Shukri, the mayor of Haifa, who opposed the strike and did not support the National Committee in Haifa, and the challenge of national sentiments has reached the point of visiting a camp for Jewish immigrants in Hadar in Haifa. And in anticipation of what was threatening his life, he sought refuge in Lebanon until the end of the strike. See Khalifa and Jabbour 1989, p. 14.

59. Zu'itir 1979, pp. 430–431; Khalifa and Jabbour 1989, pp. 15–17.

60. Khalifa and Jabbour 1989, p. 20.

61. Kayali 1985, pp. 189–200, 277; Darwazah 1984b, pp. 55–58.

62. Palumbo 1987, pp. 11–12.

63. Patai 1960, p. 88.

64. Avneri 1984, p. 130; Flapan 1979, p. 71; Lehn and Davis 1988.

65. Khilah 1974, p. 450.

66. Tamimi 2018, pp. 27–30.

67. Abu Basir 1971, p. 153; 'Ōdah 1975, p. 156; Hout 1981, p. 345.

68. Ghafani 2001, pp. 2:101–102; Salih 2012, pp. 51–55.

69. Hirst 2003, pp. 30–31.

70. Kayali 1985, p. 268.

71. Shufani 2003, p. 44.

72. Shufani 2003, p. 462; Hout 1981, pp. 299–301; Ghuri 1972, pp. 149–204.

73. Kayali 1985, p. 269.

74. Hout 1981, p. 349.

75. See Sayigh 1979.

76. Hirst 2003, pp. 236–237;

77. Swedenburg 1995, p. 233.

78. Hirst 2003, pp. 236–237.

79. Marlowe 1959, pp. 137–138.

80. Hirst 2003, p. 237.

81. Odeh 1984, p. 142.

82. Hirst 2003, pp. 238–241; see also Jarrar 2011, pp. 1:122–123.

83. Zu'itir 1979, pp. 404–405.

84. Darwazah 1984b, pp. 129–130.

85. Ghuri 1972, p. 76.

86. Hout 1981, p. 349; Safari 1937, pp. 2:48–133; Jarrar 2011, pp. 1:122–123.

87. Parsons 2016, pp. 119–125.

88. Jarrar 2011, pp. 1:122–124; Jabar 2017, pp. 145–147; Parsons 2016, pp. 93–95.

89. Parsons 2016, pp. 229–231.

90. Hout 1981, pp. 350–351; Darwazah 1984b, p. 134; Gharibah 1989, pp. 80–81; Zu'itir 1979, p. 236.

91. Qasimiyyah 1975, pp. 20–22; Barut 2013.

92. Parsons 2016, pp. 127–133.

93. Parsons 2016, pp. 110–111.

94. Raugh 2013, pp. 32–33; Snyder 1960, p. 286; Danchev 1987, pp. 21–44.

95. Darwazah 1984b, pp. 127–131; Parsons 2016, pp. 124–125.

96. Shufani 2003, pp. 464–465; Darwazah 1984b, pp. 145–146; Parsons 2016, p. 93.

97. Parsons 2016, pp. 111–112.

98. Parsons 2016, pp. 138–139.

99. Darwazah 1984b, pp. 145–146.

100. Zu'itir 1979, p. 258; Parsons 2016, pp. 138–140.

101. Parsons 2016, pp. 118–125.

102. Parsons 2016, pp. 122–123, 134–135.

103. Darwazah 1984b, p. 146.

104. Salih 2005, pp. 56–66; Parsons 2016, pp. 51–52.

105. Hout 1981, p. 352; Safari 1937, p. 2:57.

106. Hamdan 1985, pp. 145–147.

107. Darwazah 1984b, p. 133; Hout 1981, pp. 352–353; Zu'itir 1979, pp. 431–432.

108. Hughes 2019, p. 231.

109. Darwazah 1984b, p. 129; Hughes 2019, p. 223.

110. Hughes 2019, p. 234.

111. Hughes 2019, p. 220.

112. Darwazah 1984b, pp. 133–134.

113. Hughes 2019, p. 185.

114. Fahum 2012, p. 678.

115. Kayali 1985, p. 270.

116. Hughes 2019, p. 186.

117. Hughes 2019, pp. 162, 185.

118. Newberg 2012, pp. 104–105; Hughes 2016, pp. 150–151.

119. Gharibah 1989, p. 61.

120. Hout 1981, pp. 35–354.

121. Cohen 2012, p. 53; Cohen 2014, pp. 245–255.

122. Cohen 2014, pp. 245–255.

123. Cohen 2014, pp. 245–255.

124. Ghunaym 1980, pp. 64–66.

125. Cohen 2014, pp. 254–255; Khalah 1982, pp. 298–299; Hazmawi 1998, pp. 260–261; Hunidi 2003, pp. 223–227.

126. Cohen 1975, p. 242; *Palestine Post*, October 22, 1936.

127. *Palestine Post*, May 15, 1935, and August 17, 1936; Cohen 2014, p. 255; Ra'uf 1990, p. 501.

128. Allon 1970, p. 20; Tulloch 1972, p. 46.

129. Marston and Malkasian 2011, p. 33; Kumar 2012, p. 155.

130. Rossetto 1982, p. xvi; Tulloch 1972, pp. 45–46; Schiff 1985, p. 13.

131. Katz 1992, p. 12.

132. Allon 1970, p. 20.

133. Teveth 1987, p. 208.

134. Teveth 1987, p. 276.

135. Quandt, Jabber, and Lesch 1973, pt. 2, pp. 31–32.

136. Abd al-Ra'uf 1990, pp. 166–167; Fahmy 1975, pp. 172–173; Jiryis 1977, p. 2:281.

137. Safari 1937, p. 2:216; Khilah 1974, p. 777.

138. Fahmy 1975, pp. 172–173; Jiryis 1977, p. 2:281.

139. Teveth 1987, p. 216.

140. Quigley 1990, pp. 26–27.

141. Darwazah 1993, p. 845.

142. Darwazah 1984b, pp. 129–130; Jarrar 2011, p. 129; Salih 2012, p. 56.

143. Teveth 1987, p. 216.

144. Teveth 1987, pp. 216–217.

145. Teveth 1987, p. 217.

146. Rashidat 1991, pp. 92–94.

147. Darwazah 1984b, pp. 73–74; Hadi 2002, pp. 165–166.

148. Hadi 2002, p. 195; Shuqiri 1970, pp. 98–100.

149. Davis 1977, p. 25.

150. 'Alush 1967, p. 128; Zu'itir 1979, pp. 156–157; Darwazah 1984b, pp. 139–140; Kayali 1985, p. 278.

151. Wilson 1987, pp. 118–120; Tarbush 2015, pp. 151–152; Jabbar 2017, pp. 112–113; Gharib 2014, p. 260.

152. Jabbar 2017, p. 172.

153. Zu'itir 1979, p. 156; Shlaim 1988, p. 62.

154. Messiri 1999, pp. 6:265–280; 'Alush 1967, p. 127.

155. Zu'itir 1979, p. 159.

156. Shufani 2002, pp. 60–62.

157. Darwazah 1984b, pp. 139–140; Zu'itir 1979, pp. 156–157.

158. Darwazah 1984b, p. 156.

159. Jabbar 2017, pp. 135–136.

160. Darwazah 1984b, pp. 156–157.

161. Parsons 2016, pp. 133–135; Muhafazah 1989, p. 50; Shufani 2003, pp. 431–433.

162. Zu'itir 1979, pp. 156–160.

163. Darwazah 1984b, p. 140.

164. Hughes 2019, p. 102.

165. Mangold 2016, p. 145.

166. Shufani 2003, pp. 431–433.

167. Hout 1981, pp. 347–348; Parsons 2016, pp. 133–135.

168. Weizmann 1944, p. 239; Druks 2001, p. 20.

169. Teveth 1987, p. 224.

170. Hout 1981, pp. 356–357.

171. Kayali 1985, p. 278.

172. Alagha 2016, pp. 10–11.

173. See Morsy 1984, pp. 67–97; Marlowe 1954, p. 312; Crider 1978, p. iii; Abukhater 2019, p. 6.

174. Zu'itir 1979, p. 458.

175. Zu'itir 1979, p. 459.

176. Zu'itir 1979, pp. 459–460.

177. Zu'itir 1979, pp. 459–460.

178. Darwazah 1984b, p. 145.

179. Darwazah 1984b, p. 151.

180. Teveth 1987, p. 228.

181. Ḥakīm 1983, p. 4:238; Atassi 2015, pp. 131–135.

182. Zu'itir 1979, p. 309; Black 2015, p. 411.

183. Hout 1981, p. 383.

184. Hout 1981, p. 355.

185. Hout 1981, pp. 355–356.

186. 'Arif 1961, p. 407; Yassin 1992, p. 118.

187. Shaqra 1999, p. 74.

188. Hout 1981, p. 360; Goldmann 1994, p. 161; Sinanoglou 2019, p. 211.

189. Mustafa, Sha'ban, and Din 2004, p. 147; Shaqra 1999, p. 74; Menuhim 1965, p. 101; Segev 1986, p. 97.

190. McDonald 1951, p. 277.

191. Darwazah 1984b, p. 149.

192. Darwazah 1984b, p. 149; Hout 1981, p. 359.

193. Kayali 1985, p. 278; *Palestine*, December 24, 1936.

194. Kayali 1985.

195. Shlaim 1988, pp. 105–107; Barakat 2017, pp. 83–85.

196. Darwazah 1984b, pp. 152–153.

197. Darwazah 1984b, pp. 152–153.

198. 'Alush 1967, p. 133.

199. Zu'itir 1979, p. 254.

200. Zu'itir 1979, p. 254.

201. Darwazah 1984b, p. 319; Safari 1937, pp. 2:180–181.

202. Safari 1937, pp. 2:181–182.

203. Shufani 2003, pp. 468–469; Salih 2012, pp. 52–53; 'Alush 1967, pp. 140–141; 'Aqil 2017, pp. 31–32.

204. Essaid 2013, p. 94.

205. Sharett 2019, p. 473; Halul 2004, p. 110.

206. Zu'itir 1979, p. 280.

207. Zu'itir 1979, p. 280; Darwazah 1984b, pp. 151–152; Flapan 1979, p. 144.

208. Teveth 1987, p. 18; Flapan 1987, p. 22.

209. Flapan 1979, pp. 141–142.

210. Darwazah 1984b, p. 152.

211. Mahjoubi 1990, pp. 36–37.

212. Kimmerling 2005, p. 91.

213. Quigley 1990, p. 12.

214. Weizmann 1949, p. 149; Badran 2009, pp. 29–30.

215. Hout 1981, p. 361.

216. Zu'itir 1979, pp. 257–262.

217. Khalil 1998, p. 201.

218. Hadi 2002, p. 185.

219. Qasimiyah 1974, p. 230.

220. Qasimiyah 1974, pp. 262–267.

221. Qasimiyah 1974, pp. 262–267.

222. Qasimiyah 1974, p. 268.

223. Qasimiyah 1974, p. 268; Hout 1981, pp. 299–301.

224. Ibid, p. 270.

225. Ibid, pp. 274–276.

226. Ibid, p. 277.

227. Kayali 1985, pp. 279–280.

228. Kayali 1985, p. 278; Hout 1981, pp. 361–362; Darwazah 1984b, pp. 154–156; Touma 1978, pp. 132–133.

229. 'Ubaydi and Tai' 1948, p. 115.

230. Mahjoubi 1990, p. 78; Sayigh 1979, pp. 67–69.

231. Farsakh 2008, pp. 586–587; Edmunds 2000, pp. 145–146.

232. Kayali 1985, pp. 280–281.

233. Kayali 1985, p. 283.

234. Najjar 2005, p. 172.

235. Muhafazah 1989, pp. 284–285.

236. Darwazah 1984b, p. 45; Touma 1978, pp. 34–36.

237. Muhafazah 1989, p. 282; *Palestine*, Jaffa, issues 659–662, March 4–14, 1924.

238. *al-Karmel*, Haifa, no. 1406, on November 26, 1929; no. 1460, April 30, 1930; Muhafazah 1989, p. 283.

239. Darwazah 1984b, pp. 99–101; Zu'itir 1979, pp. 430–431.

240. *The Arab League*, Jerusalem, no. 1335, July 5, 1929; Muhafazah 1989, pp. 282–283.

241. *al-Karmel*, Haifa, no. 1406, January 29, 1928.

242. *al-Karmel*, Haifa, no. 1406, January 29, 1928.

243. *al-Karmel*, Haifa, no. 1406, January 29, 1928.

244. *al-Karmel*, Haifa, no. 1406, March 8, 1929.

245. Hout 1981, pp. 369–370.

246. Hout 1981, pp. 86–88.

247. Kayali 1985, p. 283; Shufani 2003, pp. 431–433.

248. 'Alush 1967, p. 137.
249. About the British Royal Commission's report, see Zu'itir 1979, pp. 308–313.
250. Stein 1984, pp. 217–218.
251. 'Alush 1967, p. 56; Shufani 2003, p. 428; Hout 1981, pp. 211–213.
252. Quigley 1990, pp. 23–26; Wright 1972, p. 13.
253. Quigley 1990, p. 20.
254. Hout 1981, pp. 211–213.
255. Zu'itir 1979, p. 296.
256. Zu'itir 1979, p. 312.
257. Darwazah 1984b, pp. 158–160; Farsun 2003, pp. 202–204; Shufani 2003, pp. 470–471.
258. Farsun 2003, pp. 202–204; Shufani 2003, pp. 470–471.
259. Darwazah 1984b, p. 74.
260. Kayali 1985, pp. 220–221; Darwazah 1984b, pp. 73–74.
261. Sulaymah 1986, pp. 30–32.
262. Turbin 1968, p. 269.
263. Touma 1978, pp. 139–140; Nuwar 2000, p. 195.
264. Darwazah 1984b, p. 125.
265. Touma 1978, p. 142.
266. Quigley 1990, pp. 23–25.
267. Hout 1981, p. 534. In High Arab Authority for Palestine 1954, pp. 75–76, the mufti of Palestine and president of the Supreme Arab Authority revealed the causes of the Palestine disaster and its relationship to international Zionist conspiracies.
268. Hout 1981, pp. 753–760.
269. Hout 1981, p. 761.
270. Touma 1978, p. 143.
271. Darwazah 1984b, pp. 142–143; Teveth 1987, p. 179.
272. Hout 1981, pp. 347–348.
273. Darwazah 1961, p. 262; Khadduri 1970, pp. 113–114.
274. Darwazah 1961, p. 263.
275. Flapan 1979, p. 144; Shlaim 2015; Masalha 1999, p. 188; Thomas 2011, pp. 19–20.
276. Touma 1978, p. 142.
277. Touma 1978, pp. 142–143; Muhafazah 2009, pp. 189–191.
278. Hadi 2002, p. 194.
279. Hout 1981, pp. 364–65.
280. Hout 1981, p. 752; Juha 2004, p. 223; Jabbar 2017, pp. 127–128.
281. Zu'itir 1979, p. 467.
282. Zu'itir 1979, pp. 467–468.
283. Zu'itir 1979, pp. 468–469.
284. Shuqiri 1970, pp. 66–68; Touma 1978, p. 144; 'Arif 1995, pp. 228–229.
285. 'Umar 1999, p. 34.
286. Hout 1981, p. 283; 'Alush 1967, pp. 102–104; Zu'itir 1979, pp. 430–431.
287. Zamili 2016, pp. 134–135.
288. Qaddurah 1993, pp. 19–20.

289. Zamili 2016, p. 134.
290. 'Alush 1967, p. 107.
291. 'Alush 1967, pp. 107–108.
292. Touma 1978, p. 153.
293. Darwazah 1984b, pp. 177–180.
294. Touma 1978, p. 153.
295. Teveth 1987, pp. 119–120.
296. Teveth 1987, pp. 121–124.
297. Darwazah 1984b, p. 181.
298. Teveth 1987, p. 249.
299. Teveth 1987, p. 250.
300. Hout 1981, p. 89; Ther 2014, p. 190; Pressman 2002, p. 24.
301. Parsons 2019, pp. 7–24.
302. Parsons 2020, pp. 8–25.

Chapter 4

The White Paper and Reviving of the Revolt, 1937–1939

The White Paper of 1939 was a policy statement issued by the British government that significantly altered its approach toward the conflict between the Jewish and Arab populations in Palestine. The White Paper proposed restrictions on Jewish immigration to Palestine and limits on Jewish land purchases, which greatly upset the Zionist movement and led to a revival of the Palestinian Arab revolt against British rule. The period from 1937 to 1939 was a time of intense conflict and political maneuvering in Palestine, as both Jewish and Arab groups struggled to achieve their respective goals. The British government, which had been administering the territory since the end of World War I, was caught in the middle of this conflict and faced increasing pressure from both sides.

In response to the escalating violence and unrest, the British government issued the Peel Commission report in 1937, which recommended the partition of Palestine into separate Jewish and Arab states. However, this proposal was rejected by both sides, and the conflict continued.

The White Paper of 1939 was seen by many as a capitulation to Arab demands and was fiercely opposed by the Zionist movement. The restrictions on immigration and land purchases effectively closed the door on Jewish immigration to Palestine at a time when Jews in Europe were facing increasing persecution under Nazi rule.

The White Paper also had wider implications for British policy in the Middle East, as it was seen as a betrayal of previous commitments made to the Zionist movement. It marked a turning point in British policy toward the conflict and set the stage for the eventual withdrawal of British forces from Palestine and the establishment of the state of Israel in 1948.

The White Paper and the revival of the Palestinian Arab revolt remain significant events in the history of the region and continue to shape the political and social dynamics of the Middle East today.

THE REPERCUSSIONS OF ENDING THE STRIKE
AND STOPPING THE REVOLUTION

In the wake of ending the strike and stopping the revolution on November 11, 1936, Palestine experienced a year of anticipation and tension. This period was a truce between the two stages of the revolution, during which two contradictory phenomena were witnessed. The Zionists began to commit criminal and provocative acts in order to bring the Arabs into conflict, until the British Royal Committee concluded that coexistence between Jews and Arabs was impossible and that the partition resolution, which was supported by the Jewish Agency, was the only solution. On the other hand, the Supreme Arab Committee adopted a policy of restraint so that the Zionists would not spoil what the intervention of the prince and the Arab kings could lead to.[1]

It was reported that a controversy erupted that day between the mandate government and the military ruler who demanded the arrest of the mufti to end his provocative activity. However, the government considered that the circumstances were not appropriate and instead preferred to exile him from the Arab region. After the decision of the Peel Commission, an attempt was made to arrest the mufti, but he managed to seek refuge in his home, near the holy mosque of al-Aqsa. At the same time, Archibald Earl Wavell was replaced by Field Marshal Sir John Greer Dill, commander of the British forces in Palestine, who failed to suppress the revolution. Arthur Wauchoupe was terminated as a high commissioner, and Sir Alec Kirkbride, who had previously served as the governor of Uganda, Acre, and the district of Galilee, as well as the commander of the British army, was appointed to succeed him in his role.[2]

At the same time, Vladimir Jabotinsky's opponent, who led the so-called Revisionist movement, believed that the Jewish state should be established on the entirety of the land that makes up Palestine. Nevertheless, he supported the concept of partition in principle.[3] Right-wing gangs began planting time bombs in Arab markets in order to disrupt the partition project, which the Royal Commission appeared to recommend. As a result, dozens of people were killed, and many more were injured. As a direct response to these massacres, Arab revolutionaries began to pick up where they left off, resuming their attacks on Zionist colonies and institutions.[4]

According to the reports filed by the police, not a single day went by without a violent or bloody incident. Although there were twice as many dead and wounded Arabs as there were dead and wounded Zionists, the procedures for prosecution and detention were limited to Arab activists, with the number of detainees held at the Mazra'a detention center near Acre reaching four hundred. This is despite the fact that the number of dead and wounded Arabs was double that of the dead and wounded Zionists.[5] The intensification of repression prompted the revolutionaries to step up their activity and led to the expansion of their activities.[6] In July 1937, the high commissioner wrote a report saying, "The number of gang operations in the country's northern and central regions has increased significantly, and it appears that the number of rebels is growing while their organization is becoming more effective."[7]

The year of anticipation and tension cast a shadow over the Arab political activity, and it completely ended what had been achieved in terms of unity of the classes in the previous year. The conflict between the two chambers and the opposition leaders worsened after the end of the strike, the end of the revolution, and the withdrawal of the Defense Party and opposition figures from the membership of the Arab Higher Committee. This coincided with the campaign of the English and Jewish newspapers, which referred to the mufti and the national elements as "extremists" and called for "moderates" to take over. The Arab Higher Committee rushed to invite Raghib al-Nashashibi to return to its membership in order for the nation to appear united in such dangerous circumstances. However, the chairman of the Defense Party did not respond, as there were no longer pressing circumstances that compelled him and his party to remain within the national ranks instead of reverting to their approach before the strike and revolution.[8]

The opposition, regardless of motives and goals, had influence among the elders of the countryside and the village leaders, inciting them to oppose the revolutionists and not cooperate with them. The revolutionaries who were active from the autumn of 1937 until the spring of 1938 were a result of the authority's pressure on the village chiefs and their leaders, as well as the opposition leaders' contacts with their supporters. In many villages, they were not welcomed; nor did they receive care and attention, as they had before the strike and revolution ended. Rather, some of the village elders and their chiefs frowned on the revolutionaries, refused to provide them with food, and asked them to leave their villages. As a result, many of them were forced to resort to the caves, as happened with the leader 'Abd al-Rahim al-Haj Muhammad, known as Abu Kamal, who was one of the first leaders of the revolution. He had no shelter when he was wounded and spent a few weeks in a cave until his wound was healed.[9] This prompted the leaders of the renewed revolution to discipline some of those notables and chiefs. With the intensification of the revolution in the spring of 1938, its leaders began to impose their presence, and the villages began to provide the required weapons and supplies and soon returned to their previous support.[10] One of the results of imposing their presence was that assassinations took place of some police officers known to be hostile to the revolutionaries and to the citizens participating in the strike. Together with a number of spies and land brokers, they sought to assassinate some of the countrymen and village leaders who were known to be loyal to opposition leaders or to act brazenly against the rebels. Such was the case in the unsuccessful assassination attempt on Suleiman Tuqan, the mayor of Nablus, a member of the Defense Party leadership.[11]

With the escalation of the revolution and the oppression operations, national sentiment grew, and with it came stern action against spies and collaborators. It is in this context that Officer Ahmed Nayif was killed in Haifa on August 7, 1937.[12] Nayif was an aide to the intelligence agent Halim Bastah and was accused of helping to track the al-Qassam activists. The public people did not pray for him in the mosque; nor was he buried in a Muslim cemetery.[13] This forced the police to bury him at night and establish a guard over his grave. This was repeated with more than one agent and spy. It was reported that a spy's wife known as al-'Abd Katsiru, when she learned of his espionage, closed the door of her house in his face, refusing to accept him; then she went to the sharia court asking the judge to separate her from him due to the charges he faced, to which the judge acquiesced.[14] The judge's ruling, divorce due to espionage in the time of the British mandate, was an indication of the power of national feeling at the time.

THE QUALITATIVE SHIFT IN AWARENESS AND GENERAL ARAB ACTION TOWARD THE ZIONIST THREAT

The Arab National Movement in Palestine retained national dimension among the national elites and the masses, despite the decline of the nationalist movement in the Levant after World War I. The Arab people in Palestine retained the strength of their national sentiments while facing the challenge of the strategic alliance between British colonialism and Zionist settlement. Most of the elites of the Levant and other Arab provinces were facing European colonialism alone.

With the increasing clarity of the extent to which the colonial powers supported the Zionists, the Palestinian intellectual and political elites felt the urgent need for Arab strength equal to colonial powers in support of the Zionist movement. One of the most prominent repercussions of the gift of al-Buraq (a winged horse, on which Muhammad ascended to heaven) was the widening circle of those demanding Arab unity and a growing sense of the urgent need for Arab support. On the other hand, the sanctity of al-Buraq and its repercussions were very clear in the Arab world, especially Egypt, which was witnessing increased Arab national awareness.

With the active Arab presence in the revolution, despite its limitations, Palestine and its Arab surroundings witnessed a qualitative shift in the feeling of unity in the protest and for the future. As the Palestinian resistance went beyond sympathy and sentimental participation to engage in revolutionary action, the report of the Peel Commission on the conclusive result indicated the position of the Arab world toward the Palestinian resistance.[15] The Arab response to the report and its recommendation to divide Palestine confirmed the result that the report referred to, which was the partitioning of Palestine into areas controlled by Jews and areas controlled by Arabs. The Arab response, not in favor of partitioning, was a direct reaction to the report presented by the committee, which included the recommendation to partition Palestine. It did not offer any support for the Palestinian Arabs' contention that they ought to have their own independent state. There was also a greater degree of interaction between the Supreme Arab Committee and both the official leadership and the Arab popular forces.[16]

It is worth noting that the committee report's conclusive result in the Arab world's attitude toward the Palestinian National Movement today was manifested in a variety of ways: popular participation in the revolution and a public perception that the Zionist threat was not limited to Palestine but rather threatened the entire Arab East, and an official intervention by the Palestinian leadership, in response to the British intervention, aimed at making it clear that the Palestinian National Movement was not a threat to the Arab world. Both of these factors contributed to the shift in the position of the Arabs. It developed a sense of having a supportive national depth to the extent that popular participation increased the sense of trust and confidence of the Arab people living in Palestine. Official Arab interventions weakened the Palestinian leadership's decision-making independence, and leadership bargaining left them unprepared to bear the consequences of the long-running conflict, which extends in nature as a struggle against the evacuation of settler colonialism, they were backed and supported by the greatest international powers and capabilities. What facilitated Arab official intervention and the response of Palestinian leaders was that Arab public thought and action, both Palestinian and private, had not come up with a comprehensive strategy for managing conflict with the Zionist-colonial challenge.

The Bloudan Conference, the National Youth Conference, the Arab Parliamentary Conference, and the Arab Women's Conference are the four Arab conferences that reflected the conclusive result of the committee report in increasing awareness and general Arab action toward the Zionist threat.

The Arab Higher Committee made a request at the Bloudan Conference for the Mandate Authority to hold a general conference in Palestine. The purpose of the conference was to investigate the conditions that were currently in place in Palestine and determine what actions were required to protect Arab rights. On the other hand, the Mandate Authority did not agree, citing the argument that holding the conference would provoke the local population. The Action Committee for the Defense of Palestine issued a call for the convening of a general Arab conference on September 8 and 9, 1937, in the resort town of Bloudan in Syria. The conference was to be attended by 411 participants from Arab countries, without a single government delegate.[17] The mufti was unable to attend the conference, as his house was besieged by the British, but he was unanimously elected as the honorary president of the conference, while Naji al-Suwaidi, the former Iraqi prime minister, chaired the conference. His office consisted of Muhammad 'Ali 'Alubah, former Egyptian minister of education and endowments; Prince Shakib Arslan and Riyadh al-Sulh, the permanent members of the Syrian-Palestinian delegation in Geneva; Archbishop Ignatius Harika, Greek Orthodox Archbishop of Hama; Syrian member of Parliament Sabri al-'Asali; Fu'ad Khalil Mufarrej, secretary of the Defense Committee in Damascus; and Muhammad 'Izzat Darwazah, representing the Higher Arab Committee. One of the most prominent manifestations of the Peel Commission report's conclusive result regarding the position of the Arab surroundings in the conflict taking place on the land of Palestine was the level of Egyptian participation in the conference and the commitment shown by Muhammad 'Ali 'Alubah, a member of the conference office, who declared, "If it is the responsibility of the Arab nation as a whole to defend Palestine, then Egypt will be the first country to fulfill this obligation."[18]

The conference unanimously passed the following decisions:

A. Palestine is an inseparable part of the Arab world.

B. Rejecting and resisting the partition of Palestine and the establishment of a Jewish state.

C. The proposal suggests the abolition of the Mandate and the Balfour Declaration, as well as the negotiation and signing of a treaty with Britain. This treaty would ensure the Palestinian Arab people's independence and sovereignty. Furthermore, it emphasizes the importance of establishing a constitutional government that upholds the rights of minorities in accordance with general constitutional principles.

D. Stopping immigration promptly, and legislation to prevent the transfer of lands from Arabs to Jews.

E. Demanding the issuance of a general amnesty for those accused and convicted during the revolution, the release of detainees and prisoners, and the return of deportees and political exiles.

F. The conference made the announcement that the continuation of friendship between the British and Arab peoples was dependent on the fulfillment of the previous demands, and that Britain's insistence on its policy in Palestine forced the Arabs as a whole to take new directions. The conference also stated that the previous demands must be met. Additionally, the only way for a coalition between Jewish and Arab people to exist is if these conditions are met.

G. Sending these decisions to the League of Nations and other relevant centres.[19]

The conference sent telegrams of acknowledgment to the Arab kings and princes and also decided to send a telegram of appreciation to the Indian leader, Jawaharlal Nehru, for his efforts in the cause of Palestine, and another to the pope, asking him to intervene to avert the catastrophe threatening the Holy Land. The conference formed an Executive Committee that included the Arab Higher Committee in Palestine, a representative from every Arab country, and the election of a Committee for the Defense of Palestine in every Arab country.[20]

Some argue that the conference established the clear scientific concept of Arab nationalism. In his speech to the conference, Nabih al-Azamih, who assumed the presidency of the Executive Committee, stressed that no Arab country could stand alone without being an integral part of a larger and stronger entity and without occupying its place in the collective system.[21]

Thus, it is clear that the conference did not close the door to friendship with the British people or coexistence with the Jews in Palestine but rather linked the two matters to Britain's implementation of the legitimate Palestinian demands and Zionist acceptance those demands. The British consul in Damascus attributed the moderation of the conference's decisions to the keenness of moderate members, especially the president of the conference, Naji al-Suwaidi.[22]

Despite the fact that many wealthy landowners, great merchants, and members of the wealthy class participated in the conference, all of whom demonstrated a strong desire to maintain the friendship between the Arab and British peoples, the conference was distinguished by the presence of elements that had a conscious vision of the scope of the conflict. More than one advocate made the following assertion: "The establishment of a colonial center in the Jewish state as a direct challenge to the continued existence of Arab and Islamic states is one of the primary goals of the British government."[23]

In spite of the fact that some participants shared this conviction, the conference did not adopt a position that was categorically anti-Jewish. Instead, it reaffirmed the Arabs' pledge in Palestine to treat Jews in the same manner as minorities in all countries that applied the principles of the League of Nations. It is clear that the distinction between Arab and general Arab and Palestinian thought was based on a human dimension when this position is compared to the racism that characterized the testimonies of the Zionist leaders before the Peel Commission months earlier.[24]

The statements that were made at the conference, as well as the comments that were made by the Arab press about the conference, reflected an advanced level of national awareness, as well as a sense of the urgent need for integration and progress on the path toward unity. After the failure of the Arab revolution in the early 1920s, which led to a decline in interest in regional thought, the colonial-Zionist challenge can be seen as a catalyst for Arab national awareness. However, despite being comprised primarily of freethinking individuals, the conference did not succeed in establishing an organization to carry out the actions suggested by its participants. Therefore, despite the adoption of Palestinian national principles, the assertion of the national dimension of the conflict, the enthusiasm of the speakers, and the generally festive atmosphere, it had no effect beyond being a phenomenon that was covered in the media.[25]

Given the outcome of the Bloudan Conference, which provided little clarity, approximately one hundred members of the national orientation, all of whom were dissatisfied with the conference, called for the holding of a secret conference on September 12 to discuss the possibility of taking effective measures to combat partition. This decision was made despite the fact that there was not a lot of clarity. They came to an agreement to organize a general conference for Arab youth and established a preparatory committee for the conference, with Damascus serving as the location of the committee's headquarters for the conference.[26] At the time, the Palestinian militants began contacting the Syrian revolutionaries and prepared to resume the revolution by collecting weapons and ammunition and storing them in the Nablus area under the supervision of the mufti.[27]

The Bloudan Conference, which is notorious for its inaction, did not go beyond the traditional methods of work used in Arab countries, which included issuing statements, sending telegrams of support and protest, and forming committees. Notwithstanding this, the National Youth Conference did carry out an analysis of the revolution and the role that the Arabs played in putting a stop to it. This analysis identified the strengths and weaknesses of Arab public and private Palestinian practice, all the way up to the identification of what was necessary to meet the challenge posed by the strategic alliance between British colonialism and the Zionist movement. In the Zionist interpretation, it was discussed how the Committee for the Defense of Palestine in Damascus should be established, and Nabih al-Azamih was given the role of chairman of the committee. The Arab uprising in Palestine was supposed to be governed by a political and military administration like this. The committee was involved in activities such as sowing the seeds of renewed unrest, collecting funds, smuggling weapons, and recruiting volunteers from Syria and Iraq.[28]

An Arab Parliamentary Conference was held in Cairo in October 1938, at the invitation of Muhammad 'Ali 'Alubah, chairman of the Egyptian Parliamentary Committee, and chaired by Bahiyu al-Din Barakat, president of the Egyptian Parliament. Present were Faris al-Khury, president of the Syrian Parliament; Mawlud Mukhlis, Speaker of the Iraqi Parliament; a number of deputies from Egypt, Iraq, Syria, and Lebanon; representatives of the Arab Higher Committee; political, social, and religious figures from Morocco, Yemen, and Palestine; Muslims of India and Yugoslavia; and representatives of the American diaspora.[29]

The conference decided to support the Palestine National Charter, reject the mandate and the Jewish national homeland, condemn the partition decision, condemn British repression measures, and demand the establishment of a constitutional government in Palestine, responsible to a representative parliament elected on the basis of proportional representation. It called for a stop to Jewish immigration and the sale of Arab lands to Jews and foreigners, demanded the cancelling of the rulings against the revolutionaries, as well as the release of prisoners and detainees and the return of exiles and deportees, and called for a treaty between Palestine and Britain ending the mandate.[30]

It was clear from previous decisions that the Arab Parliamentary Conference was committed to the Palestinian national demands. It also recognized the right to citizenship and the full political rights of Jews in Palestine, as well as the idea of a treaty between Palestine and Britain. This was at the time of the intensification of the revolution, which confirmed the positiveness of the representatives of the Arab nation toward a democratic solution to the Arab-Zionist conflict.

At the invitation of Mrs. Huda Sha'rawi, the pioneer of the women's movement in Egypt, the Arab Women's Conference was held in Cairo in October 1938, attended by a group of women's movement activists from Egypt, Iraq, Syria, Lebanon, and Palestine.[31] The conference endorsed the demands of the Palestinian Arabs to cancel the mandate and the Balfour Declaration, to stop immigration and the transfer of Arab lands to Jews and foreigners, and to reject partition and the establishment of a sovereign Jewish state. It also condemned the British repression of the Palestinian Arabs and demanded the release of prisoners and detainees and the return of deportees and exiles. It called on "every Arab and Arab to help the Palestinian revolutionists who defend their existence and the future of the Arab nation."[32]

Although the Arab Women's Conference did not go beyond a media phenomenon, it had a positive impact on the Arab people in Palestine as it was taking place at the decisive stage of the revolution. Both the Parliamentary Conference and the Women's Conference felt that the Arab revolution, aimed at achieving national aspirations, had strong national support. The significance of the four Arab conferences highlighted this support.

LOUIS ANDREWS'S ASSASSINATION, THE SUPREME ISLAMIC COUNCIL'S DISSOLUTION, AND THE MUFTI'S ASYLUM IN LEBANON

On September 26, 1937, members of the al-Qassam League assassinated the governor of the Galilee Brigade, Louis Andrews, who had been active in tracking their movement in the north. Although the Arab Higher Committee and the National Committees condemned the assassination, the mandate government saw this as an opportunity to implement the scheme to defeat the will of the national forces. On October 1, it declared the Arab Supreme Committee and the National Committees illegal and arrested four members of the Supreme Committee and exiled them to the Seychelles. These included Ahmed Hilmi Abd al-Baqi, Dr. Hussein Fakhri al-Khaldi, Fu'ad Saba, and Ya'qub al-Ghusin. Also exiled was Rashid al-Haj Ibrahim, a well-known independence figure in Haifa. Martial law was tightened, and two hundred politicians and members of the National Committees were arrested. Meanwhile, Jamal al-Husseini, the head of the Arab Party and a prominent member of the Supreme Committee, managed to disappear and seek refuge in Syria. As for the rest of the committee members who were on national missions outside the country, the mandate government issued orders not to allow them to return to Palestine. These actions were justified by claiming that Arab leaders were responsible for these events and their activities were against public security.[33] Also, the mufti was removed from the presidency of the Supreme Islamic Council, and his administration was handed over to a tripartite committee headed by the high commissioner, Alec Kirkbride, with the membership of an Englishman and a third Arab Muslim, to oversee the affairs of the Islamic endowments and Islamic courts.[34]

Thus, the mandate government returned to control the revenues of the endowments, as was the case before al-Haj Amin al-Husseini assumed the presidency of the Supreme Islamic Council. Consequently, al-Haj Amin and the National Movement lacked basic financial resources. It also meant that there was no funding for attracting employees to the endowments and sharia courts, imams of mosques, marriage celebrants, and the like. As a result of the shift in the management of the Supreme Islamic Council and Islamic endowments, loyalty switched to the mandate in the interest of preserving livelihoods.

When the mufti learned that it had been decided to bring Indian Muslim soldiers to storm the holy mosque of al-Aqsa and arrest him, he infiltrated the village of Tantturah near Haifa and then took a boat to Sidon, where the French resident prevented him from continuing his journey to Syria. He was kept in the town of Zouk Mikael under semi–house arrest. The mufti, before leaving Jerusalem, had left a pamphlet in which he called for resistance and continued struggle. As soon as the news of his arrival in Lebanon was announced, the leaflet was distributed across Palestine. He had also given permission to Agence France-Presse to air the news after his arrival in Lebanon, which stated, "We are not going to call off the jihad until we have achieved full independence. The Arab and Islamic worlds need to be told in no uncertain terms by Britain that they are not to be associated in any way with it and are a formidable force in the world."[35]

In his memoirs, al-Haj Amin al-Husseini mentioned that he suggested going to the mountains and managing the revolution from there, especially since he had military experience as he had been an officer in the Ottoman army for a time. However, those around him who were leaders of the National Movement opposed the idea on the pretext that the topography of Palestine and its limited space would not help him to secure safe and secret movement. In addition, the British would intensify their attacks in his areas of presence. Accordingly, it was decided that he would leave the country.[36]

Bahjat Abu Gharibieh states that the night of October 14–15, 1937, in which the mufti left Palestine, was "the zero hour for the revolutionaries."

> On this night, armed revolutionary groups moved all over Palestine (and our group was among them) to launch massive military attacks. In the Jerusalem area, several attacks on police and army patrols were blown up, and they were fired upon in abundance near Hebron, a train carrying British forces was attacked by heavy fire southwest of Jerusalem, a passenger train was removed from the track, railways were destroyed in several places, and telephone lines were cut on a large scale, the Iraqi oil pipeline was blown up near the Jordan River and the flowing oil caught fire. On the outskirts of Jerusalem, there were several attacks on Jewish passenger cars, and many colonies came under fire. The next day a large team of revolutionaries attacked the Lydda airport, the largest airport in Palestine, they occupied it, burned its offices, passport offices, and wireless installations completely burned, and the government forces entering the villages came under fire. Thus the revolution started and spread everywhere.[37]

The night of the mufti's departure was of zero hour for the start of the revolution, as the sheikh of the Palestinian militants decided that the mufti's exit was not an individual decision but rather the decision of the leaders around him. This confirmed the validity of what al-Haj Amin al-Husseini narrated in his memoirs.

In Damascus, where a number of members of the Arab Higher Committee and leaders of the Palestinian National Movement were present, views differed regarding the mufti's asylum in Lebanon. A group of them saw that the mufti should not have left Palestine, reasoning that harm suffered by some would stoke the revolution. The other side saw that sacrifice was not an end but rather a means and that it was more beneficial for the mufti to escape from the hands of the British and to be free to lead the National Movement from afar.[38]

When the outcomes of that asylum are taken into consideration, it becomes abundantly clear that the leader of the Arab National Movement in Palestine would not have voluntarily left the front lines and would not have sought refuge in Lebanon of his own free will. We are certain that what al-Haj Amin al-Husseini did at that time was an incorrect leadership decision made by the mufti and the leaders around him. It was perhaps the biggest mistake of his life, as it had a negative impact on the National Movement, his leadership role, and the fate of leadership. It is not to be forgotten that the Mandate Authority and its agents and representatives were from a squadron of the mufti of Palestine and the head of the Arab Higher Committee, known for bringing in Indian Muslim soldiers to storm the Al-Aqsa Mosque compound and arrest him. With the loss of Jamal al-Husseini, the second in command for Syria, the national movement lost much of the effectiveness of the two most important figures. When one reads about the experiences of national liberation movements in the third world, it becomes abundantly clear that the leaders who were responsible for arrests and forcible exiles were the same ones who imposed their influential presence on the colonial powers in their respective national arenas. Furthermore, the leaders' achievements and influence were incomparable to the achievements and influence of the perception that their presence was free outside their country in order to facilitate communication with international powers and to ensure their safety.

Even though they had ties to important people from the countryside and leaders of popular neighborhoods in cities, and even though most of the National Movement's leaders had been absent from the stage, despite attempts by leaders of the Defense Party and other opponents to fill the void left by the National Movement's leaders' absence, they were not successful. The fact that they were not arrested and prosecuted discredited them in the eyes of the public, while their withdrawal from the membership of the Higher Arab Committee ended the weak link that connected them to the National Movement. The growing revolutionary movement, in the absence of the national leadership, represented by the mufti and members of the Higher Arab Committee, is evidence of the nature of the revolution, which was, in the first place, a revolution of the peasants and the urban poor, although a limited number of intellectuals participated. As for the mufti and the other leaders, there was no doubt about their patriotism on the whole, and they were eager to reach a peaceful settlement with the colonial-Zionist alliance.

They did not take sides in supporting the revolutionary movement until after Britain failed to meet their demands and the concessions they made did not receive acceptance by the mandate government, the British government, or the Zionist leadership.

This is supported by objective foreign experts. In his testimony, Joseph Mary Nagle Jeffries states,

> The truth is that the most prominent Arab exiles and other detainees have already devoted their efforts long ago to these peaceful appeals, which have only been denied and neglected. They spent their political lives moving between the heads of the Jerusalem triangle, London and Geneva. And there was nothing in these demands hostile to the British. Indeed, their crime in the eyes of the officials was legal demands, and it was not infinite and was based on the Charter of the League of Nations.[39]

In Britain, it was clear that public opinion fully supported the escalating repressive government measures against the National Mobility activists. It was also a common belief that the Arab Supreme Committee and notables of the country were responsible for the assassination of Andrews. It seemed that the minister of colonies aimed at escalating repressive measures against national elements and increasing detention operations, preparing the stage for the British government to negotiate with people with depressed hearts and weak souls, as Prince 'Abdullah saw them.[40]

AFTER THE LEAGUE OF NATIONS ENDS, BRITAIN ASSIGNS THE PARTITION RESOLUTION TO A TECHNICAL COMMITTEE

Britain submitted to the League of Nations Mandate Committee during the first week of August 1937 a request for approval of the partition project. At the time, there were intense discussions between the British minister of colonies, the accompanying delegation, and the members of the committee on the overall recommendations of the Peel Commission, especially the issue of population exchange between the proposed Jewish and Arab countries, which constituted only 12,500 Zionist settlers compared to 325,000 Arab citizens.[41] The majority of the members of the Mandate Committee seemed uncomfortable with the idea of displacing Arab citizens from their lands.[42] As the chairman of the committee stated, "I am an old man, but in my life I have not heard of people, especially farmers, who voluntarily flee from the most fertile part of their country to the laziest parts."[43]

Although the committee approved the division in principle, it opposed the immediate establishment of the two states and proposed to prolong what it called "the period of political exercise" under the Mandate.[44]

Chaim Weizmann held a secret meeting with the British minister of colonies, William Ormsby Gore, two days before the Mandate Committee, where he called for amendments to the report of the Peel Commission.[45] These included the following: transferring the Arabs of Galilee to the Negev, or eastern Jordan, and including an area of four hundred thousand acres that was not part of the Jewish state so that it formed a third of the total land area of Palestine.[46] It also included the Jewish neighborhoods in the city of Jerusalem, the potash production centers, and the electric power station of the Rothenberg project; it stated that the customs fees and taxes that the Jewish state collected and paid to the Arab state should not be considered an aid-binding issue but rather a subject for negotiation between the Jewish and Arab countries; and it stated that the Jewish state should have full sovereignty over the cities of Haifa, Acre, Safed, and Tiberias, located in the territory of the Palestinians.[47]

At the end of the meeting, Weizmann promised that he would support the partition project at the World Jewish Congress, which was taking place in Zurich, if the necessary adjustments were made to the satisfaction of the Zionists. With the exception of the British minister's insistence on retaining sovereignty over Acre for historical reasons, he did not oppose the rest of the demands.[48] It seems that Weizmann had verified that Major Ormsby Gore would support making the required amendments, as he supported the draft partition at the World Jewish Congress, as already mentioned.[49]

During the League of Nations council meeting in Geneva in September 1937, the British foreign secretary, Anthony Eden, requested that the British government be given the authority to study and elaborate on the partition project and to limit Jewish immigration to one thousand immigrants per month for eight months.[50] Delegations from Romania, Latvia, Poland, Czechoslovakia, and Yugoslavia opposed the restriction of immigration, as all of these countries were facing the Jewish problem and saw its solution by removing their Jews to Palestine. The British request was supported by the representatives of Belgium, Switzerland, the Netherlands, the Scandinavian countries, and Portugal. The United States and the countries of Latin America that were members of the League, along with the Russian and the Turkish delegates, remained silent.[51] Consequently, opposition to the partition project was limited to Egyptian foreign minister Wasif Ghali, Iraqi minister Tawfiq al-Suwaidi, and the delegates of France, Iran, Afghanistan, Albania, and Ireland. As a consequence of this, the council gave its consent for Britain to carry out exhaustive research on the partition project. The legitimate approval that the House of Commons of the British government had given the League of Nations for its acceptance had been put on hold. As a result, the undertaking was put on hold, and the British established a technical committee to carry out the essential study. This committee, called the Woodhead Commission,[52] arrived in Palestine on April 27, 1938.[53]

THE REVOLUTION RENEWS, DEVELOPS, AND REESTABLISHES

It has already been mentioned that the terrorist operations practiced by the Zionist ultranational gangs, which rejected the partition plan, caused individual Arab reactions. Individual Arab reactions grew and developed with a growing sense of loss of hope in the British response to meet Arab demands, in spite of the cautionary approach taken by the British government. The Louis Andrews assassination was the culmination of the totality of individual operations that had not stopped since the announcement of the cessation of the revolution nearly a year before. The removal of national leaders had not paralyzed the National Movement; it had caused more revolutionary elements to take over with greater freedom of will and independent decision making. The Qassamids had a prominent role in the new stage of the revolution, as they had in the first.[54]

In addition, the ongoing arrests, dismissals, and deportations that took place in the aftermath of the murder of Louis Andrews contributed to the further escalation of the revolution, especially after Sheikh Farhan al-Sa'di, Sheikh 'Izz al-Din al-Qassam's successor, was hanged by the British on October 22, 1937 during the month of Ramadan.[55] Contrary to what the Mandatory Authority wanted with its repressive measures, the people gathered around the revolutionaries, and the British government was disappointed that removing the leadership had not led to a paralysis of political life in Arab areas and acceptance of the implementation of the partition resolution. In the face of the new reality, the British colonial secretary was forced to admit that armed resistance movements were very effective throughout the country, with dangerous consequences.[56]

Once the mufti was settled in Lebanon, he reached an agreement to form the Central Committee of the revolution with some members of the Arab Higher Committee in Damascus, most notably Muhammad 'Izzat Darwazah, as well as some leaders of the revolution and national figures. This organization had its headquarters in Damascus, and its primary mission was to secure funding and supplies for the emerging revolutionary movement. In addition, it dispatched Arab fighters to the region, working in conjunction with the Committee for the Defense of Palestine in Damascus.[57] Donations from various Arab countries were the main source of funding, after the paralysis that affected the Palestinian economy as a result of improper management of the long strike, as well as the loss of the mufti's position as head of the Supreme Islamic Council and the possibility of employing national elements in the institutions of the council and the management of Islamic endowments.[58]

The Central Committee was very effective in its investments in the conflict between the British and French mandates, in the collection of donations in Syria and Lebanon, and in the channeling of assistance from money and weapons. On that day, the national elements in Syria, Lebanon, and Jordan played reminiscent roles in enabling the revolutionaries and their assistants to facilitate the penetration of the northern and eastern borders of Palestine. This occurred as a result of the fact that the four Levant countries, in relation to the revolution and the revolutionaries, became one country. In addition, neither passage passes nor passports were required, and there were no customs checkpoints, police stations, or military patrols.[59]

The crises in Italy and Abyssinia contributed to the worsening of the situation between France and Britain. This was one of the factors that helped. During that period, a rumor circulated that the Italian Fascist regime was providing financial support for the Palestinian uprising. A number of people affiliated with the Palestinian opposition did not stop spreading rumors. This runs counter to what Benito Mussolini knew about Jabotinsky's openness to all varieties of Zionism and his support for the Zionist project. This is especially true in regard to the Revisionists led by Jabotinsky. Along with the denial of the official Israeli account of what took place, it was mentioned and stated that

> in addition, there is no evidence to support the claim that the Arabs were in receipt of actual financial assistance from Italy or Germany. The Mufti's men were soliciting financial assistance from the Arab nations that were located nearby. However, the Arabs are not used to giving targets such generous donations. The majority of the public is content with paying what they perceive to be insignificant sums, and despite this, an effort was made to impose general taxes on the Arab population.[60]

Although dozens of Arab militants joined the renewed revolution, as in the first stage of the revolution, the peasants of Palestine were its backbone and the source of its support for funding and cadres. Arab sources say that the number of revolutionaries reached about ten thousand during the peak stage in the summer of 1938, with three thousand of them coming from the countryside and about a thousand from the cities, while the rest participated on a part-time basis. This was in addition to the vast masses who possessed arms and contributed to the revolutionary work when requested to do so or deemed it necessary.[61] In terms of the Israeli story, it is estimated that by the end of

1939, there were fifteen thousand revolutionaries: ten thousand in small regular brigades that moved from village to village and the rest remaining in their homes and participating in operations as needed.

The revolution, although its backbone was a limited number of revolutionaries, was a revolution of all national forces. This was recognized by the commander of the British army in Palestine, Lt. Gen. Robert Hadden Haining, who wrote,

> Because the villagers take advantage of every opportunity to engage in sniper fire, small acts of sabotage, and the placement of mines on public roads, it is challenging for us to maintain control over the rural areas, even when there are few insurgents present. This form of resistance is difficult to overcome because it is very difficult to find a target to hit. As a result, it is difficult to find an objective to pursue. In addition, the feelings of the population are aligned with the gangs rather than with the British government.[62]

The third commander of the British army in Palestine noted the limited effect of the above-mentioned counterrevolutionary position taken by a number of village leaders and their leaders, influenced by the pressures of the Mandate Authority, along with the counterrevolutionary activities by the opposition leaders who had returned to open cooperation with the British and the Zionists.[63]

The revolution witnessed different stages of leadership and participation. In the initial stage, the urban elites played a prominent role, leading the strike in 1936 and serving as key figures in the revolution. However, as the revolution progressed, a shift occurred, and the peasantry and residents of popular neighborhoods emerged as leaders during the new stage. This change in leadership dynamics showcased the diverse support and participation across different segments of society. Not only did their numerical majority among the revolutionaries make them the backbone of the movement, but they also served as the leaders on the front lines. Every single one of them was a Palestinian farmer, with the sole exception of 'Abd al-Qadir al-Husseini, who was the most influential leader in the southern region. This, however, does not detract from the fact that members of the elite, including some intellectuals and revolutionary elements, were recruited. As a result, it was referred to as a "peasant revolution," despite the fact that it was driven by demands related not strictly to agriculture but to the nation as a whole.

The second stage of the revolution was distinguished by the fact that it engaged in conflict with the British forces and the Arab collaborators with the mandate, singling them out for the majority of its activity at a time when it was attempting to target the Zionist colonies and institutions. This was one of the defining characteristics of the revolution.[64] It was more all-encompassing and transparent in its objectives, and it contributed to the fragmentation of Arab society, particularly at the elite level. Because leaders in the field relied on the Central Committee for support and attention, not to mention the general public, the Central Committee had a significant amount of control over the leadership. On the other hand, the Arab Party and the two councils served as the Central Committee's political instruments. On the other hand, the Defense Party and those who supported it took an overtly antagonistic stance, and the majority of them did not try to hide the fact that they openly collaborated with the British and Prince 'Abdullah. They perceived the resurgence of the revolution as a powerful blow to them, which also weakened their influence.[65]

In spite of the fact that the majority of the field commanders were veterans who had taken part in the initial stage of the revolution, there was not a single individual who emerged among them as a leader who was able to win over the allegiance of every individual. As a direct consequence of this, each of them worked to a large extent independently in his sphere of influence as a ruler with absolute powers, receiving assistance from a number of faction leaders. These leaders were not appointed by the Central Committee or any other political leadership; rather, they imposed themselves on the organization by taking the initiative for revolutionary action, demonstrating courage and a willingness to take risks, as well as the strength of their leadership and the ability to gather supporters around them. All of them encircled themselves with the kind of formal trappings that served to emphasize their individuality. They had their own seals, printed papers, flyers, and rhetoric on the events of the revolution, in addition to a variety of other directives. They had their own writers, divisions, guards, and orders, all of which were under their control. They directed people based on the circumstances that required them to issue orders and instructions.[66]

A number of partisan intellectuals had joined the revolution and worked under field commanders. Among the Arab Nationalist Bloc were Wasif Kamal, Mamduh al-Sukhun, Farid Ya'ish, Rashad al-Shawa, and, from the Communist Party, Muhammad Nimir 'Uwdah, who held a leadership military position; Fu'ad Nasir, who served as a deputy to 'Abd al-Qadir al-Husseini in the leadership of the Jerusalem area; and Muhammad Duwidar, an Egyptian, responsible for the technical services. Anton Sa'adah sent a message to the members of the Syrian National Social Party, through party member 'Abdullah Na'was, asking each of them to fulfil their duty toward the revolution, even though Sa'adah did not see it as a decisive battle.[67]

The powers of field commanders were not limited to military matters but also included the administrative and judicial. A number of intellectuals who joined the revolution served as advisers to the leaders at their headquarters, and they proved to be of great help, especially when forming revolutionary courts as the leaders were issuing and ordering punishment, including death sentences. And when the government administration collapsed, the litigants frequently turned to these courts in an effort to resolve their issues. The revolutionaries, in turn, levied taxes on the residents, and each village was obliged to provide them with an adequate number of fighters.[68] It was within the jurisdiction of the revolutionary courts to stand up to agents and brokers, many of whom were sentenced to death and executed. The revolutionaries succeeded in forming a highly efficient intelligence apparatus for tracking the army's movements and alerting them to its surprise operations, which allowed the revolutionaries in many cases to disappear into the valleys and mountains and return as soon as the danger passed. During this period, regional leaders began to emerge. Each leader was accountable for a particular region, the boundaries of which the factions active within the sphere of his influence almost never exceeded.[69]

Abu Ibrahim al-Kabir, who was associated with the al-Qassam movement, emerged as the leader in the northern region with the assistance of Abu Ibrahim al-Saghir. The theater of operations was the districts of Tiberias, Safed, Nazareth, and Acre, a section of the Nablus region, and a section of the north of the Jerusalem area. In the center, there were four regional leaders in the Nablus Brigade. The region west of Jenin was led by Sheikh 'Atiyah Ahmed (from the town of al-Sheikh, Haifa district) and, succeeding him after his martyrdom, Yusuf Abu Durra (from Silah al-Hawarithiyya). The eastern Jenin region was led by Abu Khalid (Muhammad Salih al-'Abid, one of the Qassamist leaders in the first stage of the revolution), succeeded, after his martyrdom, by Abu 'Abdullah ('Abd al-Fattah al-'Abid, from the Silah of al-Dhuhir), and then after his martyrdom by Abu 'Umar (from the same village). The eastern Tulkarm region was led by Abu Kamal ('Abd al-Rahim al-Haj Muhammad, alongside his associates, who was martyred in the late days of the revolution, to be succeeded by Abu Bakir (Ahmad Muhammad al-Hassan, from Barqa, Nablus district); the West Tulkarm area was led by Abu Faisal ('Arif 'Abd al-Razzaq, from al-Taybeh, Tulkarm district). In the south, there were three regional leaderships: Jerusalem led by 'Abd al-Qader al-Husseini; the Lydda district, Ramleh, and Jaffa, led by Abu 'Ali (Hassan Salameh, Lydda district); and the Hebron region, led by 'Issa al-Battat (from Hebron), succeeded after his martyrdom by Abu Mansur ('Abd al-Halim al-Jilani, from Hebron). In Gaza, Beersheba, and al-Majdal, leaderships with regional roles did not emerge, and field commanders received guidance and support from the General Central Command or regional leaders close to their areas.[70]

However, due to the absence of centralized leadership within their homeland and the autonomy enjoyed by various factional leaders in their respective areas of influence, there were instances of mistakes, transgressions, and attempts to exploit power and settle past grievances. The majority of them were attributed to faction leaders and are still being criticized or condemned, despite a scarcity of objective readings of the circumstances at the time. The Central Committee tried to reduce errors and correct the path as much as possible. One of its actions saw that every leadership was joined by an administrative consultant, another judge, and a religious preacher. The three of them formed a committee that worked to control the practices of the faction leaders. To this end, it dispatched a number of intellectuals enrolled in the revolution, including Wasif Kamal, Mamduh al-Sukhun, Farid Ya'ish, Rashad al-Shawa, Mahmud 'Ala' al-Din, Salim al-Husseini, Akram al-Ja'uri, and Mustafa al-Tahir.[71]

In the summer of 1938, the Central Committee held a higher council for the revolutionaries, which included field leaders, where it was agreed to cooperate and escalate the struggle until Britain responded to Arab demands. To achieve the required coordination, the Office of the Leadership of the Arab Revolution was formed, which included 'Abd al-Rahim al-Haj Muhammad, 'Arif 'Abd al-Razzaq, Yusuf Sa'id Abu Durra, Hassan Salameh, and other faction leaders. It was decided that the office presidency would rotate among them, while Mamduh al-Sukhun (from Nablus) was appointed a general secretary of the office. The office's mission was to direct the activities of the leaders, to intensify operations as decided by the Central Committee in Damascus, and to control individual excesses and behavior.[72]

The revolutionaries had taken control of most of the rural areas, while city activists had largely paralyzed the effectiveness of the opposition elements and terrorized spies and brokers. In line with their class root and nationalist passions, the revolutionaries issued an order to stop paying all types of debts as of September 1, 1938, and they warned the debt collectors and land brokers not to go to the villages. The revolutionaries issued another order to the contractors, which prevented the contractors from undertaking public road and police center projects.[73] This indicates that the revolution was characterized at that time by national and social dimensions, which strengthened its position among the majority of the Arab people in Palestine.

The revolutionaries, despite their limited capabilities, developed their fighting skills and engaged in various acts of sabotage. These included blowing up bridges, roads, and railways, uprooting telephone, telegraph, and electricity poles, sabotaging airports and railway stations, as well as burning and destroying certain targets. Additionally, they launched attacks on outposts, camps, airports, railway stations, and convoys of British and Zionist caravans. The Zionist settlements and the Jewish neighborhoods in the cities, including Tel Aviv, were the target of the revolutionaries' attacks. Despite the continuous economic depression of the Iraq Petroleum Company pipeline, which extends to Haifa, the oil that flowed from it during the summer of 1938 was estimated to be thirty-two thousand tons.[74]

Initially, the revolutionaries were fighting major battles with operations spanning between ten and fifteen kilometers, while the participating British forces reached between two and three thousand soldiers equipped with aircraft, tanks, armored vehicles, and heavy and light cannons.[75] However, they soon realized that it was more beneficial to rely on small units that launched surprise attacks. This enabled them to be the initiators and to continue their operations without any hindrance. In fact, they succeeded, as the official Israeli version decided to paralyze the army, whose chief concern became protecting itself, roads, military installations, cities, and important strategic points.[76]

On the discipline and efficiency of the revolutionaries at the peak stage, the British officer, Orde Charles Wingate, who was tasked with studying the methods of the revolutionaries in northern Palestine, wrote,

> By the time night falls, things are in the hands of the revolutionary's battle group. They are free to visit the villages at night without any risk. They can move without using the main roads, and they also use them when they find them comfortable. In general, the police and the army do not move during the night. They are traveling in cars on main roads, as usual, when they do this. And when they fell into an ambush, as expected, they returned fire, which was useless at night. After the exchange of fire, the revolutionary's battle group was able to escape without chasing, and the surprise was always from the revolutionary's battle group, not from the army.[77]

As for David Hirst, he says,

> In the period when the revolution reached its peak power, and the number of its men reached fifteen thousand people, its control extended throughout most of the central mountainous region in Galilee, Hebron, Beersheba and Gaza. Indeed, the Mandate Authority in these areas did not exist. The revolutionaries (government) were collecting the taxes that they imposed, and establishing affiliated courts in which they tried the thieves who exploited the cause of the revolution or the spies and agents working against it. The revolutionaries gained the cooperation of the notables, teachers and Arab local policemen, or imposed on them this cooperation.[78]

A British military report admits that the problem facing the leadership was that the army was unable to lure the rebels into combat because of their excellent intelligence. Sometimes the rebels were attacking British soldiers from behind, especially if the army unit was small. In describing the situation that day, the official Israeli version went on to say, "During this time period, the popular saying that the British controlled the roads while the gangs, which were the revolutionaries' battle troops, controlled the mountains became popular. In other words, a new partition project would be 'a day of the government and a night of the Arabs.'"[79]

Even though there was a significant capability gap between the two sides of the military, the revolutionaries were still able to accomplish their historic goal. This was true whether one looked at it in terms of the number of elements that were trained and prepared to fight or in terms of the variety, quality, and availability of weapons. The majority of the weapons that were made available to the revolutionaries as well as the general population of Arab countries dated back to the time of World War I. Almost all of the arms came from people who sold them, and most of those people were smugglers. The following is what the official Israeli account has to say: "The weapons that fell into the hands of the Jewish army and defense personnel during the battles revealed that the guns used by gang members were Turkish and German-made, from the remnants of World War I, or British rifles that were stolen or taken away from the army and police forces in the country during the events in particular, and no new weapons or bullets were found in all searches that took place in the villages and during clashes with gangs."[80]

The Israeli narrative goes on:

> Arms smugglers brought old guns from all over the east, including Kurdistan. According to reports, the Turkish government, which has long sought to disarm Kurdish tribes in eastern Anatolia, encouraged these clans to sell weapons to gang delegates in order to get rid of illegal weapons on their territory. The gangs were particularly harmed by a lack of ammunition. Old wartime bullets were corroded and needed to be replaced. The thrill we felt after an Arab attack on a Hebrew colony revealed that 30 to 40% of the bullets did not explode. One of the factors that cooled gang activity in early 1939 was a lack of ammunition.[81]

On explosives and mines, which were the most dangerous weapons of the revolutionaries in the summer of 1938 until mid-1939, the official Israeli version says, "Gangs increased their use of homemade explosives and landmines. The rumor that the Italian and German coaches assisted in this task was greatly exaggerated. There were stone quarries, and Arab hunters knew how to use explosives. The materials were either stolen or taken from various government agencies and army depots, or they were obtained from Arab quarry workers who had access to explosives."[82]

The peak stage saw the revolutionaries make several daring acts. In Jenin, one of the revolutionaries stormed the government house, and went up to the second floor, to the office of the governor of the Nablus district, Walter S. S. Moffatt, and killed him.[83] On September 9, 1938, revolutionaries surrounded the Beersheba police station, and after seizing control and all of its weapons, they marched to the city center to occupy the various government departments. Amid the cheers and jubilation of the citizens, they were greeted and celebrated, with some even spraying them with perfumes as a sign of appreciation and joy. On April 10, 1938, about three hundred revolutionaries stormed Tiberias, raising the Arab flag on the government palace, killing and injuring a number of Jews and British, and preventing the great British garrison from protecting the city with a Jewish majority.[84] The revolution culminated in full control of Jerusalem's Old City in October 1938. In addition to burning train stations between Jerusalem and Lydda and most stations between Lydda and the Egyptian border, the revolutionaries also burned post offices, police stations, and the like in Hebron, Bethlehem, Jericho, and Ramallah.[85]

Arab society became more divided between the rich and the poor as rural revolutionaries and city activists became more powerful. Landlords and the wealthiest people in the cities and the countryside, loyal to both the government and the opposition, fled in large numbers to Egypt and Lebanon. In the summer of 1938, it was decided to abandon the *Tarbush* of Turkish origin in favor of a *Kuffiah* (a Palestinian black-and-white checkered scarf) and *al-'Iqal* (the headband) as a covering for the head in order to conceal the infiltration of villagers from the cities and their activities from the army and police.[86]

To counter the growing number of rebel operations and the clear deficit of the British army, which was bolstered by Zionist police and gangs, new forces were called in, and additional Jewish and Arab police were recruited. According to Arab sources, the British forces reached four divisions, with fifty thousand soldiers supported by approximately twenty thousand police.[87] According to an Israeli source, the army forces reached two divisions in October 1938, with eighteen infantry battalions, two battalions, an armored battalion, and an artillery battalion, as well as all the forces attached to them.[88] As of June 1938, the guardianship of the railway from Haifa to Egypt was handed over to the Zionist commanders, and later the guardianship of the Ghor region from Jericho to Tiberias was handed over to the Jordanian Border Guard, commanded by John Bagot Glubb, with mostly British officers.[89]

Under the headline "Britain Reoccupies Palestine," David Hirst wrote,

> Britain practically had to reoccupy Palestine. In the autumn of 1938 the number of British soldiers in Palestine was more than twenty thousand. The military commanders assumed responsibility for overseeing these areas while the faces of the civil authorities became political advisers to them. The revolutionaries who until that time were attacking were under attack, as the tide began to turn against them continuously. The methods adopted during the days of Robin Hood faced the logistics of one of the largest military countries at that time . . . and the rebels were subjected to large massacres from the air.[90]

According to the statistical figures of the mandate government, the revolutionaries carried out 4,969 operations during the year 1938: 986 attacks and sniper attacks against the British army and police, 335 attacks on transportation, 651 incidents of shooting at Jewish settlements and neighborhoods, 176 attacks and sniper attacks against the Zionist forces, 331 bombing operations, 215 kidnappings, 410 operations to destroy the property of the Zionist settlers, 720 wire-cutting processes, 341 railways sabotaged, 210 government properties sabotaged, 104 operations to blow up the Iraq Petroleum Company pipelines, and 490 assassinations and assassination attempts.[91]

These operations resulted in the killing of 63 British soldiers and the injury of 200, the killing of 20 British policemen and the injury of 15, the killing of 255 Zionists and the injury of 390, and the deaths of 503 Arabs and the injury of 598.[92]

The official Israeli narrative determined that at the end of the year 1937, the number of the Haganah Organization reached thirty-five thousand, including fifty-five hundred girls. Of these, nine thousand were in the cities, with the rest in the colonies. In the colonies of labor settlement, kibbutzim and moshav, almost the entire population was bound to the Haganah.[93] Added to this were members of the Revisionist gangs emerging from the Haganah. The Night Watch Force, formed by Orde Charles Wingate of British soldiers and Zionist volunteers, which had proven effective in a relatively wide area, was praised in the official Israeli report.[94]

In addition to this, the British army hired a guerrilla expert, Sir Charles Augustus Tegart, who was summoned from India, where he had proved his worth in the forests of Bengal. He took control of the organization of the undercover police, and he increased their scope of operations. In addition to this, he was well known for his proposal to construct a barrier consisting of barbed wire and a string of military posts along its length. This barrier would stretch for a total of 120 kilometers along the borders of Syria and Lebanon, and it would stretch for 40 kilometers along the border with Jordan. Its width would be three meters, and its height would be about the same. The mandate government also built fifteen fortresses, which provided it with powerful guards equipped with detection, combat, and transportation equipment in order to cut off the rebels' communication from sources of support in the three Arab countries. However, three days after the completion of the fence, which cost £1 million to build, the revolutionaries uprooted seventeen kilometers of it in several places,[95] thus confirming their ability to overcome all the siege attempts they were subjected to.

The army occupied the villages and neighborhoods in which the rebels or their areas were situated in order to exert pressure on them and disrupt their communication with their local sources of support. This was done in an effort to gain support for their cause. On May 20, 1938, military centers were established in twenty-five villages in the Galilee and Samaria regions, with twenty-five soldiers equipped with a mortar and a wireless device connected to the mobile queues in each. The goal was to prevent the infiltration of these villages by the rebels.[96] Within a short period, the number of military centers increased to sixty, supplying the outposts with food and water. However, the revolutionaries soon turned them into targets for continuous raids, so that the revolution continued its activities without any significant impact.[97]

BRITISH REPRESSION, ZIONIST TERRORISM, AND COUNTERREVOLUTIONS

In light of the developments witnessed by the growing revolution across Palestine, and in anticipation of the outbreak of war with the German-Italian Axis, the British government decided to liquidate the revolution. The liquidation plan was drawn up while High Commissioner Harold Alfred McMichael was in Britain in October 1938. Accordingly, a second division of the British army was transferred to Palestine, and the British reserve was called up for service. A telegram on the approved military measures was broadcast in London to influence morale and psychologically terrorize the revolutionaries. It was reported by the media at the time that Gen. Robert Hadden Haining would conduct a general attack in Palestine using two British military divisions, a number of squadrons of aircraft, tanks, and armored vehicles, British police, and the East Jordan Border Force, as well as Zionist organizations. High Commissioner McMichael described the plan as "a military occupation of Palestine again and the return of British rule to it."[98]

In accordance with the emergency law that had been in effect since May 1936, the government of the mandate had established military courts. The law had been changed so that anyone who carried a weapon of any kind or validity or possessed a few bullets would be sentenced to death. Additionally, anyone arrested while engaging in an act that was considered "sabotage" would also be subject to the death penalty. It was not possible to appeal these decisions, and the high commissioner's approval was required before a death sentence could be carried out.[99] The number of those executed by hanging reached 148 people, and those who were sentenced for long periods numbered about 2,000, among them sheikhs, boys, and women. Those who were arrested, regardless of the length of time detained, amounted to 50,014. Detention was carried out individually and collectively. In many cases, a hundred or two hundred people were arrested from one village or city.[100]

The judges in the military court did not follow normal trial procedures, and the procedures themselves did not follow normal standards. Lawyers did not have the ability to freely question witnesses, particularly if the witnesses were members of the military or the police, and court presidents frequently inter-jected themselves to prevent witnesses from responding to questions posed by attorneys. Among the Arab lawyers whose voluntary positions were men-tioned in defense of the detainees was George Salah, who succeeded in mak-ing friends with some military judges, so that he reached an understanding with them on the rulings in many cases.[101] Because the families of those who had been sentenced to death were informed of the dates of the executions, a significant number of those families came to receive the bodies of their loved ones who had been martyred. Women, dressed in white, lowered their heads and adorned their bodies with henna, resembling participants in a wedding celebration. As the body was brought in, a wave of murmurs and whispers filled the air, signifying the emotional response of the crowd.[102] This indicated that the death sentences, despite their abundance, did not affect the people's will and moral spirit but rather increased their determination to resist.

The detainees were hit and whipped, burned on the hands and legs, shocked in sensitive areas of the body, and even attacked by starving dogs. The people who were being held were also put through the worst kinds of physical and mental torture. Some detainees were martyred while being tortured.[103] Arab sources estimate the number of martyrs in the years of the revolution at six thousand, with tens of thousands wounded. The army continued to impose unfair sanctions without reasons. Of this, the official Israeli version stated, "Every shooting incident or attack on the soldiers resulted in severe sanctions being imposed in the wake of it, which provided the Arab villagers with the impression that the army had a powerful hold on them. Terrorists' homes are a haven for demolition, as are the orchards and vineyards where they set fire to trees."[104]

Army units that had personnel killed or injured as a result of an ambush or explosion exacted vengeance and mounted reprisals whenever possible. In the western part of the Galilee region, they did a large-scale campaign of sanctions. During this time, they went through many villages, destroyed hun-dreds of homes, and hurt many of the people who lived there.[105]

In more than one case, all the houses in a village were torn down because the people there were accused of being part of a revolution. On July 28, 1937, all ninety-three Baqa al-Gharbiyya homes in the Tulkarm district were blown up, crops destroyed, threshing floors burned, men taken to Norsham's prison, and women and children assaulted by soldiers. On the same day, the army broke into Kawkab al-Hija, burned its crops and threshing floors, and arrested most of its men. They also broke into the village of Tabrikha in the district of Acre. As a result of these atrocities committed by the soldiers in the inspection process, its people sought refuge in Lebanon, leaving their homes and fields. Whole residential neighborhoods were blown up, as happened in Jenin. Some five thousand homes and shops were blown up.[106]

During the search of their homes and businesses, crude methods were used to destroy their belongings. For example, oil and gas were poured on grain and flour and then mixed together. The soldiers would not think twice about stealing any money they came across. Even the sick and elderly were forced to stand for hours in the pouring rain or baking heat of open yards, crammed with other men. In many instances, the male residents of the village were forced to walk to the investigation centers while being whipped by the military personnel. It would be helpful to identify the rebels who had disappeared among the farmers if you had the assistance of an agent who had disappeared while riding in a military vehicle or armored vehicle. In more than one instance, the men were subjected to an attempt to humiliate them by being made to disrobe and stand naked in public.[107]

To restrict Arab citizens and paralyze their economic activity, a curfew was imposed, which expanded and intensified according to the breadth and intensity of the revolution. The curfew continued for days and was round the clock, except for two hours to meet their needs. Violators were subjected to gunfire without warning, arrests, and fines. The curfew continued in Safed for 140 days and in other cities for two to three months. Initially, it was limited to cities; then it included villages and highways.[108]

Arab citizens were responsible for the railroads and telephone and telegraph columns located in their cities and villages or that passed nearby. There were required to pay fines in the event of sabotage. The collective fine imposed on the city of Lydda amounted to £5,000 as a punishment for the storming of the Lydda airport facilities by the rebels and the burning of passports, customs offices, wireless installations, and other airport offices.[109] Arab policemen were stripped of their weapons for fear that many were not loyal and that some cooperated with the rebels.[110]

The army did not refrain from using human shields in its operations, and its convoys used Arab prisoners to remove the stone barriers, which the revolutionaries had set up at dangerous turns and where their ambushes were often located. The Arab prisoner was to declare himself in a loud voice in order not to be shot while removing the barriers. In the reoccupation of the Old City of Jerusalem on October 19, 1938, the army removed groups of Arab citizens from their homes to walk in front of its soldiers as they stormed the narrow streets. This enabled them to reoccupy the Old City, which remained under the control of the revolutionaries for five days.[111] In both cases, the army wagered on the depth of human feelings in Arab culture and that the rebels would not harm their own people.

The mandate government attempted to stir sectarian strife, which it had failed to spark since the British occupation in 1917. It removed several criminals from prisons to form armed gangs made up of twenty members. They were given salaries and documents stating that they worked for the

British so that the army would not harm them should they encounter each other. The largest of these gangs were in the Jerusalem area, Bethlehem, and Ramallah. This gang was charged with assaulting Christians in Christian and mixed towns and villages such as Beit Jala, Birzeit, and Jaffna. Workers in the Jerusalem area alone estimated a hundred criminals led by a criminal who was sentenced to life imprisonment. He was released, although it was claimed that he had escaped from prison. His gang activity continued in a theater of operations that stretched from northern Ramallah to southern Bethlehem.[112]

Under the guise of seeking medical treatment, an officer from the intelligence services of the mandate government traveled to Beirut, where he then made plans to meet with the mufti. During their conversation, the officer informed the mufti of the specifics of the episode as well as the fact that he had personally freed one of the criminals from prison and given him the mission. The mufti hastily arranged for the departure of 'Abd al-Qader al-Husseini, who was in the process of recovering from his wounds sustained in the Battle of Bethlehem, from Lebanon. He subsequently fought a battle with these gangs in northern Jerusalem, in which he succeeded in dispersing those present in the northern suburbs of Jerusalem and the Ramallah district. He set up a national military court to try its members, recovered the stolen goods they had seized, and returned them to their owners. He then went to the Bethlehem Hebron area, where he and his companions fought a battle with the hired gangs in which the British army participated with armored vehicles, infantry, heavy artillery, and aircraft. A number of revolutionaries were martyred, including the engineer 'Umar al-Husseini, and 'Abd al-Qader was seriously wounded and almost killed; his life was saved by his comrades who helped him escape the battlefield and provided him with relief. He was transferred to Damascus, where he spent a long period of treatment and recovery before returning to the battlefield.[113]

To smear the revolution's image and turn the public against it, British intelligence formed paid gangs of agents and criminals to loot at will while claiming to be raising funds for the revolution. The Central Committee for the Palestinian National Jihad issued statements warning citizens to not tolerate these criminal practices and requested the immediate reporting of their perpetrators until they could be held accountable. They made it clear that no one had the right to take anything from the citizens or impose fines and that any assistance paid must be done through the Central Committee for National Jihad or the Central Committee for Relief of the Afflicted in exchange for an official receipt. The statement was sealed with the phrase "for the benefactors of the path," which meant that paying aid was not compulsory.[114]

The Jewish Agency made another attempt to incite religious conflict between Muslims and Christians by employing third parties to disseminate leaflets. These parties were paid to do so. Additionally, in an effort to cause unrest and discord, engineer Michel Mitri, the head of the Workers Society, was murdered; however, the revolutionaries, by inflicting the harshest punishment possible on the aggressors, nipped treason in the bud.[115] According to a statement sent to faction leaders by the Central Committee for National Jihad, it was necessary to strike with an iron fist at the hands of these gangs and work to secure citizens, especially Christians, against innocent people, while being careful not to be drawn behind personal rivalries and ensuring justice among citizens.[116]

Since the start of the new revolution, Fakhri al-Nashashibi, the most active and passionate member of the Defense Party, had been fighting it. He had also been active in counteracting propaganda and undermining the revolution's intentions. He was also in constant contact with members and supporters of the opposition, as well as those whose lives were negatively impacted by the incitement against the revolution and revolutionaries by field commanders. He carried out his actions with robust protection from the authority that oversaw the mandate, and he and his companions traveled in armored cars while being escorted by military personnel. On December 12, 1938, supporters of the opposition gathered in the village of Yatta, which is located in the Hebron district. There he addressed them, invoking their animosity toward the political leadership as well as the field leaders. Those who were under his command claimed that he had armed some people to fight against the revolutionaries and confuse the revolution, and those individuals subsequently received severe punishment from the revolutionaries.[117] In reference to that meeting, the official Israeli version states, "Army officers and British officials were present, and they made a promise to anyone who participated in the gang fight that they would pardon any previous crimes they had committed."[118]

Besides the surge of opposition leaders and supporters, the mandate and opposition government took advantage of the desire for revenge rooted in Arab popular culture and the prevailing lack of awareness and knowledge. With the colonial and Zionist agents meeting with the enraged mobs to avenge their relatives who had been killed by some faction leaders, the counterrevolution gangs were formed, which worked in cooperation with the British and the Zionists under the name of Peace Factions and practiced political assassinations. This included some activists of the first stage of the revolution who were out of favor with the leadership.

In 1936, Fakhri Abdel Hadi, who served as a faction leader working under the direction of al-Qawuqaji, was perhaps the most illustrative example of one of these leaders.[119] When the revolution renewed, he was residing in Damascus, and the Central Command did not allow him to join the ranks of the revolutionaries. Frustrated, he responded to the opposition's call and joined the counterrevolution as a leader of one of the Peace Factions in the Jenin area.

As for the official Israeli account, Fakhri Abdel Hadi assumed the leadership of the Peace Factions, which included a number of those who had left the revolution, wore military uniforms, and escorted the soldiers to the mountains to guide them to the dens of the revolutionaries, whom they called bandits. In January 1939, the first search took place of the Al-Aqsa Mosque and other mosques, where many of the revolutionaries who sought refuge were arrested: "The members of the peace gang responded to the terror of the Mufti with counterterrorism, and many families who wanted revenge on the gang leaders—the leaders of the revolutionary factions—took advantage of the opportunity to settle their scores, which resulted in a civil war that undermined the strength of the Arab revolution from within."[120]

The launch of the counterrevolution coincided with the flourishing of informants, the mobilization of those seeking revenge against those who had killed their relatives without regard for the reasons for killing them, and old rivalries. This included the actions of Farid Irshaid, who, on March 27, 1939, accompanied an army force to the village of Sanour in the Jenin district. It was in Sanour where 'Abd al-Rahim al-Haj Muhammad, the commander in chief of the rebels at that time, had returned after coming back from Damascus the previous day. The village was cordoned off on all sides, and Abu Kamal, instead of leaving, insisted on a confrontation with some of his brothers and was martyred.[121] The British appreciated the heroic martyr to the extent that some of their soldiers gave a military salute to his dead body, lying on the ground.[122] The martyrdom of 'Abd al-Rahim al-Haj Muhammad had a very negative impact on the revolution, especially since it coincided with the army's development of repression and stalking operations to stop the revolution. In addition, it coincided with the exacerbation of the internal conflicts that were fueled by the start of the counterrevolution. According to official British records, the killed/martyred during the three years of the revolution numbered 5,032; the wounded, 14,760; the detained, 50,000; and those sentenced to life, 2,000; 146 people were executed and 5,000 homes destroyed.[123]

The Zionist movement saw in the revolution a dangerous and effective weapon in the hands of the Arabs, threatening the political future of its racist colonial settler project, but the Haganah faced a double problem in dealing with the Arab threat. On the one hand, the central leadership of the revolution was in Damascus, which made it unreachable. On the other hand, the Arab countryside was the stronghold of the revolution and its main source of support, which made the Haganah unable to reach the field leaders and activists of the revolutionary movement. At the end of 1938, the Haganah became involved with the British army in its war against the gangs.[124]

However, the National Military Organization/Haganah (Irgun Zvei Leumi) continued to conduct terrorist attacks.[125] It resorted to shooting Arab passersby and throwing bombs and explosives at passing cars in Jewish neighborhoods.

It also set up time bombs in Arab gathering places in Jerusalem, Jaffa, and Haifa.[126] The explosives were hidden inside milk containers or vegetable baskets, and they consisted of scrap iron and screws. The electric detonator was set to go off in an hour's time. In Jerusalem on July 3, 1939, a vegetable market and the Hebron Gate were sites of separate incidents that resulted in thirty-six Arabs killed and dozens more injured. On July 15, a time bomb that was planted in the vegetable market in the Old City of Jerusalem killed ten and wounded dozens of people. On July 25, an explosive device placed in the Jerusalem market killed fifty Arabs.[127] On August 25, 74 people were killed and 129 were injured in Haifa, with the majority of those killed being elderly people, women, and children. On August 26, a time bomb killed twenty-four people in Jaffa.[128] During July and August 1939, there was an increase in the number of terrorist incidents, which, according to the official Israeli version, were considered to be two months of Jewish terrorism.[129]

If, as Arab sources stated, the Zionist terrorist operations continued for a full year, from July 1938 until July 1939, and the process of planting the time bombs was mostly taking place during hours of curfew, it meant the occupation forces colluded with the Zionist terrorists or at least overlooked their movements. During that period, seven incidents in Jerusalem resulted in the killing of 35 Arabs and 130 injuries, and six incidents in Haifa resulted in the killing of 120 Arabs and 176 injuries, along with several incidents in Jaffa.[130]

In comparing the Zionist terrorist operations and the actions of the Arab resistance, British historian John Marlowe says, "Jews were the first to start much more active urban terrorism, which was closer to the heritage of Russian nihilists or Spanish anarchists. Arabs' preference for 'hit and run' tactics in gang warfare led to memories of assassinations or invasive tribalism in the public mind."[131]

The Israeli historian Yehuda Bauerhe maintains that the Arabs in the events of 1936 to 1939 started the unrest and that the Jews imitated them, and soon, thanks to their more sophisticated techniques, outgrew them.[132] Joseph Shechtman, Jabotinsky's biographer, stated that the terrorist operations were of inestimable political and educational value. The Yishuv (Jewish residents in the land of Israel) were protected under British rule and operated with impunity to instill the spirit of military service and sacrifice among young Jews.[133]

Shechtman claims that Jabotinsky had long struggled with his conscience over the moral nature of terrorism and found what he considered to be the political justification for revenge. At the same time, he was typical of nineteenth-century liberals who considered human life sacred but over time he fully adopted the policy of revenge. He wrote,

Despite the Arab hostility, there is a general inclination towards supporting retaliatory operations targeted at gangs rather than the entire Arab population. However, it is important to clarify that the choice is not simply between seeking revenge against the gangs or seeking revenge against the hostile population. Instead, it is a matter of deciding whether to seek revenge against the hostile population as a whole or to refrain from seeking revenge altogether. By June 1939, it became apparent that punishing only the guilty was not only difficult but also often proved to be impossible in many cases.[134]

It is noticeable that none of the Zionist organizations accepted responsibility for any of the bombings in the Arab markets, even though it was known that the Revisionist Jabotinsky group were their perpetrators. Meanwhile, the Jewish Agency and its newspapers condemned these operations, considering them outside the principle of *havelg* (self-control) rooted in official Jewish morality. Accordingly, it declared that the Jews should not respond to Arab terrorism with Jewish terrorism and demanded avoiding intrusive operations in order to preserve what it called the Jewish community's sense of moral superiority over its enemies.[135] It was clear that condemning terrorist operations against the Arabs and considering them a departure from the traditional principle of restraint was aimed at influencing European and American public opinion and not the Arab people, who considered this a kind of hypocrisy.[136]

The increasing Zionist terror operations contributed to an increase in operations against the Zionist groupings and to the persecution of Jews in a number of Arab countries, which raised the concern of the Mandate Authority. In anticipation of violence between Arabs and Jews, a large number of corrective activists were arrested and presented to the courts. Two of them were sentenced to death by hanging, and the sentence was carried out, despite Zionist and British-Zionist pressure.[137] This demonstrates the extent to which the mandate government was concerned about the impact of Zionist terrorist operations on the influence and reputation of the Arab opposition. In contrast, according to the official Israeli version, Zionist terrorist operations led to popular Arab solidarity with the revolution and national leadership.[138]

ABUSES AND ASSASSINATIONS, 1937–1939

There has never been a revolution in history that has not used violence against its opponents and those who pose a threat to its continuation, whether they are external enemies or internal enemies whose interests conflict with the revolution. There has never been a revolution in history that has not been recognized for its excesses and mistakes or that has not been accused of misjudging and producing false reports and malicious information. The leadership's share of knowledge and awareness and its competence in reading the facts of reality are the first and most important determinants of the extent and gravity, or lack thereof, of what transgressions, errors, and misjudgments occur during a revolution.

The period between 1937 and 1939 was marked by a cycle of violence and retaliation between the Jewish and Arab communities in Palestine. The conflict was fueled by deep-seated political and ideological differences and was exacerbated by the British government's inability to maintain order and find a solution that would be acceptable to both sides. The abuses and assassinations that occurred during this period left a lasting impact on the region and continue to shape the ongoing conflict between Israel and Palestine today.[139]

And because the conclusion of the revolution coincided with the absence of national leaders, it resulted in wrongdoing against innocent victims. This led to the point where it almost became a movement to settle personal accounts, with the vast majority of those killed or injured in some way being victims of the revolution. The national leadership, particularly Mufti Haj Amin al-Husseini, was held accountable for these murders and abuses of power and blamed for them. In the past, they held some historical responsibility for these events. On the other hand, the opposition, which led the counterrevolution and appeared before the peace parties as agents of the British and Zionists, was responsible for a great deal of evil, but they were referred to as "victims" instead of being held accountable for their actions.

When Fawzi al-Qawuqaji took over the general leadership in the first stage of the revolution, he formed the Revolutionary Court, which looked into cases of espionage and theft and was characterized by a high degree of justice in the investigation and issuance of judgments. That court expired with the dismantling of the strike, the end of the revolution in the fall of 1936, and the withdrawal of al-Qawuqaji from the country. The field leaders in the second stage of the revolution each had a revolutionary court in their sphere of influence, thereby multiplying the number of revolutionary courts. Because the leaders emerged with total spontaneity, and they did not follow a political organization that regulated their movement and orientations, it was natural for multiple litigation procedures to take place and for rulings to differ between one region and another.[140]

Due to the fact that the leaders of the time came from agricultural backgrounds and given the significance of the land occupied in the conflict with the colonial-Zionist alliance, the leaders of the time were adamantly opposed to selling the lands, acting as brokers in the sale of the lands, and conducting economic transactions with the Zionist settlers. The leaders did not limit their concerns to what was happening in their time. Rather, they called the brokers and clients with previous cases and subjected them to trial; a large number of them were executed as a result of the trial. It was not uncommon for a land seller to be murdered as soon as he left the Land Registry Department after completing a transaction.[141]

Perhaps the reason for the leaders of the revolution to summon and prosecute those who sold or brokered the sale of land was that there was no national procedure for their accountability by any of the executive committees of the seven national conferences or by the national leadership. Nevertheless, a fatwa[142] was issued by the gathering of imams of mosques, judges, muftis, and preachers called for by the Mufti Haj Amin al-Husseini in 1935, which prohibited the sale of land to the Zionists and considered anyone who sold or brokered the sale of land an apostate not to be buried in a Muslim cemetery.[143] This fatwa sparked significant debate in Palestinian society, as the sale of land to Jews was one of the most contentious and tense issues in Palestine at the time. Many Palestinian Muslims relied on this fatwa to avoid selling their land to Jews. It should be noted that this fatwa was issued in the context of the political and social situation in Palestine at the time, and it cannot be interpreted in any other way. It is worth noting that this fatwa is still a source of contention and debate in Palestine and other Arab countries today.

District leaders bore direct responsibility for the assassinations they ordered and carried out, even if the political leadership was responsible for keeping quiet about what was going on. One of the reliable historical sources indicates that the mufti was encouraged by Dr. 'Umar al-Khalil, the delegate of some Haifa youths, to issue a directive prohibiting the assassination of an Arab by an Arab, but he refrained from doing so. Jamal al-Husseini, the head of the Arab Party, admitted that the leadership ordered the assassination of between thirty and forty landlords who had not been dissuaded from completing their sales.[144]

Political assassinations were very limited, and the most prominent politician assassinated, Hassan Sidiqi al-Dajani, was one of the leaders of the Defense Party. As a consequence of the memorandum that 'Arif 'Abd al-Razzaq delivered to the high commissioner, Fakhri al-Nashashibi was sentenced to death by 'Arif 'Abd al-Razzaq. He had said in the memorandum that he would be willing to cooperate with the British. 'Arif 'Abd al-Razzaq asked every Arab to implement the ruling if he could. However, this was not achieved at the time, although al-Nashashibi was later assassinated in Baghdad.[145]

Muhammad 'Izzat Darwazah states that some opposition leaders were ambushed, some wounded, and some killed. The leaders and men of the Defense Party were not harmed during the first phase of the revolution, when they were at that time participating in the Arab Higher Committee and the National Committees. This indicates that the assassination and wounding of some of them in the second stage of the revolution stemmed from their antirevolutionary stance and active public participation in the counterrevolution.[146] Moreover, Darwazah categorically denies that the mufti or the Central

Committee issued orders to do so. He says, "For our part, we only assert that we had no prior knowledge of such incidents and that we were not instructed in any way similar to them. We condemned their occurrence and emphasized the importance of abstaining from them with all of our efforts, as well as attempting to avoid their consequences."[147]

What Darwazah says in this regard does not contradict the fact that the mufti refrained from issuing a statement prohibiting the assassination of an Arab by an Arab. Because such prohibition, despite the good-will of those requesting its issuance, was pouring into the channels of agents, spies, and brokers, and because the mufti was not naive, he did not want the revolution-aries to be bound by what no revolution in history had committed to. It is abundantly clear that hostile practices on the part of the revolutionaries were the cause of the deaths of some opponents and the destruction of property belonging to others, rather than the liquidation of old party accounts being the cause of these events.

Besides field commanders, excesses and assassinations were attributed to the secret al-Qassam League, which assassinated traitors, spies, and brokers. According to its directives it undertook extensive investigations to verify the charges of treason, espionage, and land sale. After confirming the conviction of the accused, it resorted to religious scholars known for their piety in issu-ing the legal ruling. Besides its assassination of Louis Andrews, it carried out a death sentence on Halim Bastah, the assistant police chief of Haifa, who was known to pursue Palestinian fighters day and night.[148] It also assassinated the officer Muhammad Nayif, who was working with Halim Bastah in track-ing down the Qassamids.[149] It has already been mentioned that the public refused to pray over his body and bury him in a Muslim cemetery. There were several smaller secret societies dedicated to identifying the suspects involved in certain activities and sending intimidating letters to individuals who pro-vided evidence of their involvement. Among these secret societies, the ones formed by residents of Saffuriyya and Ijzim, including some workers from Haifa, were particularly notable. One of these revolutionaries conducted an investigation into the allegation that Abdullah Mukhlis, one of the opposition figures, had sold some of his land to Jews.[150]

The Mandate Authority and the Zionist movement both had a minimal hand in carrying out the killings, which affected a number of patriots with the intention of getting rid of them properly and, at the same time, aimed at deepening conflicts between Arab authority and constituents, spreading confusion, and raising mutual accusations among Arabs. The partisan fam-ily disputes and internal divisions that existed among the Arabs made it easier for the British and the Zionists to accomplish their goals. "There is no doubt that the authority used political and fundamental partisan division as a destructive device in assassinations and sedition to eliminate the revolution.

The atmosphere of anxiety among citizens, regardless of the restrictions and extent of responsibility for all parties, eventually leads to the withdrawal of the revolutionary trend."[151]

ZIONIST DECISION CAUSED LONDON
ROUND TABLE CONFERENCE FAILURE

As a consequence of the escalation of individual operations during what was considered the year of the armistice, in the wake of ending the strike and stopping the first stage of the revolution and Britain feeling unable to impose the partition project, Herbert Samuel, the first high commissioner, proposed in the House of Lords on July 26, 1937, a contract between Arabs and Jews to limit immigration in such a way that the percentage of Jews did not exceed 40 percent. His proposal was met with opposition from Zionists, which ultimately led to his downfall. In October 1937, Lt. Col. Stewart Francis Newcombe, from the remnants of the Arab Office in Cairo, and Albert Montefiore Hyamson, the former director of the Immigration Service in Palestine, drafted a proposal to establish a Palestinian state that included eastern Jordan, in which Arabs and Jews would enjoy autonomy and the percentage of Jews would not exceed 50 percent of the total population. Negotiations on this proposal took place between Dr. Judah Magnes and 'Izzat Tannus as an envoy to the mufti, who demanded that the immigration cease and the sale of lands be stopped and that the number of Jews in the future not exceed their current percentage. Negotiations did not continue, and the proposal fell through like the previous one.[152]

On April 27, 1938, the British Technical Committee arrived in Palestine to study the division project headed by Sir John Woodhead, which the Arab Higher Committee decided to boycott. And since the revolution was at its peak and the Arab regimes rejected the partition resolution, they did not exert pressure to discourage the Palestinian leadership from its decisions.[153] Consequently, no British Arab was interviewed by the Technical Committee. However, the Defense Party submitted to it a memorandum refuting the partition project and saying that the solution lay in establishing a single country linked to Britain by a treaty. Some scholars and notables of the northern region submitted a memorandum saying that they would accept what Prince 'Abdullah accepted.[154]

The lack of security made it very difficult for the Technical Committee to take action, and the extent of its connections was limited to meetings with senior British officials and leaders of the Zionist movement. The committee departed Palestine on March 8, 1938, with the intention to release a report on September 10, 1938, questioning the validity of the partition project. The report emphasized the challenges of having three hundred thousand Arabs under Jewish rule and concluded that their voluntary evacuation from the land was unlikely and forcibly evicting them would be a risky proposition.[155]

In the summer of 1938, Colonel Newcombe carried a British proposal to Baghdad.[156] He asked Nuri al-Sa'id and Tawfiq al-Suwaidi, on behalf of the British government, to mediate with the High Arab Committee.[157] This was at a time when the committee had been dissolved by the decision of the high commissioner and its members were residing in Lebanon, Syria, and Europe or in exile in the Seychelles. This request indicates that the mufti and the men of the National Movement were still, in the eyes of Britain, the leadership of the Arab people in Palestine.[158] The main points of the Newcombe settlement project were the following:

A.   The establishment of an independent state in a sovereign Palestine.
B.   Every Palestinian has a political and civil right to the state, without discrimination on the basis of gender and religion.
C.   Sects are given powers to care for sectarian matters.
D.   Jewish immigration will cease, given that the largest number of the Jewish population is considered its current number.
E.   Municipalities in Arab and Jewish cities and villages will have broad decentralization powers that enable them to control education and various personal, civil, and administrative matters.
F.   The British government will guarantee the interests of the different sects in clear clauses in the constitution of the next country.
G.   Britain's legitimate interests will be safeguarded.

Newcombe also suggested holding an Arab-Jewish conference and allowing Arab countries to accept a reasonable number of Jewish immigrants. However, his proposed project did not fulfill the key demands of the Palestinian National Movement, which sought the establishment of an independent Arab state in Palestine, potentially united with other Arab countries. Nevertheless, his proposal stood out from previous British suggestions by advocating for political equality between Arab citizens and Zionist settlers, which was seen as a progressive step. However, due to a lack of trust in the British government's policy towards the Arabs at the time, Newcombe's proposition was ultimately rejected.[159] The Israeli version stated that mediation failed because the two men in Britain insisted on stopping immigration and freezing the proportion of Jews in Palestine.[160] This request also indicated that the solidarity of the national position of the Arab people in Palestine imposed itself on Nuri al-Sa'id and Tawfiq al-Suwaidi and prevented them from achieving Britain's goals, as was achieved by the kings and presidents via Nuri al-Sa'id in the fall of 1936.[161]

This was followed by a series of British contacts with a number of Arab leaders, which ended with a British proposal to hold a round table conference in London, to which a delegation representing the Palestinian Arabs, representatives of the Arab governments, and the Jewish Agency would be invited. Britain tried to exclude the mufti and the Arab Supreme Committee from participating in the delegation of the Arabs of Palestine, as they were the group keenest on national demands and less prepared to bow to pressure from Arab governments, which were very loyal to Britain and were willing to put pressure on the Palestinian leadership to accept what Britain imposed. The mandate government encouraged the opposition to be active in winning over the largest possible number of members in the Palestinian delegation, especially its leadership.[162]

Fakhri al-Nashashibi delivered a memorandum to the high commissioner in which he accused the mufti and his men of masterminding the revolution and being responsible for the assassinations. He also asserted that the opposition represented more than 50 percent of Arab citizens and 75 percent of those citizens' interests.[163] His opposition, he asserted, was ready to cooperate with the British government toward peace and understanding with the Jews living with them. The memo provoked a patriotic response and led to pro-mufti telegrams, denouncing the memo. Despite this, we find that the leadership of the party, headed by Raghib al-Nashashibi, in the presence of the members Suleiman Tuqan Ùuqan, 'Asim al-Sa'id, 'Abd al-Rahman al-Taji, and Ahmed al-Shaka'a, held a meeting in Cairo on January 24, 1939, decided to assign the party's secretariat to Fakhri al-Nashashibi, and sent him to Jerusalem accordingly.[164] Several prominent figures in the Defense Party and its supporters expressed their commitment to what was decided by the Arab Higher Committee regarding participation in the membership of the Palestinian delegation to the round table in London.[165]

Britain opposed the mufti's leadership of the Palestinian delegation, claiming that his participation would lead to the failure of the conference. In response to the intervention of the Egyptian prime minister, Muhammad Mahmud, Britain agreed that the mufti would lead the delegation, but he apologized profusely for not being able to travel to London and suggested that Jamal al-Husseini be delegated on his behalf. As a result of the mediation of Nuri al-Sa'id, the mufti agreed that the delegation would include Raghib al-Nashashibi, leader of the Defense Party, and Ya'qub Farraj, its leading member.[166] Thus Britain had succeeded in excluding the mufti, the leader of the National Movement, and including the opposition leader loyal to the delegation by harnessing the mediation of Arab rulers. The participating Arab countries were represented by strong delegations, headed by Egyptian crown prince 'Abd al-Mun'im, Prince Faisal ibn 'Abd al-'Aziz on behalf of Saudi Arabia, Iraqi prime minister Nuri al-Sa'id, Jordanian prime minister

Tawfiq Abu al-Huda, and Prince Saif al-Islam Hussein from Yemen.[167] It also appointed as its adviser 'Abd al-Rahman 'Azzam, who was soon appointed as a member of the official delegation.

The Arab delegations convened in Cairo on January 17, 1939, reaching an agreement on the general principles of the Arab position. The key elements included the establishment of an Arab government with a treaty-based connection to Britain and the election of a Palestinian constituent assembly to determine the system of governance. The constitution would ensure the rights of Jewish settlers and their participation in government based on their proportionate representation. The Palestinian delegation was designated as the primary negotiator, authorized to speak on behalf of the Arab delegations. This arrangement aimed to ensure the Palestinian delegation's acceptance of favorable terms and the rejection of anything deemed unsuitable, meeting their specific demands.[168]

The progressive Palestinian forces considered the acceptance of representatives of some Arab governments in the conference a very serious issue:

> These governments, to one degree or another, coexisted and cooperated with British imperialism, and blessed their presence in the region. And later, each according to its location, it was active in containing the Palestinian Arab National Movement and solving the Palestinian problem in accordance with its objectives. The revolutionary national forces realised the importance of the solidarity of the Arab peoples with the people of Palestine, but they categorically distinguished between Arab participation in the framework of cooperation with British imperialism, and the unity of the organic struggle of Arab nationalist movements against imperialism.[169]

In London, the conference was held at St. James's Palace in February 1939. Because the Arab delegations refused to sit at the same table as the Zionist delegation, the negotiations were led by a British woman, who met with each party separately. Chaim Weizmann and David Ben-Gurion believed that the negotiations were doomed to failure from the start. In a previous interview, Weizmann told James G. McDonald that the British government was yielding to the Arabs and giving them a state or something similar, which would invite them to take a tougher stance on the issue of immigration, which was at the heart of the conflict.[170]

Jamal al-Husseini reaffirmed Arab demands for independence, the end of the mandate, the establishment of a constitutional government and an elected parliament on the basis of proportional representation, the refusal of the Jewish national homeland, and a halt to Jewish immigration and the sale of land to the Jews. He did not object to a transition period between the end of the mandate and the establishment of the independent state.[171]

The demands of the head of the Zionist delegation, Chaim Weizmann, on the other hand, were summarized as follows: a return to the idea that a country's economy should be able to absorb immigrants, assistance with immigration and settling immigrants by giving them all the land in Palestine that the government said wasn't good for farming, and a Jewish defense force to take some of the pressure off the British army.[172]

Faced with the opposing demands, British Colonial Secretary Malcolm MacDonald declared that there were two necessary steps: first, ending the mandate, establishing an independent Palestinian state linked to an alliance with Britain, and seeking to implement that immediately upon the arrival of peace in Palestine; second, that the British government during the transition period had a role in administering the state and establishing its institutions, ensuring British interests, preserving the holy places of all sects, and guaranteeing the rights of the Jewish minority.[173] The Palestinian delegation saw this this as a sign not of willingness to end the mandate but rather of desire to continue it and the continuation of Jewish immigration. MacDonald made it clear that he was ready to accept the continuation of the mandate for a period of ten years, after which British responsibility would end and Palestine would become completely independent. A spokesman for the Palestinian delegation added,

> If it is not feasible for supernatural reasons and the mentioned time frame has passed, a British-Arab Palestinian conference will be convened to discuss necessary actions. The delegation also reached an agreement that immigration would continue for a period of five years, at a rate of 12,000 individuals annually, with the condition that no further migration would occur without the consent of the Arabs. Additionally, it was stipulated that an independent Palestinian government would be established, comprising Palestinian ministers, and would enact its own constitution, establishing an independent Palestinian entity or association.[174]

The Arab proposal was modified by Britain to include an assurance that the British government would do everything in its power to facilitate the establishment of an independent Palestinian state within the next ten years. In the event that it becomes apparent that certain circumstances would require the establishment of the state to be delayed, the representatives of Palestine, the League of Nations, and the Arab countries would first be consulted.[175]

The Zionists were not satisfied with the proposed formula, and Weizmann responded by saying that the Jews did not agree to an independent state in Palestine without a prior agreement between the Jews and the Arabs that guaranteed the continuation of Jewish immigration, the development of the country, and the development of autonomous institutions. In addition, the state must be based on the principle that one of the two peoples would not dominate the other. While the Arab delegations insisted that Palestine was an Arab country, they expressed their willingness, as a concession for peace, to accept all the Jews in Palestine as citizens of the new state.[176]

However, the Zionist delegation decided to withdraw from the conference on February 27, 1939,[177] claiming that the British project was an indication that Britain was siding with the Arabs to appease them while they were on the threshold of a world war.[178] Weizmann issued a statement on that day saying that the proposals ignored the principles that the Jews had relied on during their twenty years of cooperation with the mandate government in the land of Israel, totally disregarded the Balfour Declaration and the mandate, and overlooked the historical link between the people of Israel and the land of Israel. According to the Zionists, there were no guarantees of or directives for the continuation of Jewish immigration, and there was no mention of immigration in the Jewish Agency, which was clearly defined by the mandate as the body that represented the Jewish people in matters related to the national homeland.[179]

The statement also asserted that the proposal to establish an independent state did not include a guarantee that Jews would not remain a minority in the country forever. As Weizmann went on to say, "This proposal is a denial by His Majesty's government of the solemn promises that were given to the Jewish people in the Balfour Declaration,[180] and the British government that followed came to it, and the League of Nations approved it in the Mandate Instrument, and the United States of America." This political line was proposed at a time when the Jews were subjected to an unprecedented persecution, and hundreds of thousands of them saw in the land of Israel their only hope and only refuge. During the conference, the Jews showed good-will, but it was not possible to reach any arrangement if the national homeland remained subject to Arab rule or if it meant the Jews living as a minority in the land of Israel.[181]

In Palestine, the Zionist National Council called for a meeting of the representatives of the Yishuv settlement from all over the country, including those who made a statement warning about the British government's intention to liquidate the policy of the national homeland and hand over the Yishuv to Arab rule. The Zionist National Council called on the Zionist militants not to submit to this, to mobilize all their forces for the battle, and to organize illegal immigration campaigns, until what was called the conspiracy was thwarted. The Zionist delegation was keen during the conference and its aftermath to hold meetings with members of the Arab delegations, with the aim of appearing to be looking for understanding and peace as a weapon to win public opinion. The St. James negotiations were also the final chapter in Ben-Gurion's attempts to obtain Arab recognition of the right of the Jews to be a majority, not a minority, in a Palestine part of an Arab federation. And Ben-Gurion concluded with the certainty that peace with the Arabs would be achieved when they realized that they were powerless to defeat the Zionist force.[182] Because many ships were landing migrants on the shores of Palestine despite the regulations set by the mandate government and contained many people who were ready to fight "for their right to seek refuge in the land of their fathers and grandfathers," Ben-Gurion put into place a policy to combat migration in order to accomplish this goal.[183]

After the Palestinian delegation returned to Beirut, the mufti dispatched a delegation to Cairo, stressing the necessity of establishing a Palestinian government as soon as the revolution ceased. He demanded, if possible, the establishment of a constituent assembly that would draft a constitution within three years. The Higher Arab Committee also proposed to keep the issue of lands suspended subject to an agreement between the high commissioner and the Palestinian ministry.[184]

THE INTERNATIONAL POSITION AND ITS IMPLICATIONS FOR THE ARAB-ZIONIST CONFLICT

Given the importance of Palestine's strategic location on the one hand and the fact that the Zionist settlement project occupies an important position in the global strategy of the colonial powers, particularly the British, there is a dialectical relationship between the international situation and the Arab-Zionist conflict. This relationship is reflected in the fact that there is a conflict between Arabs and Zionists. As a result, it is of the utmost significance to give careful consideration to the international situation during the years 1935 to 1940.[185]

Adolf Hitler, after he had succeeded in suppressing internal opposition in Germany and consolidated the Nazis' position, had in the spring of 1935 cancelled Germany's commitment not to create a large army within its borders, as was required by the Versailles Treaty. Compulsory recruitment was announced, and a large German army was established. In the spring of 1936, German forces entered the demilitarized zone in the Rhine, violating the Treaty of Versailles for the second time. In the beginning of October of the same year, Hitler announced the establishment of the Berlin-Rome Axis, which Japan joined a month later. The tripartite Axis declared its intention to redivide the world and not to leave the world's wealth in the hands of the imperialist states: Britain, France, and the United States.[186]

In the spring of 1938, Hitler finished adding Austria to Germany. This made Germany a stronger rising colonial power. The Nazi regime in Germany used Czechoslovakia as a benchmark to measure its power and ability to take action. In addition to its strategic location in the middle of Europe and the naturally fortified borders that separated it from Germany, Czechoslovakia was also home to a highly developed military industry. France was a member of a military alliance with Romania and Yugoslavia, and the three countries also had a defense treaty in place. In addition, the Soviet Union made clear that it was prepared to assist Czechoslovakia in the event that Poland and Romania allowed German armies to pass through their countries.[187]

When attempts to set up a European counterfront failed, Britain and France agreed, at the Munich Conference in late September 1938, to Hitler's demands, which saw Czechoslovakia forced to cede to Germany its German-majority border region, including the defensive lines and fortifications separating the two countries. This paved the way for the occupation of Czechoslovakia on March 15, 1939, while Italy occupied Albania without any resistance from the Allied countries. On August 20, 1939, Moscow and Berlin announced the signing of the Molotov-Ribbentrop Pact, followed by Germany's invasion of Poland on September 1 and the division of the country between Germany and the Soviet Union. This precipitated Britain and France's declaration of war on Germany.[188]

As has been mentioned before, the rapidity with which events transpired in Europe had an effect on Britain's attitude toward the revolution in Palestine. People in Britain were concerned about the effects that the revolution in the Levant would have on their country as well. A report dated April 14, 1939, stated,

> Egypt is a transportation node, and the port of Alexandria is the largest port in the eastern Mediterranean. Also, Iraq is close by, and the Habbaniyah base looks out for British interests in both Iraq and Iran. And then there's Saudi Arabia, which could be dangerous if it joins with Germany and Italy to make a coalition. Because Aden is considered the base of the British fleet, the sheikhdoms that are located along the Trucial Coast and Kuwait will be in danger as a result of the oil supply to Britain.[189]

The Committee of Imperial Defence (CID) report in Palestine in early January 1939 stated, "We feel the need to clearly refer to the patriotic senti-ment that prevails in all Arab countries about British policy in Palestine, and accordingly we assume the necessity of taking the necessary measures to find calm. To public opinion in Palestine and in the neighbouring Arab countries, if we fail to win the trust of the Arabs in the event of war, we announce that we have no measures or proposals that we recommend to take regarding this country."[190]

The British Imperial Staff seemed eager to promote calm in the area given the impact of the rise of Nazism, the increase in anti-Semitism, and the persecution of the Jews in Germany and central Europe. The result of this was increased Jewish immigration to Palestine, which was one of the greatest achievements of the Zionist movement after the tragedy of the Jews of Germany and central Europe. The Zionist leadership tried to exploit the alarming international situation to enhance the position of the Zionist settlement grouping and to limit the effectiveness of the escalating calls in Britain to take Arab grievances into account.[191]

On the initiative and assistance of Chaim Weizmann, the Haganah called the attention of the British High Military Command to the importance of the strategic location of Palestine and to the military and logistical capabilities of the Zionist Caucus regarding British defense plans in the Middle East.[192] A memorandum was sent to a number of English military experts, including Basil Henry Liddell Hart,[193] which included a statement outlining the importance of Palestine for transportation between London and India if Italy proceeded to block British transport routes in the Mediterranean.[194] The memo said that the need for a British military base in Palestine would depend on what the Zionists could do. There were enough drivers, mechanics, and tractor drivers who both were technically skilled and had worked in defense-related fields in the past. There was a foundation for the development of industries that could be used for military purposes. There was also a foundation for the growing Zionist military force, which could boast the ability to defend against air strikes and secure transportation.[195]

The official Israeli narrative states, "The memorandum was heard in a number of influential military circles, but it was clear that the implementation of the projects contained therein is linked to the general political decision regarding the fate of the country."[196]

When Theodor Herzl outlined the strategy of the Zionist movement, he emphasized the significance of developing closer ties with the imperial power. The presentation of the memo was another indication that serving the interests of colonial power is at the core of the Zionist movement's strategy. In addition, the location of the Zionist project within the strategy of the colonial powers in the Arab East, the Mediterranean basin, West Asia, and East Africa is another indication. The official Israeli account of how the memo met with influential British military circles is just one indication.

It was clear at the time that Britain was determined to cancel the political role of the Palestinian National Movement and the leadership of Haj Amin al-Husseini. This was shown not only by insisting that the Arab delegation not head the London conference but also by rejecting all reconciliation attempts initiated by Musa al-'Alami and George Antonius, then Nuri al-Sa'id.[197] The contacts made by Musa al-'Alami during his visit to Berlin in September 1937 and then by 'Awni 'Abdel Hadi, who was returning from the London conference, as well as his meeting with the Nazi Party philosopher Alfred

Rosenberg, the assistant secretary of the foreign minister Foreman, and a number of employees of the Nazi Party Office for Foreign Policy, made it abundantly clear that the stakes were unsuccessful. This demonstrated that they had failed to gain German support for the Palestinian cause.[198]

THE 1939 WHITE PAPER AND ARAB/
ZIONIST REACTIONS

Despite the decline of the round table conference following the withdrawal of the Zionist delegation, separately discussions continued in London between representatives of the British government and the Arab and Zionist delegations. The British government appeared ready to show a degree of positivity toward Arab demands in anticipation of a shift by Arab leaderships toward supporting German imperialism. This shift was anticipated by the British government. It declared that it had fulfilled its commitment to the establishment of the Jewish national home because it had enabled three hundred thousand Jews to immigrate to and settle in Palestine. Additionally, it stated that its obligations did not stipulate the establishment of a Jewish or Arab state, and for this reason it saw the establishment of an independent state and the end of the mandate.[199] A secret meeting was held on March 16, 1939, to talk about a British plan to set up an independent Palestinian state after a transitional period of ten years, which would start when Arabs and Jews worked well together on a board of directors. The meeting was called to discuss the proposal that the state's constitution would include guarantees for the minority, that the state would be divided into Arab and Jewish cantons, and that the immigration of Jews would be capped at seventy-five thousand over the course of the next five years, until the percentage of Jews reached one-third of the population. In certain regions, selling land to Jews would be strictly prohibited, while in others, land sales would be severely restricted.[200]

The British proposal was not submitted to the Higher Arab Committee but rather to the Egyptian government, whose Cairo ambassador to London, Nash'at Hassan, brought it to Cairo. Muhammad Mahmud, the prime minister, decided to hold a special Arab conference to discuss the proposal, in which Muhammad Mahmud, 'Ali Mahir, and Nash'at Hassan came from Egypt, Tawfiq al-Suwaidi and 'Abd al-Qadir al-Kilani came from Iraq, and Prince Faisal—later King Faisal—and Sheikh Hafiz Wahbah came from Saudi Arabia. The Palestinians did not participate in the conference given that the proposal was submitted to Arab countries through Egypt. However, Muhammad Mahmud took the opinion of a number of Palestinian figures who were residing in Cairo, including Ahmed Hilmi 'Abd al-Baqi, 'Awni 'Abdel Hadi, Amin al-Tamimi, and Ya'qub al-Ghussin, who would not decide anything before consulting the mufti in Beirut.[201] The Arabs expressed their willingness to consider the British proposal on three conditions: immediate cessation of immigration and the sale of lands, determination of the exact length of the transitional period, and a clear decision that the Zionists could not impede the establishment of the independent state.

As for the Jewish Agency, on March 16, 1939, it was informed of the details of the British proposal, and on April 18, 1939, it attempted to present or postpone its issuance. Weizmann telegraphed to the British prime minister, "The survival of the Jewish presence in Palestine, by a third of the population, the reduction of the area of Jewish settlement in a small area is considered in our view a destruction of the Jewish actions, and the handing over of the Jewish presence in Palestine to the rule of the Arab gangs."[202] As a consequence of this, the announcement of the project was put off until May 17, 1939. At that time, it was published in the form of a White Paper that had been prepared by Sir Malcolm MacDonald.[203]

On May 23, 1939, the White Paper was approved by the British House of Commons with a majority of 179 votes out of a total of 268 votes cast, and it was subsequently passed without opposition by the House of Lords the following day.[204] As a consequence of this, the British government was compelled by the constitution to put it into effect. The statement that Britain had reached the conviction that it had fulfilled its commitment to the Jews in accordance with the Balfour Declaration and the mandatory instrument was included in the third White Paper that was published after the mandate. The White Paper also had a brief history of the committees that came before and the round table conference.[205] The Arabs' rights were no longer being violated, and their very existence was no longer in danger as a result of the continued immigration of Jews and the transfer of Arab lands to Jewish ownership. Moreover, since the mandate was temporarily based on it, the destiny of Palestine is independence, provided that this is done in partnership between Arabs and Jews. This could only be accomplished if there was compelling evidence that they had the potential to mix with one another and collaborate with one another. Accordingly, the establishment of self-government would take place within the next ten years, during which time Palestinians would play an increasingly active role in the management of their affairs. This would be followed by the termination of the mandate and the formation of an independent state.[206] The White Paper included three chapters.[207]

The first, concerned with the constitution, stated,

1. The goal of His Majesty's government is to establish within ten years an independent Palestinian government, linked with the United Kingdom with a treaty that guarantees the two countries their commercial and war demands in the

future in a satisfactory manner. The proposal to form an independent state would involve consulting the League of Nations with a view to ending the Mandate.

2. The independent state must be a state that Arabs and Jews contribute to its rule in a way that guarantees the maintenance of the basic interests of both parties.

3. The formation of the independent state will be preceded by a period of transition during which His Majesty's government retains responsibility for governing the country. During the transition period, the people of Palestine are given an increasing share in the government of their country. Both teams of residents will have an opportunity to participate in government administration, and the process will take place whether or not both teams seize this opportunity.

4. Once security and order have been sufficiently established, take the necessary measures to take over the Palestinian leadership in some quarters, with British advisers. Palestinian heads of departments are members of the Executive Council, which provides advice to the High Commissioner. Representatives from the Arabs and the Jews are invited to assume the presidency of the departments in proportion to the number of the population, and looking at the conversion of the Executive Council into a cabinet in the future.

5. During this stage, His Majesty's government does not submit proposals to form an elected legislative body. If the public opinion in Palestine expresses his favour of such a development, the King's government will be ready to form the necessary tool, provided that the local conditions allow this.

6. When five years have passed since the consolidation of security and order, an appropriate body of representatives of the people of Palestine and His Majesty's government is formed to consider how the constitutional arrangements will proceed during the transition period, and to search for a constitution for an independent Palestinian state and to provide recommendations in that regard.

7. His Majesty's government will be required to include the expected constitution and put in place protective texts to protect:

A. Holy places, facilitating access to them, and protecting the interests and properties of various religious bodies.

B. The various sects in Palestine in accordance with the obligations of His Majesty's government towards Arabs and Jews, and with regard to the special status of the Jewish national homeland in Palestine.

C. Concerning the matters required to meet the war situation, which His Majesty's government may consider necessary in light of the conditions prevailing in the country.

D. Increase the powers and responsibilities of municipalities and local councils during the transition period.

8. If it appears to His Majesty's government at the end of ten years that the circumstances require postponing the formation of the independent state, contrary to what it hopes for, it shall consult with representatives of the people of Palestine, the Council of the League of Nations, and the neighbouring Arab countries, before making a decision on this measure.

The second concerned Jewish immigration during the transition period, where during the first five years, fifty thousand immigrants were allowed to enter, at a rate of ten thousand annually, in addition to twenty-five thousand refugees from Nazi persecution, taking into account the country's economic capacity to absorb.[208] During the next five years, immigration would depend on the Arabs' willingness to accept this. His Majesty's government declared its determination to suppress illegal immigration and to take the necessary measures against that.[209] If the illegal immigrants succeed in entering the country and could not be removed, their number would be deducted from the annual quota.[210]

The third concerned the land. The reports put forth by the various committees of experts indicated that, given the growth of the natural Arab population and the continued sale of lands from the Arabs to the Jews in recent years, there was now no room in any area for the transfer of lands from the Arabs to the Jews, while restrictions on the transfer of land from the Arabs in some other regions must be established if the Arab farmers were to maintain their current standard of living and prevent the formation of a large group of Arabs with no land. Given these conditions, the high commissioner would be granted powers to prevent and regulate the transfer of lands; these powers would be effective the day the statement was published, and the high commissioner would retain them throughout the transition period.[211]

Arab, Palestinian, and national views differed on the White Paper. On the day following its issuance, the Arab Higher Committee announced its rejection in a quick and comprehensive statement, in which it clarified that it was hoping to ensure the formation of a national government immediately after stopping the disturbances, issuing a general amnesty, canceling all that occurred under the emergency law, and guaranteeing the completion of the following constitutional steps: that the structure of the national government would be formed by its constitution, parliament, and head of state within three years and that the White Paper guaranteed the termination of the mandate within a reasonable period.[212]

Despite Britain's acknowledgment of the theoretical right of the Palestinian people to independence and the establishment of a state with an Arab majority, its recognition seemed to be limited to the gains achieved by the Palestinian delegation during the round table conference in London. In other words, while Britain acknowledged these rights in principle, it did not fully recognize or appreciate the broader implications of its own acknowledgment. The British perspective viewed the progress made by the Palestinian delegation as a specific achievement within the conference, rather than a comprehensive recognition of the Palestinian people's rights to self-determination and statehood.

A comprehensive briefing was provided on the stages of implementing the ambiguous and absolute measures.

The foundation of the matter lies in the mandate instrument, which includes the Balfour Declaration as an integral part.

> D. Connecting Palestine's independence to Zionist approval and consent by requiring Jewish participation and contribution to the establishment of an independent state.

> E. Failure to fully specify the transition period. The British government has the option of extending the ten-year period. Also, not giving a clear time frame gives the Zionists a way to stop the plan to set up a state and get independence.

As for the rebel leaders, they were shocked by the absence of the amnesty they had hoped for, and they did not see in the White Paper a tendency to reconcile with the mufti. They therefore immediately announced their rejection of the British proposals.[213] It was stated in the report of British wing commander Lt. Gen. Neil Ritchie assessing the situation after the release of the White Paper that, although the Palestinian Arabs were exhausted by the unrest and anxious for peace, their vast majority did not trust the intentions of the British government.[214] As a result of the propaganda that the revolutionaries were broadcasting, their intransigence increased against the White Paper.[215] This became apparent in the second half of May 1939, when great efforts were made to continue the revolution.[216] After the White Paper was made public, various parts of Palestine began sending in their reports. The fact that several incidents have taken place within the last ten days serves as additional evidence that supports this argument.[217] The White Paper, which was met with opposition from the majority of the Palestinian Arab population, was seen by the Palestinian Arab leadership as a betrayal of their aspirations for independence and self-determination.[218] They rejected the proposed establishment of a Jewish national home and the continuation of British rule in Palestine.[219] In response, the Arab Higher Committee declared a six-month general strike to exert pressure on the British government to withdraw the White Paper and affirm the Palestinian Arab demand for independence.[220, 221]

This strike not only demonstrated the continued support for the revolution and the leadership of the mufti and the rebels, but also highlighted the suffering endured by the citizens amidst British repression and the declining effectiveness of the revolution.[222]

On the level of partisanship, the defense parties and the National Bloc singled out the support of the White Paper under the guise of realism and staging. Additionally, on May 30, 1939, Raghib al-Nashashibi issued a statement in which he expressed his party's willingness to cooperate with Britain and his hope to shorten the transitional period.[223] He also condemned what he called terrorism and the position of the Supreme Arab Authority in opposing the White Paper.[224] Based on the evidence given by Emile Touma, it looks like this was also the position of the Communist Party. It was decided that the national forces saw in the White Paper a British concession to the national armed struggle, that they saw a positive valuation as a positive value, and that it was necessary to take advantage of the opportunity available, regardless of British imperial intentions. He accused the Supreme Arab Committee of having rejected the White Paper due to the increasing influence of Arab governments on Palestinian decision making.[225]

In evaluating the White Paper, Muhammad 'Izzat Darwazah wrote,

> Whatever it is, the White Paper, in some ways, gave in to the Arabs' demands, and their charter went a long way. The fact that Britain agreed to a Palestinian state with a majority of Arabs was a huge success and a significant shift that would not have occurred two years ago. This could not have happened. In other words, the Arab uprising was victorious, and the revolution was successful in achieving its goals, both practically (by abolishing partition) and theoretically (by finding a general solution to the Palestine question in accordance with the Arab Charter). Both of these accomplishments were the pinnacle of the Arab uprising. Despite the setback of the establishment of a Jewish state in Palestine, the Palestinian Arab leadership found some degree of satisfaction in recognizing the accomplishments of the Jewish community. This sentiment was further fueled by the British government's presentation of the White Paper to Parliament, which signaled an official endorsement of the document's policies. However, the Palestinian Arab leadership remained determined to pursue their own aspirations for independence and continued to advocate for the withdrawal of the White Paper's provisions.[226]

With the agreement of both Emile Touma and Muhammad 'Izzat Darwazah on the positive view of Britain's theoretical recognition the Arab rights, there is a clear differentiation between historians on the position of the White Paper. While Touma viewed it in the light of the impasse in the Arab situation and believed that the positives required its acceptance, Darwazah viewed it in the light of the international climate and the bitter Arab experience with

British colonialism burdened with initiatives to circumvent the Palestinian National Movement.

In a statement made in Egypt, Prime Minister Muhammed Mahmud quickly stated that he was unable to provide the Arabs of Palestine with guidance that they would be content with and accept.[227] Meanwhile, Muhammad 'Ali 'Alubah issued a statement against the White Paper and appealed to Arab and Islamic countries to redouble their efforts to support the Arabs of Palestine. The British initiative encountered fierce opposition from the Iraqi government. Simultaneously, the Committee for the Defense of Palestine in Syria and Lebanon opposed the White Paper of 1939 because they believed it was biased against the Palestinians, restricted free Jewish immigration, and deprived the Palestinians of their land rights.[228] In contrast, the Jordanian government, headed by Tawfiq Abu al-Huda, announced its official acceptance.[229]

The Zionist leaders' rejection of the White Paper was clearer and more decisive. Ben-Gurion described it as "the book of treachery and betrayal" and said, "It was a true copy of the Munich Agreement, whereby the young Czech people were handed over to Hitler and his soldiers, and here Britain surrenders the weak Jewish people to the Mufti and his terrorist gangs."[230]

Ben-Gurion was in no way objective in his comparison; nor did he express the facts of the reality. The Arab side was not heavily armed and possessed a trained army whose number of officers and soldiers of both sexes was not less than forty thousand. Nor was Arab resistance to the British occupation and the Zionist settlement project a terrorist act; it was rather a legitimate national struggle in accordance with the international law that permitted resistance against the occupiers and aggressors by all available means, including armed struggle.

Also, had Ben-Gurion had moral courage and been honest, he would have said that the Arabs of Palestine were the ones who were attacked and that they, like the Czech people, were facing a similar form of racism, which did not see the self or the other any differently than Nazi racism did. In addition to this, he was unable to recall anything constructive that the nearly one hundred years of British colonialism had brought to the Zionist movement. According to his views, he had a very pessimistic outlook on the nation that had supported Zionists in the lands of Arabs and brought international legitimacy to the endeavor of colonizing Arab lands. He said, "Britain has not just renounced its pledges to aid Jewish immigration, she even took on a completely further task as she forcibly prevented immigration."[231]

On the day following the issuance of the White Paper, the Zionists declared a general strike, held mass meetings, and issued statements confirming that they would violate immigration land laws and would never cooperate with institutions established based on what was stated in the White Paper. During a Zionist demonstration in Jerusalem, a British policeman was killed. The demonstration was not limited to politicians and the politicized public, but it was attended by the chief rabbi, Yitzhak Isaac HaLevi Herzog, who stood on the steps of the Hurva Synagogue in Jerusalem and tore up, before the crowd, a copy of the White Paper.[232] An angry crowd burned down the immigration administration building, and government offices in Haifa and Tel Aviv were stormed on order to tear up all the files of illegal Jewish immigration. In Jerusalem, Arab shops were looted.[233] The Irgun undertook a series of bombings aimed at Arabs in movie houses, coffeehouses, and public squares. It set a time bomb at the vegetable market in Haifa, killing eighteen Arabs.[234] The next day, Gen. Sir Robert Hadden Haining, commander of the British army in Palestine and Transjordan, summoned the Zionist leaders and warned them that he would respond to force with force and held them responsible for any bloodshed. Ben-Gurion sent him a written response in which he said, "The demonstrations that took place yesterday indicate the beginning of the Jewish resistance to the criminal policy proposed by the government of His Majesty, and that intimidating the Jews will not force them to surrender even if their blood is shed, and that responsibility for what may happen lies with the government."[235]

The Zionists made a fuss in the international press, condemning Britain and the White Paper. On June 26, 1939, a Zionist conference was held in New York, attended by delegates from across the United States, chaired by Rabbi Shlomo Goldman, who said in the opening speech that Palestine was not Arab and that the White Paper could only be explained on the basis of international anti-Semitism against the Jews. Weizmann sent a telegram to both conferences, in which he stated that the Jewish people had made the decision to arrive at the point of full implementation of the Zionist idea—that the Zionist movement as well as Jews all over the world needed to fully participate in taking responsibility and making sacrifices in order to maintain immigration to Palestine, Jewish colonialism, and opposition to the White Paper.[236]

In late 1939, Weizmann did not hesitate to take an escalatory stance, declaring that a Jewish state must be established, even if it meant pitting Zionism against Britain. Ben-Gurion declared that the Zionists were entering a new stage of development: after the stage of Zion's beloved ones and the political stage of Zionism, a new page in the history of Zionism, the page of fighting Zionism, was opened. Zionist work could only be accomplished through struggle. The positions of Weizmann and Ben-Gurion were chanted in Geneva on August 16, 1939, condemning the British betrayal.[237]

The official Israeli version concluded its comment on the events of the years 1936 to 1939 by saying,

> After twenty years of working together and forming an alliance, the relationship with Britain has come to an end. It was a partnership that made it possible for the

Yishuv to grow in the country on both the economic and political fronts, despite the limits and restrictions that its interpretations put on it. Since then, a policy of closing the gates and stopping the growth of the Jewish national homeland has taken its place, and the Hebrew Yishuv has only stayed in the lead because of its efforts to make sure it stays alive.[238]

Once the White Paper was issued, a number of US senators representing both Republicans and Democrats rushed to request the Foreign Affairs Committee in Congress to discuss an urgent proposal to immediately cancel the White Paper and declare Palestine a Jewish state.[239] As soon as the news of the American proposal was broadcast, the British Labour Party initiated a conference of its Parliament Party to discuss the issue, which issued the following decision: The White Paper's policy represented surrender to aggression and was a setback for the progressive forces. The party demanded that the British government bypass this policy and reopen the doors of Palestine to Jewish immigration.[240]

ZIONIST MILITARY DEVELOPMENT DURING THE ARAB REVOLUTION

Ben-Gurion did not waver in his determination to put an end to the revolution and end the strike on December 10, 1936. He did this on the basis that he saw the intervention of the Arab kings as involving them in the affairs of Palestine and recognizing Palestine as a part of the Arab countries and that the Arab countries bordering Palestine had the authority to intervene in its fate and pass legislation. In his view, this meant undermining the foundations of the Balfour Declaration and the British mandate.[241] In December 1936, he told the members of the Zionist Executive Committee, "We must not delude ourselves and believe that the events of 1936 have already ended. Almost every Arab opposes Zionism, because it contradicts Arab and Muslim identity, and and harbors a general aversion towards outsiders due to our cultural differences. Therefore, the events of 1936 represent merely a chapter in an enduring conflict that may persist for hundreds of years. It is a genuine war, a struggle for survival and existence."[242]

In light of this conviction, he demanded that the position of European Jews be used in a propaganda campaign to compel the mandate government to open the doors of Palestine to immigration for a million Jews. He thought that this was the only way to make sure that the Jewish people would stay alive. He listed the things he thought were important to reach the following three goals:

First: The Arabs gave their approval to the peace plan proposed by the Zionists after they heard them say, "We must first and foremost build up a large Jewish force in this country." It is in the best interest of everyone involved for the Zionist Movement to organize this army as quickly as humanly possible. It was widely acknowledged in Palestine that the peace negotiations had been productive and that a settlement had been reached.

Second: So that they can protect the Jews who live in Palestine from an all-out Arab attack, which could include the surrounding Arab countries. According to what he said:

1. We must control the sea, not only the coast but on the sea altogether. We have speed boats and ships that we use in the days of calm for transportation purposes and in crises for security purposes.

2. Control over the mountains.

3. To create within the nation an adequate military industry, so that we are not reliant on the sources of weapons that come from outside the country.

4. Vanguard numbers are military.

Third: The bargaining power of the Zionist Movement. Britain seeks to gain friendship with the Jewish force, which has trained youth and military factories.[243]

When he tried to get the Arabs to turn down the Zionist project, Ben-Gurion ignored both the facts of history and the facts of the present. This is something that should be noted. Arabs and Muslims have been known throughout history for their unrestricted openness to the Jews. There have been times and places where Jews and Muslims have lived together in harmony and shared cultural and intellectual traditions.[244] For example, during the golden age of Muslim Spain (eighth to fifteenth centuries), Jews played important roles in fields such as medicine, philosophy, and poetry, and there was a flourishing of Jewish scholarship and creativity.[245] Historians and orientalists, especially Jews, acknowledge this, as was the reality in all Arab-Islamic countries before the emergence of the Zionist movement and the uprooting of Arabs from Palestine to form a foreign human barrier to separate the wings of the Arab world, to be a tool of colonial and exploitative powers, and to maintain fragmentation, backwardness, and Arab dependency.[246]

Ben-Gurion knew that the Zionist project was just a plan for racial settler colonialism, and he used the phrase "the real war," which could last hundreds of years, to show that he knew this.[247] And because it also triggered a zero-sum battle, it was not possible to reach a settlement based on mutual concessions; rather, it was necessary for one of the two sides to decide in order to reach a conclusion.[248] Based on this conviction, he decided to adopt a strategic option to impose surrender on the Arabs, and he rejected all of the generous settlement initiatives that the Arabs had offered him only two years prior to his speech in front of the Zionist Executive Committee.[249]

In light of this, the leadership of the Zionist movement interpreted the end of the revolution on October 12, 1936, as a temporary truce that gave the heads of the Haganah and its officials the opportunity to assess their performance and get ready for the next round of fighting.[250] The Haganah leaders concluded that the readiness during the years 1933 to 1936 was not at the level required to face the dangers posed by the Zionist project, nor the degree of motivation and strength of Arab society during the events of 1936.[251] In addition, the Zionist group Yishuv and the Haganah had not prepared enough from a psychological point of view for effective defense, and the levels of training of individuals and groups, which were inherited from the training of the Hebrew battalion in World War I, were not appropriate for the emerging situations.[252]

The observers made sure to point out the good things about the way the settlement grouping did its job, which showed resilience and self-control in the face of what happened. In addition to this, they made note of the fact that no settlement site was evacuated, with the exception of Hebron after the events that took place in August 1929 and the Ruhama colony in the northern Negev. At the end of the evaluation process, it was decided that the Yishuv settlement bloc ought to be able to defend itself in a number of different situations, particularly when there was no other light infantry support. Based on this information, a lot of people joined the Haganah's regional leadership in 1936. This was meant to bring about a big change in how they planned to protect the colonies and the area around them.[253]

Ben-Gurion had announced at the beginning of the events of 1936 the necessity of uniting defensive organizations on the basis of two conditions. The first was that unification be effective and not legitimize division under the guise of unification.[254] The second was political submission to the management of the Jewish Agency regarding security matters. To achieve this, the agency appointed a Committee for the Unification of Security Organizations. It established a political program for unification based on the principle that defending the Yishuv would be unified, comprehensive, and fully subject to the supervision and control of the National Council and the Zionist Administration. The parties pledged to exercise their full influence and loyalty to establish a single defense organization. On August 6, 1936, the agreed political program was signed.[255]

In the spring of 1937, Abraham Tehoumi, his colleagues, and a number of the men of the National Military Organization announced their union with the Haganah, which constituted a division in the Revisionist camp, which opposed unification.[256] However, Organization B, which was led by Jabotinsky, was divided in April 1937, with approximately fifteen hundred out of three thousand members joining the Haganah.[257] This was a very important achievement on the path to the unification process that Ben-Gurion had called for at the beginning of the events.

Unification removed many obstacles to the Haganah and the recruitment of individuals, so that it witnessed a rapid growth in the number of its affiliates, as well as in its armament. In addition, during the years of the Arab revolution, it had witnessed a qualitative development in its relations with the British army, so that by the end of the year 1937, the members numbered thirty-five thousand, among them fifty-five hundred girls. Of these, nine thousand were in the cities and the rest in the kibbutzim and moshav settlements, almost all of whose residents were affiliated with the Haganah. The Haganah also witnessed the transition of its leaders from volunteers to full-time employees, and many organizational changes occurred in the various branches. Beginning in the spring of 1937, armed patrols were conducted in the Galilee, the coastal plain, and Marj Ibn Amir.[258] During the year 1937, fifteen new settlement points were established, including five in the Besan Plain.[259]

In November 1937, the Jewish Agency and the regional leadership of the Haganah commissioned a committee tasked with studying the development of proposals to defend the Jewish state in the event of the implementation of the partition project. It also formed two subcommittees. The first to draw up plans for the police and the gendarmerie and the second for the militia and army. The commissioned committees discussed security plans and established budgets to implement them. The formation of the commissioned committees demonstrated the Zionist leaders' awareness of the necessity of advancing from the stage of allied local organizations to the level of an organized popular army. This realization was expressed by Yisrael Galili in one of the commissioned committee's sessions, saying, "The education of a fighting people who are always ready to defend themselves should be our primary focus as a nation. I also think that the country should take a more all-around approach to military training. Aside from the militia, there are also groups for sports, crafts, and other activities. We won't be able to defend ourselves against a regular army, so it's important that we raise a population that can fight."[260]

In 1937, Haganah members made up 8.75 percent of all Zionist settlers, a number that did not exceed four hundred thousand individuals. When other gang members and policemen who were completely independent of British control are added to those who served in the Haganah, it becomes abundantly clear that the number of Zionists who served in military formations exceeded 10 percent of the total number of settlers. This is an early indication of the trend toward militarization of the Zionist-colonial settlement grouping that was at the core of the Zionist strategy. This high percentage separates the experiences of Zionist settlement colonialism from those of European colonialism in North and South America, Algeria, and Rhodesia.[261] Even though many countries, like Britain and the United States, supported the Zionist project, which had no legal rights as early as the early nineteenth century, Arabs and Palestinians were against it because they saw the creation of a Jewish homeland as a threat to their own aspirations for self-determination. This tension ultimately led to conflict between Jews and Arabs in Palestine, which continues to this day.

When it came to buying weapons, the envoy of Yehuda Arazi Haganah to Poland was able to work out a deal with a regime that was known for being hostile to Jews. The Yehuda Arazi Haganah envoy paid for these weapons with the Zionist funds that were collected in Poland. Between the years 1936 and the outbreak of World War II, 2,750 rifles, 225 machine guns, 10,000 grenades, 700 tons of ammunition, and 2 million rounds were purchased and smuggled into Palestine. Additionally, two light planes, six gliders, and two million rounds were brought illegally into Palestine. The Polish secret police covered up illegal arms purchases and smuggling, and the Polish authorities gave the green light for the formation of the vanguard organization Halutz, as well as the training of its members and the facilitation of illegal immigration operations into Palestine.[262]

Eliyahu Golomb, the Haganah official, was able to conclude agreements with arms dealers and smugglers in Belgium to buy weapons and smuggle them from the port of Antwerp, including German-made weapons. The money of German Jews smuggled into Belgium was used to pay for the weapons and the smuggling costs. Finland was the source of the weapons for Organization B affiliated with the Revisionists under the leadership of Jabotinsky, and agreement was reached with the Finnish authorities to buy and export weapons, provided that an import permit was obtained from one of the countries. This was also agreed with the Czechoslovak government.[263]

Arabs also bought weapons from dealers and smugglers in Palestine and the areas around it because the prices were so high. Additionally, weapons and ammunition were purchased from British authorities, who were in charge of the police warehouses. According to the Israeli version, one official was responsible for selling fifteen hundred bullets each week. One night, the officers who guarded the Central Police Command in Jerusalem were bribed by the British police, and as a result, fifty thousand bullets were taken from the building. Over the course of the three-year period, these acquisitions allowed the Arab factions to procure arms and provide training to settlers, enabling them to wield these weapons effectively.[264]

Before 1936, the arms industry had been confined to small workshops. An agency developed so that within three years, a section for manufacturing explosive materials, another for packing hand grenades, and a third for installing explosives and bombs were set up. The Haganah owned the factories producing hand grenades and rifle grenades. In 1937, the military industry was concentrated, and an advisory committee composed of chemical experts and a chemical-technical factory were formed. In 1938, 17,500 grenades and 16,000 rifle grenades were produced, as well as stores for machine-gun ammunition. The Regional Command of the Haganah decided to distribute weapons production centers so that each region could secure its needs as much as possible in an emergency. Forty-eight mortars of 3-mm caliber were produced in 1938, and by the end of 1939, ammunition-production machines with a capacity to produce fifteen thousand bullets a day had been imported. The Haganah envoys took advantage of the existing agreement with the British army so that manufacturing machines could be introduced with the help of British intelligence, which did not want to know the contents of the boxes in which these machines were shipped. At the end of 1939, fifty chemists worked in the arms industry.[265]

The Haganah's most significant accomplishment was the combat experience it gained over the course of the three years of the Arab revolution. During that time, the Haganah shifted from inactively guarding fixed locations to actively working in fields and on roads, and the experience was invaluable. Motorized units penetrated deeply into the hostile Arab areas, initially with the assistance of the British and later on without their assistance. The combat effectiveness achieved by the defense units under Orde Charles Wingate's command as the British intelligence officer rose to an excellent level. The Haganah members, in whom they had full confidence, participated in these activities because they were in their best interest.[266]

As a direct result of the actions taken by the Mandate Authority, the Zionists' combat prowess saw significant improvement. In 1936, it gave the go-ahead for the recruitment of a Jewish militia, and it informed the leadership of the Zionist movement that they would permit a special force of policemen to keep their weapons in the settlements where they were stationed. In spite of the fact that it was stipulated that the Haganah organization would be dissolved and the handing over of weapons would adhere to this condition, it abandoned it without making an announcement. By 1939, this army had approximately 14,500 men under its command. Orde Charles Wingate, a British officer, was an important figure in the history of the Special Night Squads, which he helped organize and train. Moshe Dayan was among the top Israeli officers who saw action against Arab forces while he was in command, and they did so under his direction.[267] David Hirst states, "The British civil authorities have objected to political reasons for this rapid development of Jewish military capacity, but the army leadership, whose only concern was the elimination of the Arab revolution, supported Jewish demands to promote recruitment and training."[268]

THE REALITY OF THE ZIONIST SETTLEMENT GROUP AFTER THE PUBLICATION OF THE WHITE PAPER

In explaining the reasons for the refusal of the White Paper, especially the issue of restricting immigration and the sale of land, the official Israeli version stated,

> The rights of minorities, including the guarantee of peace and stability for a specified duration, are crucial. Without an independent political framework, the small Jewish minority that exists among the sea of millions of Arabs in and around the country will degenerate and transform into another community of miserable and humiliated Jewish sects in Islamic countries, and they will vanish from the stage of history over the course of time. This will happen because the Arabs will dominate the political system.[269]

When it was stated that Jewish communities in Islamic countries were miserable and made to feel as if they were nothing, the official Israeli version, similar to the statements made by Ben-Gurion, did not take the facts of history into account. Also, it showed that Arab society still did not want to live together in a democratic way. After explaining the Zionist movement's strategic position on immigration and the redemption of the land, which was the reason the Zionist movement rejected the White Paper in 1939, there was a public display of what the Zionist movement perceived as the accomplishments of the Yishuv (Jewish community in pre-state Israel).

> At the time, Yishuv had reached a high level of organization, similar to organizing a state that was about to be established. It had central institutions (the Jewish Agency), the Elected Association (Hanifharim's Assifat), the National Council (Hava'ad Haleiumii), a branched education system, its own health services, and security organisation at the country level. It is Haganah. The authorities were forced to admit all of this publicly albeit reluctantly, even though they frequently expressed their concerns about the Jewish community's autonomous presence and influence in the country.[270]

The mandate for Palestine was granted to Great Britain by the League of Nations in 1922, and one of the terms of the mandate instrument was the establishment of the Jewish Agency. The Jewish Agency was tasked with promoting Jewish immigration to Palestine and developing the infrastructure necessary for the establishment of a Jewish national home. During the early years of the mandate, the British colonial government did indeed work closely with the Yishuv, the Jewish community in Palestine, to develop the country's infrastructure and economy. The British authorities saw the Yishuv as a potential ally against Arab nationalism and were keen to support the development of a Jewish homeland in Palestine. In addition, none of the institutions that were a part of the Zionist settlement were targeted by the British in an attempt to sabotage them, as was the case with the institutions that were a part of the Arab community in Palestine.[271] Also, when the official Israeli story talked about the achievements of the Yishuv, it didn't mention at all how the British war machine helped the Zionist-colonial settlement group survive and stay together over time.

Furthermore, the official Israeli version ignored the effect of the Arab revolution on the Zionist achievements. Despite the escalation of Nazi Germany's terrorism of the Jews of Germany, Austria, and Poland and Nazi cooperation with the Zionists in facilitating the process of Jewish immigration from the three countries, as previously explained, immigration figures declined during the three years of the revolution from 61,854 immigrants in 1935 to 29,727 in 1936, 10,536 in 1937, 12,868 in 1938, and 11,405 in 1939.[272] Meanwhile, illegal immigration decreased from sixty-two thousand in 1935 to fifteen thousand during the three years of the revolution. The number of counterimmigrants who emigrated from Palestine reached ten thousand, as the official Israeli version stated.[273]

The revolution was most influential in terms of the Zionists' possession of land, as the total bought during the four years of the revolution (1936–1939) reached 112,766 dunums.[274] When comparing the numbers of what the Zionists had acquired by way of purchase and from state lands, it is clear that in 1935 they acquired 72,905 dunums, while their possession was 18,146 dunums in 1936, 39,367 dunums in 1937, 27,280 dunums in 1938, and 27,973 dunums in 1939,[275] at a rate of 28,191.50 dunums annually during the four years, while the average rate of purchase for the four years prior to the revolution was 47,725 dunums.[276]

The Zionist industrial sector witnessed a peak in 1935, when many factories were established in various fields of production. However, the Arab revolution had had an impact on industrial progress. A report by the Jewish Agency indicated that the economy in Palestine suffered deflation after a period of expansion and recovery. The report attributed this to the impact of the Arab revolution, lack of confidence in Palestine's economic future, and decline in immigration. This had a severe impact on Jewish industry, especially newly established institutions, some of which were forced to close or were sold to other investors.[277]

However, the Zionist settlement bloc managed to mitigate the negative impact of the revolution. The unemployed were absorbed into the security forces, whose number multiplied. For security reasons, the size of the public works sector also expanded significantly. The mixed agricultural sector occupied new markets because of the broken link with Arab production sources. This was in addition to the increased flow of aid from the Keren Kayemet (Jewish National Fund), the founding fund Keren Hayesud, and the German Jews Aid Fund.[278] Weizmann commented on the events: "No longer is a colony or a Yishuv here. . . . It is a nation in the full sense of this concept." "The past three years of events, along with their victims of expensive daily labor, night shifts, and constant tension, have brought about a sense of national cohesion and a level of resolve that we have never witnessed before; iron has caused this people to lose their soul."[279]

The achievement of the Zionist settlement bloc in effectively responding to the challenges it faced is undeniable. However, in order to accomplish this goal, not only did its leadership make great efforts and sacrifices (which are perhaps indisputable), but it also had the sponsorship and protection of the British government, as well as the support and funding of Jews all over the world, particularly in the United States.[280] Furthermore, the unfortunate rise of anti-Semitism in Nazi Germany and Italian fascism played a role in providing additional support to the Zionist cause.

During the course of the revolution, which lasted for four years, it became abundantly clear that both the Balfour Declaration and the mandate instrument were founded on lies, as was the assertion that the Arab citizens of Palestine were merely members of religions that were not Jewish who resided in Palestine. If Britain had promised Weizmann that Palestine in 1935 would be Jewish, as Britain is English, then it was the will of the people, who known for their great generosity and amazing resilience, that caused the British promise to be emptied of its content.

As the Arab National Movement in Palestine did more and more, the relationship between the British intelligence services and the Zionist intelligence services got stronger. Arab buyers and brokers were also taken advantage of. They were forced to sell because they didn't like the National Employment Movement. The Israeli intelligence services were not able to get into the leadership of the revolutionaries, but they were able to get into the Mandate Authority and its circles and organs. In 1935, it installed a system that could listen in on telephone conversations and read telegrams. When the police increased the number of radio stations they used, the Zionist intelligence services increased their activities to listen in on them and figure out messages. During the autumn of 1939, there were a total of thirty-four Haganah radio contact centers. The British eavesdropping centers and spying on other agencies played a big role in the illegal immigration that happened.[281]

Avraham Stern was successful in making contact with the Jews who had integrated into Poland, particularly those who had connections to the officers of the Polish army and the secret police. He was able to broker deals to buy weapons, provide training for pioneers, and assist people in illegally entering the country. In the spring of 1939, Stern established a training camp for explosives specialists at the Andrikov resort in the Zakopane Mountains in the southwest of Poland with the assistance of the Polish army. This camp was located in Poland. The men who worked for Etzel received instruction in various aspects of military strategy, including sabotage, clandestine communication, and the planning of terrorist operations.[282]

EVALUATION OF THE GREAT ARAB REVOLT, 1936–1939

According to the accurate calculations made by Dr. Walid al-Khalidi, the number of martyrs during the revolution years exceeded five thousand, while the wounded exceeded fourteen thousand. "If we apply these numbers to Britain or the United States based on their respective populations, it would mean killing approximately two hundred thousand Britons and injuring approximately six hundred thousand more people in Britain, or it would mean killing one million Americans and wounding three million people in the United States."[283] Such is an indication of the great price that the Arab people paid in Palestine because of its revolution. Despite this, the revolution was aborted, and the historical question is what factors caused the abortion?

Arabs and Palestinians talked to each other in the same way on the international level about a number of things related to conditions in the region and around the world, the Arab reality at the official and popular levels, and the objective and subjective conditions of the revolution and the Palestinian National Movement. However, everything changed on the day after the start of World War II in September 1939. At that point, a nearly complete halt was imposed on the revolution. On November 23, 1939, the British colonial secretary, MacDonald, used this information to announce that Britain would be slowly returning to Palestine with force.[284]

The following is a concise summary of the factors that contributed to the inevitability of the revolution's failure:

First, the Asian and African national liberation movements didn't have much support from the rest of the world. This was true despite the fact that conflicts between countries that had been colonized became worse. The colonial phenomenon was still prevalent in international relations, and the countries that had previously held colonial positions continued to wield the most power. The Soviet Union adopted Joseph Stalin's strategy, which was based on the policy of building socialism in one country. On the other hand, the Zionist movement was supported by a variety of capitalist states, including the regimes of the German Nazis and the Italian Fascists, despite the contradictions that exist between these countries.

Second, the most significant flaw in the revolution was that the majority of its field leaders were al-Qassamids, people from agricultural backgrounds working as laborers. The countryside was the primary source of support for men and a safe haven for the revolution. The political leadership, on the other hand, reached a compromise with the urban bourgeoisie, which was the element of the movement that was the least revolutionary and the most willing to compromise. In addition, the establishment of peasant committees did not serve as the revolutionary cadre's backbone. Because of this, the revolution was unable to provide the kind of self-support it required in order to develop and spread its message. Fear was used in situations where it was necessary to try to be spontaneous and provide relief rather than organizing supplies and maintaining communication.

Third, the political and military leaders of the time did not understand how complicated the fight between the colonial alliance and Zionism was. This showed that they were always open to the idea of finding a middle ground or taking a settlement offer. In addition, neither the Arabs nor the field commanders possessed the skills that would have enabled the Arab people living in Palestine to make the most of the people and things at their disposal. This was a major obstacle for the Arab people. Even though unbiased historians agree on everything, the vast majority of political and military leaders were not able to handle the conflict with the colonial-Zionist alliance well. This was the case despite the fact that historians agree on everything. This was one of the factors that prevented the revolution from making any headway, which ultimately led to its demise occurring much more quickly. These leaders, despite their sincerity and enthusiasm, were not successful in managing the conflict.

Fourth, there is no doubt that, with the help of the mufti, the country's leaders were able to build good relationships with the different national and Islamic forces in the Arab world and the Maghreb. Because of this, they were able to get material and moral support from most of these forces, which helped the revolution succeed. However, this support was not enough to develop and maintain the revolution in the face of the growing escalation of the forces and means of British repression and the rapid development of the capabilities of the Zionist settlement group. Both of these factors made it impossible for the revolution to develop and continue. In addition, there was no official Arab system that provided any kind of material support for the revolution. On the other hand, the regimes that were in place at the time, particularly the two monarchies in Riyadh and Baghdad, put pressure on the Palestinian leadership to get them to accept the British offers of calm. As a consequence of this, the shortcomings of the Arab world were considered to be among the first and most important factors that required the conclusion of the revolution by both the official government and the general populace.

Fifth, there was an insufficient amount of political leadership present in the arena to make the appropriate decisions at the times when they were required. This was due to the fact that the Central Committee was located in Damascus, which was a significant distance from the actual battlefield. In addition, there were no political leaders present who were able to take charge of the situation on the ground. The results that the envoys sent by Central Command had achieved with the field commanders were limited. Because there was a lack of direct political leadership that was also effective, there was an inability to mobilize the popular support that was available, to effectively lead them, and to fully benefit from all of their potential. As a result, the actions taken by the nation were restricted to impulsive, spur-of-the-moment decisions or actions of a limited scope, and the military, which lacked prior experience in political or mobilization matters, assumed significant responsibilities for which it was unprepared.

Sixth, there was a lack of unity among those in charge of the military. In spite of the Central Committee's efforts to unify and coordinate, the field leaders continued to enjoy a large degree of independence in decision making. This did not prevent them from competing to the point where conflict erupted, however. The Central Committee made the following observation in relation to this topic: "Guerrilla leaders usually enjoy a great degree of independence, which is not enjoyed by regular army leaders; however, guerrilla warfare requires a central leadership that sets the general plan, supervises implementation and mobilization, and commands major operations."[285] This was not available for the Palestinian revolution.[286]

Seventh, given the limited armed and training capabilities, we have provided an explanation of the magnitude of the disparity between the revolutionaries and the forces belonging to the British colonial alliance and the Zionists in terms of their training and their ability to acquire weapons. The lack of ammunition was one of the contributing factors that led to the revolution's eventual defeat. The attempts to obtain arms by taking advantage of the inconsistency that existed among the industrialized countries of Europe were unsuccessful. In the year 1937, al-Haj Amin al-Husseini reached out to the German consul in Jerusalem as well as the German ambassador in Baghdad in an effort to solicit support. Both of these requests were for additional devices. Through the German ambassador in Beirut, the Syrian Committee for the Advancement of the Palestinian National Movement made a purchase request to acquire German weapons; however, the German ambassador did not respond to the request. Mussolini, the leader of Fascist Italy, maintained close ties with the founding fathers of the Zionist movement, despite the fact that the Israeli government consistently denied receiving assistance from Italy.

Eighth, the impact of the deteriorating economic conditions and the fatigue caused to the citizens by the British repression during the years of the revolution, as well as the repercussions of the six months of the strike, had a significant effect. On May 26, 1939, 'Ajaj Nuwihid connected with 'Awni 'Abdel Hadi and sent him a telegram in which he reported the weakness of the situation throughout the country. This included the city, the village, the coast, the mountains, the northern and southern areas, and the southernmost region. He made a strong plea to the Arab Higher Committee to consider the country's current circumstances.[287]

Ninth, one of the results of the underdevelopment of the Palestinian Arab community and the scarcity of conscious elites committed to the National Movement was that the existing political organizations were unable to provide an effective response to the existing challenges. Because of this, none of the existing political parties were able to fill the void left by the lack of leadership and make up for the problems with their own platforms and the fact that their supporters couldn't get involved, even though this was possible. Nor were they able to limit the devastating influence of the opposition forces, especially those closely related to the colonial circles that enrolled these factors to sabotage the revolution. In the beginning, these factors rallied their friends against the developing revolutionary movement. These cronies included the elders of the villages and the mayors of the villages. As a result of these factors, activists resorted to the use of force to assert their presence and bolster their influence. On the one hand, this led to mistakes and overreactions, and on the other, it made leaders feel even more in control of their actions, especially on the political side. The forces of the opposition also started a counterrevolution, which involved spreading rumors, stirring up hatred, getting the owners of revolutions to work together, and surprising the revolution from the inside by using the methods of the Peace Factions.

David Hirst notes that there existed little separation between the politician and the fighter and between the city and the countryside. While the revolution, which was the first Palestinian attempt to organize armed violence, represented a growth of resistance to the Zionist invasion, it did not keep pace with the parallel and necessary growth of social, political, and organizational capabilities. As a result, the fighters were unable to overcome religious, regional, or familial ties. As a result, many of them were unwilling to join groups based in other cities. Those who did participate in the activity sometimes saw the other groups as disruptive outsiders. There was no national strategy, and there were numerous military leaders; however, the most problematic aspect of this situation was the weakness caused by inherited tribal differences and revolutions that were mixed with political differences. Because of these differences, one village sided against another, and in some cases, two villages were split apart.[288]

Tenth, the international crisis ended when British prime minister Neville Chamberlain and Adolf Hitler reached an agreement in Munich. This allowed Britain to deal with the volatile situation in Palestine. Additional forces, backed by warplanes, were brought in to weaken the revolution in order to create the atmosphere for a political solution that corresponded with its strategic interests in the region. After regaining control of Jerusalem's Old City, the army began the process of regaining control of the remaining cities, as previously explained. As a result, the revolutionaries' activities were limited to the countryside, where they shifted from attack to defense in the face of the combined forces of the army, the Haganah, and the Peace Factions. As a result, as their victories dwindled, so did the revolutionaries.

Eleventh, the British army imposed road passes, and the Central Command refused to comply. However, car owners transporting citrus needed to move quickly, and the Central Committee was forced to allow the drivers to apply for permits. The British army took advantage of the situation by requiring that the required permits be issued only if the Arabs applied for a similar number of permits for noncitrus car drivers. As a result of this, the Arab leadership's decision to refuse to apply for permits failed. This exacerbated the negative effects of the decline in revolutionary operations, precipitating a deterioration in revolutionary prestige, the Central Committee's prestige, and the national leadership's prestige.

Twelfth, Britain and France formed a coalition with Nazi Germany and Fascist Italy. The French mandate authorities in Syria and Lebanon had become very active in pursuing Central Committee members as well as Palestinian, Syrian, and Lebanese national elements. Many of them were arrested and imprisoned in Palmyra's desert prison, including Central Committee secretary Muhammad 'Izzat Darwazah. As a result, the two brotherly countries severely limited their means of support.[289]

Even if the revolution was ultimately unsuccessful, it had accomplished much. When it increased its promises at the start of 1938, it affected those British involved in the partition project and the immigration issue. British newspapers and political figures began to discuss the difficulty of implementing the partition resolution and the need to consider the Arab position when considering Britain's interests in the Levant. In order to appease Britain, the Colonial Ministry announced in a 1938 White Paper the abandonment of the principle of "economic assimilation" as a basis for determining the number of immigrants permitted to enter Palestine and the adoption of the principle of "political assimilation" as a substitute. Around twenty members of Parliament in the House of Commons proposed a complete halt to immigration until the Palestinian issue was resolved.[290] According to David Hirst, a number of British politicians began to have second thoughts about the policy of reoccupying Palestine and the stringent measures and high costs that it required.

He said that these worries came from "the late realization by some powerful parties that this desperate Palestinian resistance, even though it didn't work out in the end, must have deeper causes than what is known and understood." Malcolm MacDonald, the British colonial minister, said in front of the House of Commons that most of the revolutionaries were motivated by national causes, that if he were an Arab citizen, his feelings would be similar to theirs, and that politics based on power might be successful in establishing security, but it would not be successful in establishing peace.[291]

The Zionist movement and the Jewish forces in Britain had been prepared as a result of the growing sentiment in the political sphere of Britain. While the Jewish Agency attempted to capitalize on the plight of Jews in Germany, central Europe, and eastern Europe, as well as the dissemination of racist Nuremberg anti-Jewish directives, these events occurred simultaneously. A total of thirty-three countries attended the conference in Evian, France, called for by US President Franklin D. Roosevelt to discuss the issue of refugees. The Jewish Agency presented proposals and projects to accommodate one hundred thousand immigrants in Palestine within a short period. However, the British delegate to the conference opposed this. Britain had stipulated that the conference would refrain from discussing Palestine as a refuge for Jewish refugees.[292] The British delegate, Lord Earl Winterton, who chaired the Governmental Refugee Committee, was successful in distancing Palestine from the problem and holding the conference as if it were a global problem that could only be solved with the cooperation of countries and opening borders to refugees. This was due to the fact that Palestine was unable to accommodate new immigration and that the circumstances in which it found itself at the time were not exceptional. It paved the way for research to be carried out on the subject and for adjustments to be made to the policy that the British were enforcing.[293]

What had been accomplished along the axes of the division and emigration project demonstrates that the Arab revolution and the popular response to it had a greater influence on the unofficial British position at the time than they did. Both the interventions of British politicians who supported the Zionist project and the Jewish pressure group, which had a great traditional influence in British political, economic, and media circles, had the effect of causing the situation to deteriorate further. According to Ilyas Shufani, the revolution was the factor that prevented the establishment of a Zionist state at that time. "The revolution was responsible for the Arabs not achieving their goal of independence. However, it was also responsible for preventing the establishment of a Jewish state then."[294]

DID THE MUFTI MAKE A MISTAKE IN
REJECTING THE WHITE PAPER?

The mufti was not the only one who rejected the White Paper immediately upon its release; nor was it the political leadership and rebel leaders alone who shared in the refusal of that day. On the side of the political leadership and revolutionary leaders, there was Arab public consensus on the refusal, as evidenced by the previous report by the British wing commander Ritchie, Alan Patrick.[295] The majority of Palestinian parties and Arab political organizations unanimously rejected the White Paper, as did most prominent Arab ruling regimes.[296] This is in addition to the decisive rejection that the Zionist leaders unanimously agreed upon in Palestine and abroad, especially in the United States.

Nevertheless, allegations abounded later that the mufti lost a golden opportunity when he rejected the White Paper in the spring of 1939. 'Awni 'Abdel Hadi's private papers stated that Nuri al-Sa'id and representatives of the Arab countries at the round table conference, in which the ideas contained in the White Paper crystallized, supported those ideas, but they followed the Palestinian leadership in rejecting them.[297] It is a saying that is uncomfortable because the formation of the Palestinian delegation to the conference took place according to the British requirements and as a result of the pressures and interventions of the regimes of Baghdad, Riyadh, and Cairo. It is also contrary to the fact that the proposals contained in the White Paper had been rejected by the Palestinian delegation to the round table conference, which also included in it Raghib al-Nashashibi, leader of the Defense and Opposition Party. It was also rejected by representatives of Arab governments, before the White Paper was issued and approved by the British House of Commons.[298] In addition, the White Paper was presented to Arab governments through the Egyptian government, which held a conference attended by representatives of the governments of Iraq and Saudi Arabia.[299] This conference was the initiator of the rejection, not the Higher Arab Committee, whose role had been marginalized since it issued the statement ending the strike and stopping the revolution in the fall of 1936.

On the private Palestinian level, Bayan Nuwihid al-Hout attributed a position of acceptance of the White Paper to 'Awni 'Abdel Hadi. Bayan also added,

> It is also evident from the papers of Dr. 'Izzat Tannus that most members of the Higher Arab Committee have approved the White Paper after they carefully researched it in a special meeting in Qarnayel the Mufti's headquarters in Lebanon but the Mufti rejected it because of the ambiguity in a number of its clauses. Therefore, the committee sent Dr. 'Izzat Tannus to London to discuss

the ambiguous points with the Minister of Colonies, and the Minister replied to him in the interview by saying: Return to the Higher Arab Committee and advise it on the necessity of accepting the White Book immediately because the acceptance of the British House of Commons to the new policy in Palestine was only made with extreme difficulty the Arabs should not neglect this golden opportunity, and Dr. 'Izzat Tannus returned to Qarnayel with this message, but the Mufti insisted on rejecting it.[300]

Bayan Nuwihid al-Hout resorted the leadership to putting the mufti's opinion back on top as the standard for how the leaders should act. The majority of those who rejected it did so as a result of the deteriorating living conditions in Palestine. Although the mufti was physically located in Lebanon at the time, he was aware of all of these conditions. Rather, he built his rule on a number of interconnected factors. The most important of these was the small percentage of Palestinian national demands and rights that were approved by the White Paper, the lack of trust in the British government to carry out even this, the fact that the establishment of the independent state depended on the decision of the Zionist leaders, and the fact that setting up a democratic state in Palestine was at odds with the racist views of the Zionists.[301] As a result, the mufti provided evidence that he had a greater familiarity with the facts of the conflict than the other members of the Higher Arab Committee and the other leaders of the National Movement. He exemplified the highest levels of honesty, and he was most committed to the principles that guide the nation.

Also, the claim that Arab government representatives and some members of the Higher Arab Committee respected or feared the mufti over their own beliefs is an argument that denies the mufti's exclusion from the Palestinian delegation's leadership of the round table conference and the participation of opposition leader Raghib al-Nashashibi in the delegation as a response to Britain.[302] It is impossible for those who accepted this and imposed it on the mufti to have rejected the White Paper out of fear or respect for him because they accepted it. Let's say, for the sake of argument, that this were true, that these representatives and members were not at the level of responsibility entrusted to them, and that they were historically responsible for the loss of the golden opportunity, assuming there was a golden opportunity available to be lost.

Moreover, the revolution had ended in the fall of 1939, and nearly all of the leaders and men of the National Movement described as militant had left the stage and made room for those who were considered "moderate." Despite this, the British government did not implement any of the terms of its White Paper, contrary to what it had announced before its publication that it would go ahead with implementing what it contained regardless of the position of the Arabs and Jews.[303] Nuri al-Sa'id had envisioned that Britain would directly implement some of the provisions of the White Paper, which would satisfy Haj Amin al-Husseini, a refugee in Baghdad at the time, and would prevent him and some Iraqi politicians from communicating with the Axis powers.[304] Lord Halifax, Edward Frederick Lindley Wood, informed him that his government's intention to establish national government institutions in Palestine to qualify its citizens for independence was postponed until the end of the war and that it refused to stop immigration until the implementation of the terms of the White Paper.[305]

Moreover, in July 1940, Colonel Newcombe—a member of the House of Commons with extensive Arab contacts—was dispatched to Baghdad to reach an understanding with Haj Amin al-Husseini and his companions. After Newcombe contacted Nuri al-Sa'id and conveyed the message of the British government to him, the prime minister of Iraq contacted Jamal al-Husseini and Musa al-'Alami and presented them with the proposal that Newcombe carried, based on what was included in the White Paper.[306]

With the participation of Nuri al-Sa'id and Naji al-Suwaidi, Newcombe held extensive talks for two weeks with Jamal al-Husseini and Musa al-'Alami about the proposal that he brought. It was agreed to implement the White Paper immediately, by gradually replacing the heads of government departments in Palestine with Arab directors, and for the high commissioner to remain president of the state for the duration of the war and for six months after its end.[307] Although the mufti did not meet Newcombe, the participation of Jamal al-Husseini, head of the Arab Party, and Musa al-'Alami, his political adviser, meant his acceptance and acceptance by the Palestinian leadership of what was agreed upon.

In the event that the agreement was carried out as planned, the government of Iraq committed to putting one-half of its military at the disposal of the British Middle East Command for operations outside Iraq.[308] Also, the Iraqi government said that as soon as the agreement was signed, it would declare war on the Axis powers.[309] Newcombe left Baghdad and went to Cairo to sign the agreement that the top British officials had made, but he didn't tell the Arab side what he was doing. Then Nuri al-Sa'id traveled to Cairo to follow up on the matter, where he met with Lt. Gen. Archibald Wavell, the commander of the British army, and explained the matter to him, but he did not receive anything from him. Winston Churchill and the British high commissioner in Palestine prevented the implementation of what was agreed with Newcombe and Wavell.[310] As 'Ali Muhafazah stated, "This was one of the reasons that prompted Haj Amin al-Husseini and some Iraqi leaders to contact the two Axis countries."[311]

Churchill opposed the White Paper when it was issued and strongly criticized it.[312] Even though he did not object to the lawful distribution of land or immigration, when he took over the ministry on May 12, 1940, he refused to allow any step that might contribute to building governmental institutions that could be a basis for the independence of Palestine.[313] This was despite the fact that he did not object to the legal issuance of land. In an attempt to show Britain's commitment to the Arabs to pacify them, and in confirming his conviction,[314] he wrote thirteen days after assuming the ministry, to Lord Lloyd, the colonial minister who succeeded MacDonald, saying, "Right now, our only goal in Palestine is to get eleven battalions of our best soldiers out of the area as soon as possible. Because it is impossible to leave the Jews defenseless, they have to be organized and armed as quickly as possible. Furthermore, they cannot be left without a weapon."[315]

On criticizing the refusal of the White Paper, Bahjat Abu Gharibieh said,

> In my opinion, as well as the stance of the revolution's leaders, led by Haj Amin al-Husseini, we rejected the White Paper in 1939. Over the past half-century, I have repeatedly reaffirmed this position. It was not a matter of accepting the policy of the White Paper while working to develop it. We scrutinized certain sections of the White Paper that appeared to recognize our rights outwardly while denying them in practice. This deceptive approach was something we had experienced and learned from our dealings with Britain, and it led us to distrust their announcements and promises. It should be noted that the Arabs of Palestine did not take any action that hindered the implementation of the White Paper. Yet, Britain, which had declared its determination to implement this policy regardless of whether Arabs and Jews accepted or rejected it, backtracked on its implementation as if it had never existed. This was exactly what we had anticipated.[316]

The international situation on the eve of World War II made it clear that the White Paper of 1939 was necessary.[317] The goal was to fulfill the aspiration of the British Imperial Staff to provide calm in Palestine and the Arab East, and the reason for this was to avoid responding to the demands that were being made by the Arabs.[318] Even though the British position was very important, Churchill stopped any of its parts from being put into action the day after he became prime minister.[319] On the other hand, he gave off the impression that he was interested in securing the Zionist project, which confirmed that his sponsorship was at the center of the British colonial strategy and that he was committed to it.[320]

In conclusion, the 1939 White Paper had a profound and devastating impact on the Palestinian people. By limiting Jewish immigration to Palestine and imposing restrictions on land purchases by Jews, the British government effectively shut down the Zionist project of creating a Jewish homeland in Palestine. But this decision did not come for free. It left the Palestinians to deal with the effects of continued British colonial rule and a growing Jewish population.

The 1939 White Paper marked a turning point in the history of Palestine and set the stage for decades of conflict between Israelis and Palestinians. The restrictions on Jewish immigration and land purchases were seen as a betrayal by the Zionist movement, which had worked tirelessly to create a Jewish homeland in Palestine. At the same time, the Palestinian people were left to deal with the reality of British colonial rule and the displacement caused by the influx of Jewish immigrants.

The impact of the 1939 White Paper on the Palestinians cannot be overstated. It contributed to the displacement of hundreds of thousands of Palestinians and set the stage for the conflict that continues to this day. It also serves as a reminder of the importance of respecting the rights and aspirations of all people, regardless of their ethnicity or religion. As we look to the future, it is essential that we work toward a just and lasting solution that recognizes the rights of both Israelis and Palestinians to live in peace and security.[321]

Despite the fact that there are still those who believe that the Palestinian national leadership during the time of the mandate squandered a number of promising opportunities, including the White Paper, due to their pessimistic outlook, there are others who do not share this view. This point of view completely ignores the fact that the White Paper was just one of a number of compromise plans that were made to get around the Arab National Movement and make its leaders fight among themselves. The White Paper was one of the proposals that was rolled out. This disregards the fact that the United Kingdom failed to mention in its White Paper that it had already accomplished its objective, as was the case with every one of the previous suggestions for a settlement. Sadly, some of the most prominent leaders of Palestinian organizations in the period after 1962 have recently denied certain allegations made in the past. These statements contradict some of their earlier claims. During the fruitless negotiations that took place prior to the signing of the Oslo Accords on September 13, 1993, and afterward, a good number of them discovered their justification for cost-free concessions. These negotiations took place after the signing of the Oslo Accords.

NOTES

1. 'Alush 1967, p. 127.
2. Rogan and Shlaim 2001, pp. 168–169.
3. Schechtman 1956–1961, p. 1:437.
4. Hirst 2003, pp. 165–168; Flapan 1987, pp. 87–89.
5. Touma 1978, p. 151.
6. Quigley 1990, pp. 30–31.
7. Touma 1978, p. 151.

8. Shufani 2003, pp. 431–433; Hout 1981, pp. 347–348.

9. Darwazah 1984a, p. 184.

10. Darwazah 1984a, pp. 193–195.

11. Hout 1981, pp. 301–307; 'Alush 1967, pp. 102–204; Abrash 1987, p. 61; Morris 1999, p. 124.

12. Zu'itir 1979, p. 287.

13. Zu'itir 1979, p. 148.

14. Zu'itir 1979, p. 161.

15. Hout 1981, pp. 301–307; 'Alush 1967, pp. 361–362; Zu'itir 1979, pp. 262–276; Kayali 1985, pp. 297–280.

16. Flapan 1987, p. 144; Quigley 1990, pp. 23–27.

17. The attendees were 160 Syrians, 128 Palestinians, 65 Lebanese, 39 Jordanians, 12 Iraqis, 6 Egyptians, and 1 Saudi; see Kayali 1985, 286.

18. Touma 1978.

19. Zu'itir 1979, pp. 462–467.

20. Zu'itir 1979, p. 467.

21. Mufarej 1937, p. 370; Hout 1981, p. 365.

22. Kayali 1985, p. 286; Muhafazah 1989, p. 83.

23. Touma 1978, p. 145.

24. Touma 1978, p. 145.

25. Hout 1981, p. 369.

26. Zu'itir 1979, pp. 462–467.

27. Kayali 1985, p. 286; Muhafazah 1989, p. 287.

28. Khalifa and Jabbour 1989, p. 149.

29. Zua'iter 1958, pp. 112–113; Jabbour 1970, p. 124.

30. Zu'itir 1979, pp. 463–467; 'Umar 1999, p. 41.

31. Khalifah 1973, p. 187.

32. Zu'itir 1979, pp. 470–492; Muhafazah 1985, p. 447.

33. Jeffries 2000, p. 4:209; Hadi 2002, p. 50; 'Umari 1969, p. 198.

34. 'Umar 1999, p. 36.

35. Zu'itir 1979, p. 332.

36. 'Umar 1999, p. 36.

37. Gharibieh 1993, p. 99.

38. Zu'itir 1979, p. 336.

39. Jeffries 2000, pp. 4:211–212.

40. From a message sent by 'Adil Arsalan in London to 'Awni 'Abdel Hadi in Paris. See Hadi 2002, p. 50; 'Umari 1969, p. 198.

41. Quigley 1990, pp. 24–25; Segev 2000, pp. 401–408; Sakhnini 1985, pp. 64–65.

42. Stein 1984, p. 91; Gilmour 1980, pp. 40–41; Flapan 1979, p. 69.

43. Jeffries 2000, pp. 4:191–192.

44. Jeffries 2000, pp. 4:191–192.

45. Weizmann 1949, p. 535.

46. Khalidi 1998, pp. 234–235.

47. Segev 2000, p. 110.

48. Jeffries 2000, pp. 4:193–198; Quigley 1990, p. 24.

49. Segev 2000, p. 113.
50. Quigley 1990, p. 27.
51. Jeffries 2000, pp. 4:203–207.
52. Hout 1981, p. 372; Darwazah 1984a, p. 172; Touma 1978, p. 155.
53. Zu'itir 1979, p. 328; Hout 1981, p. 371; Darwazah 1984a, pp. 181–182.
54. Hout 1981, pp. 375–377.
55. Kessler 2023, pp. 117–118.
56. Hout 1981, pp. 375–377.
57. 'Umar 1999, pp. 38–39; Kayali 1985, p. 286; Muhafazah 1989, p. 378.
58. Darwazah 1984a, p. 741.
59. Darwazah 1984a, p. 209.
60. Khalifa and Jabbour 1989, p. 156.
61. 'Alush 1967, p. 142.
62. Touma 1978, p. 151.
63. Touma 1978, p. 151.
64. Touma 1978, p. 151.
65. Kayali 1985, p. 286.
66. Darwazah 1984a, p. 215.
67. Hout 1981, pp. 480–505.
68. Kayali 1985, p. 290.
69. Kayali 1985, pp. 291–293.
70. Darwazah 1984a, pp. 211–212.
71. Darwazah 1984a, p. 217.
72. Khalifa and Jabbour 1989, p. 164.
73. Kayali 1985, p. 293; Gharibieh 1993, p. 119.
74. Darwazah 1984a, pp. 197–198.
75. Darwazah 1984a, 195.
76. Khalifa and Jabbour 1989, p. 161.
77. Khalifa and Jabbour 1989, p. 161.
78. Hirst 2003, p. 246.
79. Hirst 2003, p. 162.
80. Hirst 2003, p. 157.
81. Hirst 2003, p. 158.
82. Hirst 2003, p. 158.
83. Hirst 2003, p. 163.
84. Zu'itir 1979, pp. 438–458.
85. Khalifa and Jabbour 1989, p. 152.
86. Kayali 1985, p. 293.
87. 'Umar 1999, p. 40.
88. Khalifa and Jabbour 1989, p. 167.
89. Khalifa and Jabbour 1989, p. 162.
90. Hirst 2003, p. 248.
91. Gharibieh 1993, p. 125; Hamudi 2008, p. 318.
92. Gharibieh 1993, p. 125.
93. Gharibieh 1993, p. 125.

94. Khalifa and Jabbour 1989, p. 167; Segev 2000, pp. 430–432.

95. Darwazah 1984a, p. 282.

96. Khalifa and Jabbour 1989, p. 161.

97. Darwazah 1984a, p. 203.

98. Gharibieh 1993, pp. 126–127.

99. Khalifa and Jabbour 1989, p. 159.

100. Hout 1981, p. 382.

101. Cohen 2015, pp. 157–158.

102. Hout 1981, pp. 117–118.

103. Zu'itir 1979, pp. 434–438.

104. Shufani 2003, p. 40.

105. Shufani 2003, p. 40.

106. Hout 1981, p. 380.

107. Zu'itir 1979, pp. 438–440, p. 425; Darwazah 1984a, pp. 197–200; Touma 1978, pp. 150–152; Khalifa and Jabbour 1989, pp. 159–173.

108. Darwazah 1984a, p. 202; Kayali 1985, p. 288.

109. Kayali 1985, p. 288; Darwazah 1984a, p. 202; Kayali 1985, p. 288.

110. Khalifa and Jabbour 1989, p. 163.

111. Khalifa and Jabbour 1989, p. 165.

112. Barakat 2018, pp. 84–97; Nafa' 2009, pp. 109–110; 'Umar 1999, pp. 42–43; Darwazah 1984a, p. 202; Kayali 1985, pp. 210–211.

113. 'Umar 1999, pp. 42–43.

114. Darwazah 1984a, p. 202; Kayali 1985, pp. 210–211.

115. 'Umar 1999, p. 42.

116. Darwazah 1984a, p. 202; Kayali 1985, p. 210.

117. Kayali 1985, p. 238.

118. Khalifa and Jabbour 1989, p. 170.

119. Parsons 2016, pp. 119–125.

120. Khalifa and Jabbour 1989, pp. 170–171.

121. Yassin 1967, pp. 157–158.

122. Hout 1981, p. 408.

123. Khalidi 1971, pp. 848–49; Sayegh 2002, p. 39.

124. Khalifa and Jabbour 1989, p. 198.

125. Hirst 2003, pp. 80–83; Flapan 1979, p. 116; Segev 2000, p. 441.

126. *New York Times*, May 30, 1939, p. A11; June 1, 1939, p. A17; June 3, 1939, p. A3; June 20, 1939, p. A4; July 4, 1939, p. A4.

127. Mardor 1964, pp. 3–16; Flapan 1979, pp. 62–63.

128. Segev 2000, p. 441.

129. Khalifa and Jabbour 1989, pp. 212–214; Flapan 1979, pp. 62–63.

130. Gharibieh 1993, p. 127.

131. Marlowe 1946, p. 244.

132. Bauer 1995, p. 26.

133. Schechtman 1961, p. 483.

134. Schechtman 1961, p. 485.

135. Hirst 2003, p. 258.

136. Hyamson 1942, pp. 129–130.

137. Darwazah 1984a, p. 236.

138. Khalifa and Jabbour 1989, p. 164.

139. Quigley 1990, pp. 16–22.

140. Parsons 2016, pp. 111–112, 146–148.

141. Hout 1981, pp. 401–402.

142. A fatwa is a legal ruling or opinion issued by a qualified Islamic scholar (a mufti) on a specific question related to Islamic law (sharia). The mufti derives the fatwa from Islamic sources such as the Quran, the Hadith (sayings and actions of Prophet Muhammad), and the consensus of Islamic scholars.

143. Shaqra 1999, p. 156; 'Ashur 2022, pp. 35–36; Hout 1981, p. 740.

144. Hout 1981, pp. 402–403.

145. Hout 1981, p. 402; 'Alush 1967, pp. 102–104; Abrash 1987, p. 61.

146. Darwazah 1984a, p. 218.

147. Darwazah 1984a, pp. 218–219.

148. Sanagan 2020, pp. 93–94.

149. Hout 1981, pp. 405–406; Zu'itir 1979, pp. 438–440, p. 148.

150. Hout 1981, p. 407; Shufani 2003, p. 454.

151. Hout 1981, pp. 407–408.

152. Khalifa and Jabbour 1989, p. 180.

153. Hout 1981, p. 383.

154. Darwazah 1984a, p. 228.

155. Touma 1978, p. 156.

156. Khalaf 1991, pp. 77–79.

157. Darwazah 1984a, p. 225; Hout 1981, pp. 386–387.

158. Khalaf 1991, p. 78.

159. Hout 1981, p. 387.

160. Khalifa and Jabbour 1989, p. 180.

161. Khalaf 1991, p. 78.

162. Hout 1981, p. 387.

163. Nashashibi 1990, pp. 87–88.

164. Nashashibi 1990, pp. 378–388.

165. Nashashibi 1990, p. 389; Khalaf 1991, p. 79.

166. Hout 1981, pp. 195–198.

167. Hout 1981, p. 390.

168. Hout 1981, p. 390; Quigley 1990, p. 27.

169. Touma 1978, p. 257.

170. Teveth 1987, p. 245.

171. Segev 2000, pp. 409–410.

172. Khalifa and Jabbour 1989, p. 185; Quigley 1990, p. 25.

173. Khalifa and Jabbour 1989, p. 186.

174. 'Alush 1967, p. 145.

175. 'Alush 1967, p. 145.

176. Quigley 1990, pp. 26–27.

177. Khalifa and Jabbour 1989, p. 186.

178. Quigley 1990, p. 27.
179. Quigley 1990, pp. 10–11.
180. Parisien 2010, p. 240; Faruqi 2003, p. 23.
181. Quigley 1990, pp. 186–187.
182. Teveth 1987, p. 255.
183. Teveth 1987, p. 256.
184. 'Alush 1967, pp. 145–146.
185. Messiri 1999, pp. 6:13, 46–47.
186. Ghani 1995, pp. 15–17.
187. Khalifa and Jabbour 1989, pp. 175–176.
188. Hirst 2003, p. 105.
189. Bathel 1979, p. 60; Hussein 1984, p. 25.
190. Cohen 1978, p. 14; Hussein 1984, p. 27.
191. Weinstock 1979, p. 204; Teveth 1987, p. 125; Stein 1984, pp. 173–211.
192. Teveth 1987, pp. 175–176; Mardor 1964, p. 24.
193. Segev 2000, p. 402, p. 430.
194. Touma 1978, pp. 113–118.
195. Segev 2000, pp. 436–437.
196. Khalifa and Jabbour 1989, pp. 173–174.
197. Musa al-'Alami and George Antonius attempted it in July 1939, while Nuri al-Sa'id attempted it in February 1940.
198. Ghani 1995, pp. 231, 466; Muhafazah 1980, pp. 209–211; Yisraeli 1975, p. 143.
199. Touma 1978, p. 161.
200. Nicosia 2015, p. 136; Watson 2014, p. 126.
201. Hout 1981, p. 395.
202. Teveth 1987, pp. 257–258.
203. Khalifa and Jabbour 1989, pp. 186–187.
204. Galnoor 2012, p. 54.
205. Galnoor 2012, p. 255.
206. Zu'itir 1979, p. 594; Darwazah 1984a, pp. 244–245; Kayali 1985, pp. 302–303.
207. Kayali 1985, pp. 353–365.
208. Sabbagh 2006, p. 220.
209. Laqueur and Schueftan 2016, pp. 48–50.
210. Taylor & Francis Group 2003, p. 54.
211. Laqueur and Schueftan 2016, p. 49; Bunton 2009, p. x.
212. Hout 1981, pp. 395–396.
213. Kayali 1985, p. 302.
214. Jeffery 2014, p. 108; Miller 2010, p. 181.
215. Tamraz 2018, p. 321.
216. Salih 2012, p. 61.
217. Khalidi 2007, p. 117.
218. Etheredge 2011, pp. 51–52; Newsinger 2016, p. 6.
219. Kayali 1985, pp. 302–303.

220. Khalidi 2007, p. 90.

221. Ben-Gurion 1963, pp. 378–386; Hunidi 2003, pp. 246–261; Wasserstein 2001, pp. 83–91; Zweig 1987, pp. 46–52.

222. Mattar 1988, pp. 50–80.

223. Cohen 2008, p. 126;

224. Muhafazah 1989, p. 76.

225. Touma 1978, pp. 163–164.

226. Darwazah 1984a, pp. 244–245; Kayali 1985, p. 246.

227. Darwazah 1984a, p. 245.

228. Segev 2000, p. 456; Khalidi 1997, esp. chap. 6, where Khalidi discusses the reactions of various Palestinian political groups to the White Paper of 1939. He notes that the Committee for the Defense of Palestine in Syria and Lebanon opposed the White Paper because they believed it was "fundamentally biased against the Palestinians" and would "deprive them of their rights." Khalidi quotes a statement issued by the committee that called on Palestinians to reject the White Paper and continue their struggle for independence; Sayigh 1997, p. 18.

229. Hout 1981, p. 396.

230. Teveth 1987, p. 258.

231. Teveth 1987, p. 258.

232. Hertzberg 1969, p. 566; Hazony 2001, p. 123.

233. Hirst 2003, p. 254.

234. Quigley 1990, p. 27.

235. Teveth 1987, p. 258.

236. Hout 1981, p. 399.

237. Farsun 2003, p. 208.

238. Khalifa and Jabbour 1989, p. 188.

239. Roosevelt 1948, pp. 2:1–16; Ovendale 1984, p. 47.

240. Rashidat 1991, p. 120.

241. Teveth 1987, pp. 236–237.

242. Teveth 1987, p. 242.

243. Teveth 1987, pp. 246–247.

244. Abitbol 2000, pp. 1–13; Ben-Sasson 1977, pp. 862–878; Stillman 1979; Zaken 2011.

245. Fierro 2009, pp. 297–315; Gerber 1998, pp. 24–50; Goitein 1967.

246. Roberts-Zauderer 2019, pp. 2–3.

247. Bell 1977, p. 317.

248. Avineri 2016; Black 1991; Laqueur 1972; Pappe 2006.

249. Katz 2016, p. 36.

250. Cohen 2013, pp. 95–97; Karsh 2010, pp. 47–52; Rogan and Shlaim 2001, pp. 22–26.

251. Morris 2012, p. 91.

252. Morris 2008, p. 134.

253. Khalifa and Jabbour 1989, pp. 78–80.

254. Laqueur 1972, pp. 469–470.

255. Khalifa and Jabbour 1989, pp. 78–80.

256. Such as Yaakov "Yashka" Eliav, who joined the Irgun at a young age and in 1938 was in charge of the Irgun's operations in Jerusalem. Eliav took part in the Irgun Commander Course in Poland, organized and directed by the Polish Army. He returned to Eretz Israel after the publication of the British White Paper and took part in the operations against British targets in Jerusalem. During the split in the Irgun (in 1940), he sided with Avraham Stern (Yair) and was one of the founders of Lehi. See Do'ar 2004, pp. 16–19, 38–39.

257. Khalifa and Jabbour 1989, pp. 109–11; Eliav 2016, pp. 1:25–30.

258. Khalifa and Jabbour 1989, p. 131.

259. Khalifa and Jabbour 1989, pp. 143–145.

260. Khalifa and Jabbour 1989, pp. 143–145.

261. Rose 2007, p. 98.

262. Khalifa and Jabbour 1989, pp. 400–405; Segev 2000, p. 395; Brenner 2015, p. 116.

263. Khalifa and Jabbour 1989, pp. 406–407; Ra'uf 1990, pp. 494–497; Shufani 2003, p. 360; Segev 2000, p. 386.

264. Khalifa and Jabbour 1989, pp. 407–408.

265. Khalifa and Jabbour 1989, pp. 408–418.

266. Khalifa and Jabbour 1989, p. 532.

267. Ben-Ami 2012, pp. 57–58; Black 1991, pp. 29–31; Halevi 1995, pp. 60–62; Katz 1988, pp. 37–39.

268. Hirst 2003, p. 262.

269. Khalifa and Jabbour 1989, p. 526.

270. Khalifa and Jabbour 1989, p. 528.

271. Khalidi 2020, pp. 38–40.

272. Ra'uf 1990, p. 209.

273. Khalifa and Jabbour 1989, pp. 528–529.

274. A unit of measurement of land area equal to one thousand square meters or about a quarter acre.

275. Ra'uf 1990, p. 285.

276. Khalidi 1977, pp. 44–60; Morris 2008, esp. chap. 2, titled "The Jewish Yishuv and the Arab Rebellion, 1936–1939."

277. Ibid, pp. 311–312.

278. Lehn and Davis 1988, p. 192.

279. Khalifa and Jabbour 1989, pp. 520–521.

280. Realizing how the Zionist project fits into the global colonial strategy and getting involved with the fight against it. Compare what you have done and what you continue to do with other Zionist collection institutions and activities at various facilities in Europe and the United States for more than a century with the process of drying the springheads, which includes all Arab and Islamic charities that support social services in occupied Palestine.

281. Khalifa and Jabbour 1989, pp. 528–531.

282. Khalifa and Jabbour 1989, pp. 581–521; Bell 1977, p. 62.

283. Khalidi 1971, pp. 846–849; Hirst 2003, p. 251.

284. Kayali 1985, p. 315.

285. 'Alush 1967, p. 143.

286. Rogan 2009, pp. 219–228; Khalidi 2006, pp. 65–77; Kimmerling and Migdal 1993, pp. 94–113.

287. Hadi 2002, pp. 249–250; Nuwihid 1981.

288. Hirst 2003, p. 251.

289. Darwazah 1984a, pp. 244–245.

290. Darwazah 1984a, p. 244.

291. Hirst 2003, p. 253.

292. Khalifa and Jabbour 1989, pp. 177–178.

293. Darwazah 1984a, p. 255; Cell 2002, p. 240.

294. Shufani 2003, p. 484.

295. Hughes 2019, p. 203.

296. Khalidi 2001, pp. 21–44; Shlaim 2000, p. 126.

297. Hout 1981, p. 146.

298. Darwazah 1984a, p. 252.

299. See Muslih 1981, pp. 3–22; Khalidi 2006, pp. 40–61.

300. Hout 1981, p. 397.

301. Hout 1981, p. 399.

302. Elpeleg and Himelstein 2012, pp. 26–27.

303. Elpeleg and Himelstein 2012, p. 54.

304. Elpeleg and Himelstein 2012, p. 60.

305. Ghani 1995, pp. 237–238.

306. Ghani 1995, pp. 238–239.

307. Muhafazah 1989, p. 83.

308. Izzeddin 1981, p. 218.

309. Nicosia 2015, p. 163.

310. Segev 2000, pp. 158–159.

311. Izzeddin 1981, p. 218.

312. Khadduri 1960, p. 171; Cohen 2014, p. 312; Kolinsky 2016, p. 10.

313. Ghani 1995, p. 239.

314. Kolinsky 2016, p. 10.

315. Pearlman 1965, p. 103.

316. Gharibieh 1993, p. 133.

317. Kolinsky 2016, pp. 134–136.

318. Kolinsky 2016, p. 132.

319. Kolinsky 2016, p. 240.

320. Khalidi 2007, p. 35.

321. Khalidi 2006, pp. 263–280; Pappe 2006, pp. 31–45; Segev 2000, pp. 386–401.

Conclusion

As stated in the introduction to the book and detailed in the successive chapters, the interwar period had profound effects on shaping the rest of the twentieth century in general and the subsequent course of the Arab-Zionist conflict in particular. First, this was because, despite the idealist theoretical and practical atmosphere of the interwar period, power-interest-centered tendencies came to the fore regarding the Arab-Zionism conflict. It is possible to see an illustration of this in the approach that Britain took toward the conflict, in the alliances that it created, and even in the ambiguous nature of the relationships that existed between these parties.

Second, before the establishment of the state of Israel, the conflict was dealt with by states like Britain and France, which were in decline after World War I and contributed to the insolvency of the conflict. Because, in this new era, the global power structure had started to progressively shift to the United States and the Soviet Union, countries like Britain and France did not have the same power that they once had to influence how the conflict was resolved. The fact that United States stayed away from international relations and the Soviet Union failed exclusion caused states such as Britain and France to no longer have their old power to have a say in the resolution of the conflict.

Third, during the interwar period, opposing ideological currents regarding the Arab-Zionist conflict started to develop gradually, and these movements are still in effect today: socialism against capitalism and Islamism against secularism. In this respect, the current of socialism against capitalism is largely related to the worldwide impact of the October Revolution of 1917. Secularism versus Islamism, on the other hand, stems from the theological aspect of the Arab-Zionist conflict itself. However, the most important polarization in the intellectual sense was experienced between Zionism and Arab nationalism. At this point, it is worth noting that Arab nationalism has matured as a reaction to Zionism, but at the point of its emergence it flourished by targeting the hegemony of the Ottoman Empire and subsequently the British-French mandate governments. Fourth, and concerning the second point, the Arab-Zionist conflict began to take shape around the US-USSR struggle in the period between the two wars and the end of the Cold War. This is because, as previously stated, although the period after World War II is accepted as the beginning of the Cold War, it is possible to argue that a global struggle between the United States and the Soviet Union, which also affected other states and international conflicts, started as of the October Revolution of 1917.

Fifth, the point made above can be seen in the main goals of Western imperialism in the years before World War II. To phrase it another way, the objectives of Western imperialism in Palestine had an effect on the nature of the conflict between Arabs and Zionists. These goals were to carry out the Balfour Declaration of November 2, 1917, which promised all Jews in the world a "national homeland" in Palestine; to make sure that the Middle East would stay under European control after the fall of the Ottoman Empire; and to stop the Soviet Union from spreading its communist ideas in the Middle East and the Arab world. Even though people at the time were very idealistic, how they felt about the Arab-Zionist conflict was based on their realist goals and their desire to keep a balance of power. As a consequence of this, it is essential to take into account the history of the interwar period because of the way in which it shaped the nature of the Arab-Zionist conflict. The purpose of this research has been to pursue that. As a result, I believe that it is essential to place a strong emphasis on the findings that have surfaced as a result of this study. The origin of the Arab-Israeli conflict, which is widely regarded as one of the most significant conflicts in the field of international relations, has always been a contentious topic. Palestine as a whole and Jerusalem in particular served as the epicenters of not just one but three religions that are acknowledged as having originated from a divine source. This is significant because many different schools of thought contend that the fundamental reason for this conflict was differences in religious beliefs. Judaism, Christianity, and Islam are the religions that fall into this category. The Palestinian-Israeli conflict will never be easily resolved because of the fundamental nature of the rift, which is made worse by the fact that religious and ideological differences contribute to the rift. When the current nature of the conflict is taken into consideration, as well as when we believe that the conflict will not end until the status of Jerusalem is resolved peacefully, this claim makes sense. Another school of thought maintains that the instrumental relationship that existed between Western colonialism and Zionism was the primary driving force behind the Arab-Zionist conflict. Particularly, the founders of Zionism, who ironically and tragically received support from Western states that had historically persecuted Jews, and the transnational nature of both Zionism and Western colonialism, reveal shared interests and an ongoing conflict in the Arab homeland. Specifically, the main arguments of those who make these claims center on the tendency of Western colonialism to be continually involved in the Arab world as a permanent problem, with the primary purpose here being to absorb the human, energy, and geopolitical potential of the region. When one takes into account the support that imperialist states have provided to Zionism, one can see a reflection of this argument in both reality and the argument itself.

According to others, the main root of the Arab-Zionist conflict is the fundamentalists on both sides. The holders of this claim discard a very important point because even though Zionism has embraced some fundamentalist ideas, such as establishing a state in the lands they claim to have been promised in the Old Testament, Arab nationalism emerged with similar motives to those of other nations seeking independence in the interwar period. Zionism, though, assumed an anti-Zionist face within the framework of its attacks. In other words, Arab nationalism turned first to the Ottoman Empire, then to the mandatory states of Britain and France, and then to Zionism, which again meant the independence of the Arabs. As such, it is an ahistorical approach to consider Arab nationalism as equivalent to Zionism and to turn it into a fundamentalist movement. However, the intellectual and practical roots of Arab nationalism started while the hegemony of the Ottoman Empire prevailed in Arab lands. Therefore, it is not possible to draw a similarity between Zionism and Arab nationalism in terms of either fundamentalism or their emergence processes. Undoubtedly, such approaches aim to give the Arabs some responsibility for the current situation of the conflict, taking the responsibility off the Zionists.

This study agrees that all of these claims, except for the last one, have some truth to them. However, the events that transpired during the time between the wars are seen as the most important cause of the ongoing conflict. In other words, theological approaches and Western colonialism in the Arab-Zionist conflict are indeed well known and rooted in certain conditions. This is the situation in the conflict. My first book on the topic, which focuses on the early history of the conflict, emphasizes this point. The purpose of this investigation is to highlight how the events that occurred during the interwar period had a significant impact on the nature of the Arab-Israeli conflict to the present day. These developments included the rise of anti-Semitism in Europe as well as the rise of Zionism; the emergence of Arab nationalism as well as the call for independence by Arabs; the destruction of the Ottoman Empire during World War I; the emergence of a truly modern geography of the Middle East; and the occurrences that took place during the British mandate in Palestine. Although Great Britain served as a moderating influence between the two societies during the aforementioned mandate rule, in the end neither community was convinced that the mandate was one of the factors that contributed to the formation of the Arab-Zionist conflict in its earliest stages.

Even though idealist theory and practice show how things were during the interwar period, it was the events before the end of World War I in the context of the conflict between Arabs and Zionists that showed how the situation would actually play out based on the balance of power interests and alliances. This is because idealist theory and practice show how things were during the time between the two world wars. Both the war itself and its aftermath had a significant impact on the regional power structure. The Ottoman Empire began to punish Arab nationalists and Zionists harshly and to subsidize the burden of the war on the Arab geography just as the war was beginning. The Ottoman Empire believed that these actions could trigger separatist movements throughout the region. As a result of this, both organizations discovered the opportunity to strengthen their existing positions within the context of Britain's policy regarding alliances. Because of the involvement of the Ottoman Empire in the conflict, Britain found itself in this predicament in the Middle East region. Simply put, the participation of the Ottoman Empire in the war provided the opportunity for Arab nationalists and Zionists to declare their independence from the Ottoman Empire, albeit in very different ways. As a result, Great Britain had two primary allies to fight alongside it against the Ottoman Empire in the Middle East. Before the end of World War I, the issue of an alliance with Britain, which would have been detrimental to Arabs, began to emerge as a problem. This was the case even though it was not possible to say the same thing about Zionism. Because, as was stated previously, the most deplorable option was for the Ottoman Empire to maintain its hegemony over the Arab lands while they continued to be exploited and persecuted. When we consider history in terms of the conditions of the period rather than those of today, of course, it is understandable why this occurred.

But Britain wasn't just interested in making alliances with these two groups. Instead, its relationship with Arab nationalism and Zionism shed light on two of their most important ideas. To begin, I would like to touch on other alliances that Britain established with Russia and France with the Sykes-Picot Agreement of 1916. These alliances were signed in 1916. This document proposes that after the conclusion of the war, the countries of the Middle East would be governed by mandated regimes supervised by England and France, respectively. Two documents describe Britain's alliance with Arab nationalism and Zionism; both of these documents are comparable to one another in terms of the ambiguity they contain and the outcomes they produced. The first one is the Hussein-McMahon Correspondence, which took place between Britain's high commissioner in Cairo, Sir Henry McMahon, and Sharif Hussein, the leader of the Hashemites as well as the defender of holy places such as Mecca and Medina. The second document is a letter written by British foreign secretary Arthur James Balfour to the Zionist Lord Rothschild. This letter is now commonly referred to as the Balfour Declaration.

As was already said, these two documents were similar in how they were made and what happened as a result. These similarities can be explained by the position that Britain took: that it did not want to lose either side but rather wanted to consolidate its power and presence in the Middle East. Simply put, Britain acted in line with the realist balance of power and tried to keep both groups on its side by acting in a way that wasn't clear so as not to turn either of them against it. To begin, neither of these papers is formal; the first one is a correspondence, and the second one is a letter. Second, despite the nature of the documents, the fact that they were found out through letters to Britain gave them a sense of being more important than casual things. This was due to the fact that formality was the subject of the correspondence. Third, both documents are ambiguous. Accordingly, there are no regions in today's geography known as Syria and Lebanon, which were said to be under the control of the sovereignty of Arabs in the correspondence between Hussein and McMahon; however, Great Britain did not mention Palestine or Jerusalem in this correspondence at any point. Arab nationalists thought that Britain's decision to keep the Arabs out of Palestine and Jerusalem after the war was a clear betrayal of the Arabs' trust. The land that was promised to Zionists in the Balfour Declaration was not bounded in any way, and the very idea of a "national home" was left open to interpretation. This creates a similar kind of ambiguity. Zionism, on the other hand, was able to find the opportunity to be internationally recognized thanks to this document, in contrast to the Arabs and despite the uncertainty. The fact that the document had its beginnings in the United Kingdom was, without a doubt, the determining factor in ensuring that it would eventually receive international recognition at this point.

The fourth thing about the current state of the Arab-Zionist conflict is that both of these documents have something in common with one another. Despite the ambiguity surrounding the land that was promised to both communities in these documents, it has been determined that the same lands were promised to both communities. Today, if a question is asked about the borders of a Palestinian country or a Zionist country, the answer will be given as a region on the map that falls within the same geographical borders. These documents played a role not only in the formation of a large number of partnerships but also in the character of the conflict in terms of the results. When the Hussein-McMahon letters couldn't be resolved, the Arabs felt betrayed, but the Zionists saw an opportunity to be recognized on the international stage. Chaim Weizmann, who was a professor of chemistry at Manchester University at the time, made a big difference in this success. Weizmann was more astute than Theodor Herzl, who had previously taken actions that were comparable, due to the fact that he utilized his political connections in addition to his background as a scientist in a field that would be useful during the war. For instance, his work on the production of acetone from the starch found in cereal grains may have prevented defeat for the nation that he had adopted. Another circumstance that had an impact on these accomplishments of the Zionists was connected to Britain's priorities in the power balance. After the October Revolution, Great Britain did not want Russia to withdraw from the war because it had previously shown support for the Zionists. In addition to this, it aimed to undermine Germany from within and make it simpler for the United States to join the conflict. The Zionist cause made progress in the eyes of Britain as a result of all of these goals.

Arabs and Jews both had greater hope for independence as a result of the shift in the power dynamic that occurred after World War I. Following the conclusion of World War I, the Ottoman Empire was finally brought to an end, marking the beginning of the modern Middle East. As a result, the conclusion of the war gave both camps increased hope for achieving independence. These anticipations were, however, rendered meaningless when, in the aftermath of the war in Palestine, Britain established a regime that was subject to a mandate. As a result of the division that took place in San Remo in 1920 regarding the Arab lands that had been governed by the Ottoman Empire, those lands were assigned to the mandates of France and Britain. However, when the League of Nations approved the division in Arab geography, this showed a serious similarity with the division that was envisioned by the Sykes-Picot Agreement in 1916. This took place in 1916. This situation essentially brings attention to two different points. First, when the United States and the Soviet Union were absent from the organization, what was once considered one of the most idealistic and flamboyant institutions changed into an organization that served the interests of Britain and France. Second, as the example shows, the general trend in international relations during this time was not idealism but realism, which put things like the balance of interests and power first. This was the case because realism prioritized these factors. Two of the United Kingdom's primary goals became clear after the mandate governments in the area were approved by the British and French governments. The first of these was to continue to have a presence in the Middle East and even to strengthen that presence. The second objective was to lessen the influence that competing European powers, particularly France, had in the area. Within the context of these two goals, the United Kingdom provided support for the uprisings of Arabs, Armenians, and Zionists. To summarize, the process regarding the Arab-Zionist conflict was not carried out with an idealistic view but rather within the framework of the interests and balance-of-power calculations of the British Empire.

However, despite the calculated policies of Britain, the British mandate administration in Palestine started to face difficulties. This situation had an internal reason, related to Britain, and an external one, the view of the Arab and Zionist societies toward the British. According to the internal reason related to the domestic policy of Britain, different points of view began to form between the local representatives of the British mandate administration and the British government. Accordingly, the local British rulers were sympathetic to Arab society and skeptical of the Zionists' goals. Whenever the Zionists ran into issues with regional authorities, they attempted to exert pressure on them by making direct contact with the British government in an effort to get their attention. But the Zionists' claims that the local rulers had the same rights as they were met with a lot of doubt from both sides. Some of the demands made by the Zionists extended beyond the borders of Palestine and had a disruptive impact on the societies that were still governed by the British mandate. On the other hand, according to the British government, the British presence in Palestine was based on the Balfour Declaration. At the same time, the British government had placed itself under a legal obligation by adding the aforementioned declaration to the mandate constitution. Therefore, according to the British government, the demands of the Zionists should have been supported by the British local administrators. Simply, the British government and local British rulers in Palestine held differing views regarding the administration of Palestine, and this situation created an administrative crisis in the mandate.

The changing perceptions of Arabs and Zionists by the British government made it difficult for the British to remain in Palestine. While the British administration favored the Jews over the Arabs in Palestine, it favored the Arabs over the Zionists. As a result, the management crisis that emerged in Britain became unmanageable because, while Britain's presence in Palestine was supposed to be a balancing factor, it began to appear as a problem in and of itself. As a result, Britain's ambiguity, which it had maintained from the start, began to disrupt the balance rather than being a tool for diplomatic gain and stability. Therefore, in the early stages of the British mandate in Palestine, Britain's main goal was to realize what was promised to the Zionists by the Balfour Declaration but also to protect the civil and economic rights of the Arabs. To put it simply, the main tendency of the British mandate government, which believed that the two communities could live together, was to establish a balance between them.

The outcome of this policy was the restriction of the Zionists' land area and migration to the region by the British mandate. The British mandate administration also thought that the Arabs should have a say in the mandate. However, when the emerging conflicts confirmed that the two communities could not live together, Britain realized that this policy could no longer be carried out. The first major conflict between the two communities, the Nebi Musa uprising, took place in 1921. This uprising saw clashes in Tel Aviv and Jaffa, and retaliatory attacks began between the two communities. Britain's policy toward this situation and the subsequent uprisings was to investigate the conflict and temporarily stop the Zionist immigration to Palestine. Likewise, the British followed a similar policy in the Buraq (Wailing Wall) uprisings in 1928 and 1929. In response, Britain set up the Shaw Commission in 1929. It started with sacred sites in both communities and got worse as people worried that the other community would take control of these sites. According to the commission, Arab society's unrest was caused by two factors: First, the Arabs were concerned about being left without land as a result of the Zionists' uncontrolled land acquisition. Second, the Arabs were concerned about their economic future as a result of the uncontrolled land acquisition by the Zionists. As can be seen, the British mandate administration, in attempting to strike a balance between the two communities, began to recognize that one society's problem was caused by the existence of the other, and thus the two communities couldn't coexist.

With similar motives, Britain, which first established the Hope-Simpson Commission in 1930 and then published the Pass field report of the same year, restricted the Zionists' immigration to Palestine and land purchases with these initiatives. Therefore, in this 1930 report, Britain blamed the Zionists for the source and development of the conflict and almost forced the Zionists to make some concessions to establish a national home. However, the division of Palestinian lands was not recommended until the Peel Commission of 1937. For the Arab-Zionist conflict, division and separation would not be preferred for the British administration until 1947. Therefore, and as can be seen, in this process, the idea of two ethnic groups together, which the British mandate administration initially hoped for, began to collapse, and the British protectorate began to be viewed with suspicion by both Arabs and Zionists. With this understanding, the Zionists preferred to put pressure on the British mandate through the British government by establishing their own self-defense organizations in Palestine. However, it is not possible to see a similar political trend among Arabs because Arabs did not have a direct connection with the British government like the Zionists, and Arabs thought that Britain would always side with the Zionists. Currently, the most important indicator justifying this opinion of Arabs is the interest-based orientalist perspective of Britain toward the Arab lands.

In spite of this, the Arab community, upon realizing that the British had not stood still in the face of their uprisings, rebelled the following year, in 1936. The Peel Commission was established in 1937 in response to this uprising; however, the riots transformed into a rebellion between the years 1937 and 1939 because Arab society did not provide a satisfactory result. In this period, the nature and scope of the uprisings, as well as the date they emerged, were influential in determining British policy. This was because the British feared the Arabs supporting the Axis powers in the impending European conflict, thus endangering British colonies. It is possible to see this concern, especially in the 1939 McDonald Report. Therefore, the result that emerged from the report, shaped by these concerns, was a victory for the Arab community, in that it was decided to restrict immigration to Palestine and land acquisition and to establish an Arab-Palestinian state in Palestine within ten years. Thus, the Arab uprisings ceased, and the Zionists began to think that they had been betrayed by Britain. As can be seen, the only factor that determined the attitude of Britain toward the conflict was the interests of the British Empire and the minimizing of damage to these interests in a possible world war.

The rest of the process is known to everyone who has already studied the Arab-Zionist conflict. In my next book, I will try to examine the process after World War II. However, I think it is useful to highlight a few points to reach more specifically: although some focuses on the post-establishment of the state of Israel, the established elements that determine the character of the Arab-Zionist conflict mostly focused on are inherent to the historical process. Therefore, to specify respectively: The emergence of anti-Semitism in the West, the maturation of Zionism, the emergence of the identity of the transnational natures of Western colonialism and Zionism and the unity of purpose, the instrumentalization of Zionism by Western colonialism in response, the awakening of Arab nationalism that had already begun to mature, partly decked with Islamist elements, and the fact that Britain only took its own interests as a political motivation in solving the crisis have deeply affected the present character of the conflict. Therefore, it is almost impossible to address the Arab-Zionist conflict and even hope for a solution while dealing with it without grasping this historical process.

Bibliography

A'zami, Ahmad 'Izzat al-. 1934. *The Arab Cause: Its Causes, Premises, Developments and Results* (al-Qadiyyah al-'Arabiyyah: Asbabaha, Muqadamataha, Tatawurataha, wa-Nata'ijaha). Baghdad: Matba'at al-Sha'b.

'Abd al-Ra'uf, Salim Muhammad. 1990. *The Activity of the Jewish Agency for Palestine from Its Inception until the Establishment of the State of Israel from 1922–1948* (Nashat al-Wikalah al-Yahudiyyah li-Falastin mindh Insha'iha hata qiyam al-Dawlah, 1922–1948). Cairo: al-Mu'assasah al-'Arabiyya lil-Dirasat.

Abitbol, Michel. 2000. "The Jews of the Arab World: A Millennium of Coexistence." *Jewish Social Studies* 6, no. 4: pp. 1–13.

Abrash, Ibrahim. 1987. *The National Dimension of the Palestinian Issue: Palestine between Arab Nationalism and Palestinian Nationalism* (al-Bu'd al-Qawmi lil-Qadiyah al-Falasiniyah: Falastin bayn al-Qawmiyyah al-'Arabiyyah, wa-l-Wataniyya al-Falastiniyyah). Beirut: Markiz Dirasat al-Wahdah al-'Arabiyyah.

Abu Basir, Salih Mas'ud. 1971. *The Battle of People of Palestine during Half a Century* (Jihad al-Sha'b al-Falastini khilal nisf Qarn). Beirut: Dar al-Fath.

Abu Shaqra, Ibrahim. 1999. *Mufti Falastin al-Hajj Amin al-Husseini wa-Thawrat 1936–1939* (The mufti of Palestine, Hajj Amin al-Husseini, and the 1936–1939 revolution). Damascus: Dar Al-Numeir.

Abu-Lughod, Ibrahim A. 1971. *The Transformation of Palestine: Essays on the Origin and Development of the Arab-Israeli Conflict*. Evanston, IL: Northwestern University Press.

Ahmad, Hisham. 1996. "The Roots of Denying the Right: The American Attitude towards the Right of Self-Determination for the Palestinians—from the Balfour Declaration to the Second World War" (Judhur Inkar al-Haqq, al-Mawqif al-Amriki mi Haqq Taqrir al-Masir lil-Falastiniyin-min Wa'd Balfour 'ila al-Harb al-'Alamiyyah al-Thaniyyah). In *Palestine and American Policy from Wilson to Clinton* (Falastin wa-l-Siyasah al-Amrikiyya min Clinton 'ila Wislon), ed. Michael Sulaiman, pp. 60–123. Beirut: Markiz Dirasat al-Wahdah al-'Arabiyya.

Ahmed, Hisham H. 1990. "From the Balfour Declaration to World War II: The U.S. Stand on Palestinian Self-Determination." *Arab Studies Quarterly* 12, no. 1/2 (winter/spring): pp. 9–41.

Alagha, Malath. 2016. *Palestine in EU and Russian Foreign Policy: Statehood and the Peace Process*. London: Routledge.

Allawi, Ali A. 2014. *Faisal I of Iraq*. New Haven, CT: Yale University Press.

Allon, Yigal. 1970. *The Making of the Israel's Army*, forward by Michael Howard. London: Valentine Mitchell.

'Alush, Naji. 1967. *Arab Resistance in Palestine, 1917–1948* (al-Muqawamah al-'Arabiyyah fi Falastin, 1917–1948). Beirut: Dar al-Tali'ah.

Ambrosius, Lloyd. 2002. *Wilsonianism: Woodrow Wilson and His Legacy in American Foreign Relations*. New York: Palgrave.

Antonius, George. 1961. *Arab Awakening: The History of the Arab Nationalist Movement* (YaqÐit al-'Arab: Tarikh Harkat al-'Arab al-Qawmiyyah), presented by Nabih Fares. Translated by Nasir al-Assad and Ihsan 'Abbas. Beirut: Dar al-'Ilm lil-Malayin.

'Aqil, Muhammad. 2017. *Sijil al-Mahkumin bil-I'dam fi Falastin fi 'Ahd al-Intidab al-Britani* (Record of those sentenced to death in Palestine during the British mandate era). London: E-Kutub Ltd.

"Aqil, Nabih. 1990. 'Palestine from the Arab Islamic Conquest to the Middle of the Fourth Century AH' (Falastin min al-Fatih al-"Arabi al-Islama 'ila al-Qarn al-Rabi' Hijri). *Palestinian Encyclopedia*—Special Section 2: pp. 289–299.

'Arif, 'Arif al-. 1961. *Al-Mufasal fi Tarikh al-Quds* (The Detailed in the history of Jerusalem). Jerusalem: Maktabat al-Andalus.

'Arif, Jamil. 1995. *Secret Records of the Role of Egypt, Syria, and Saudi Arabia: A Witness to the Birth of the League of Arab States* (al-Watha'iq al-Siriyyah li-Masr, Suriya wa-l-Su'udiyyah). Cairo: al-Duwaliyyah lil-I'lam wa-l-Nashir.

Arna'ut, Muhammad M. al-. 2020. *Min al-Hukuma 'ila al-Dawlah* (From government to state: The experience of the Arab government in Damascus 1918–1920: Studies and reviews). Amman: al-'Ann lil-Nashir.

'Ashur, Muhammad Abdul Rahman. 2022. "Al-Tatni' fi al-ShariÑah wa-Akhtaruhu 'ala al-Qadiyah al-Falastiniyyah w-al-Shu'ub al-'Arabiyyah w-al-Islamiyyah" (Subordination in Islamic sharia and its dangers to the Palestinian cause and the Arab and Islamic peoples). In *Studies in Normalization with the Zionist State*, edited by Muhsin Muhammad Salih, pp. 17–48. Beirut: al-Zaytouna Center for Studies and Consultations.

Atassi, Nashwan al-. 2015. *Tatawor al-Mujtama' al-Suri* (The development of Syrian society). Beirut: Atlas Publishing.

Avineri, Shlomo. 2016. *The Making of Modern Zionism: The Intellectual Origins of the Jewish State*. New York: Basic Books.

Avneri, Arieh L. 1984. *The Claim of Dispossession: Jewish Land-Settlement and the Arabs, 1878–1948*. New Brunswick, NJ: Transaction Books.

'Awad, 'Abd al-'Aziz. 1983. *Introduction to the History of Modern Palestine, 1831–1914* (Muqaddamat Tarikh Falastin al-Hadith, 1831–1914). Beirut: al-Mu'asassah al-'Arabiyyah lil-Dirasat.

'Ayid, Khalid. 1990. "Zionist Expansionism and Greater Israel" (al-Tawasu'iyah al-Sahyuniyah wa-Isra'il al-Kubra). In *The Palestinian Encyclopedia*, pp. 550–552, pt. 2, vol. 6. Beirut: Mu'asassat al-Mawsu'ah al-Falastiniyya.

Badran, Amneh. 2009. *Zionist Israel and Apartheid South Africa: Civil Society and Peace Building in Ethnic-National States*. London: Routledge.

Badur, Suleiman al-. 2004. *Palestine in the Umayyad Era, Economic Life and Social Aspects*. Amman: Wizarat al-Thaqafah.

Bahjat, Sabri. 1982. *Palestine during the First World War and Its Aftermath* (Falastin khilal al-Harb al-'Alamiyyah al-'Ulah wama ba'daha). Jerusalem: Jam'iyat al-Dirasat al-'Arabiyah.

Barakat, Rana. 2018. "Criminals or Martyrs? Let the Courts Decide! British Colonial Legacy in Palestine and the Criminalization of Resistance." *al-Muntaqa* 1, no. 1 (April): pp. 84–97.

Barakat, Zeina M. 2017. *From Heart of Stone to Heart of Flesh: Evolutionary Journey from Extremism to Moderation*. München: Herbert Utz Verlag.

Barghuthi, 'Umar al-, and Khalil Tutah. 2006. *History of Palestine* (Tarikh Falastin). Cairo: Maktabat al-Thaqafah al-Diniyyah/Religious Culture Library.

Baron, Xavier. 1978. *Les palestiniens un people/The Palestinians . . . a people* (al-Falastiniyun Sha'ban). Translated by 'Abdullah Iskandar. Beirut: Dar al-Kitab al-'Arabi.

Barr, James. 2012. *A Line in the Sand: Britain, France and the Struggle That Shaped the Middle East*. London: Simon & Shuster.

Barut, Muhammad Jamal. 2013. *The Recent Historical Formation of the Syrian Island: Questions and Problems of the Transition from Nomadic to Theoretical Urbanization* (al-Takawun al-Tarikhi al-Hadith lil-Jazirah al-Suriyyah). Beirut: Arab Center for Research and Policy Studies.

Bathel, Nicolson. 1979. *The Palestine Triangle: The Struggle for the Holy Land, 1935–48*. London: Weidenfeld & Nicolson.

Bauer, Yehuda. 1995. "Holocaust and Genocide Studies." *New Outlook* 9, no. 7 (July-August).

Beckford, James A., and Jay Demerath, eds. 2007. *The SAGE Handbook of the Sociology of Religion*. London: SAGE.

Bell, John Bowyer. 1977. *Terror Out of Zion: Irgun Zvai Leumi, LEHI, and the Palestine Underground, 1929–1949*. New York: St. Martin's Press.

Ben-Ami, S. 2012. *Scars of War, Wounds of Peace: The Israeli-Arab Tragedy*. Oxford: Oxford University Press.

Ben-Gurion, David. 1963. *Rebirth and Destiny of Israel*. New York: Philosophical Library.

Ben-Sasson, H. H. 1977. "The Jews in the Muslim World." In *The Cambridge History of Islam*, edited by P. M. Holt et al., pp. 2:862–878. Cambridge: Cambridge University Press.

Berdine, Michael D. 2018. *Redrawing the Middle East: Sir Mark Sykes, Imperialism and the Sykes-Picot Agreement*. London: Bloomsbury Publishing.

Berlin, George L. 1970. "The Brandeis-Weizmann Dispute." *American Jewish Historical Quarterly* 60, no. 1 (September): pp. 37–68.

Biru, Tawfiq 'Ali. 1960. *Arabs and Turks in the Ottoman Constitutional Era, 1908–1914* (al-'Arab wa-l-Turk fi al-'Ahd al-Disturi al-'Uthmani, 1908–1914). Cairo: Ma'had al-Dirasat al-'Arabiyyah al-'Alamiyya.

Bisisu, Fu'ad. 1990. *The Arab Economy in Palestine during the British Mandate Period from 1920–1948* (al-Iqtisad al-'Arabi fi Falastin fi 'Ahd al-Intidab al-Britani 1920–1948). Beirut: al-Mawsa'ah al-Falstiniyyah.

Black, Ian. 1991. *Israel's Secret Wars: A History of Israel's Intelligence Services.* New York: Grove Press.

———. 2015. *Zionism and the Arabs, 1936–1939.* RLE Israel and Palestine. New York: Routledge.

Brenner, Lenny. 2015. *The Zionist Revision Movement from Jabotinsky to Shamir: Zionist Personalities* (Harkat al-Tashih al-Sahyuniyyah min 'ahd Jabotinski 'ila Shamir: Shakhsiyat Sahyuniyyah). Amman: Dar al-Jalal.

Bunton, Martin P. 2009. *Land Legislation in Mandate Palestine.* New York: Cambridge Archive Editions.

Butenschøn, Nils A., Syvind Stiansen, and Kåre Vollan. 2016. *Power-Sharing in Conflict-Ridden Societies: Challenges for Building Peace and Democratic Stability.* London: Routledge.

Caplan, Neil. 1983. "Faisal Ibn Husain and the Zionists: A Re-examination with Documents." *International History Review* 5, no. 4 (November): pp. 561–614.

Cell, John Whitson. 2002. *Hailey: A Study in British Imperialism, 1872–1969.* New York: Cambridge University Press.

Cohen, Hillel. 2008. *Army of Shadows: Palestinian Collaboration with Zionism, 1917–1948.* Berkeley: University of California Press.

———. 2015. *Year Zero of the Arab-Israeli Conflict: 1929.* Boston: Brandeis University Press.

Cohen, Michael J. 1975. "Direction of Policy in Palestine, 1936–45." *Middle Eastern Studies* 11, no. 3 (October): pp. 237–261.

———. 1978. *Palestine, Retreat from the Mandate: A Study of British Policy, 1936–45.* New York: Holmes and Meier.

———. 2012. *Palestine to Israel: From Mandate to Independence.* London: Routledge.

———. 2013. *Churchill and the Jews: A Lifelong Friendship.* London: Routledge.

———. 2014. *Britain's Moment in Palestine: Retrospect and Perspectives, 1917–1948.* London: Routledge.

Crider, Elizabeth Fortunato. 1978. "Itailo-Egyptian Relations in the Interwar Period, 1922–1942." PhD diss. Ohio State University.

Danchev, Alex. 1987. "'Dilly-Dally,' or Having the Last Word: Field Marshal Sir John Dill and Prime Minister Winston Churchill." *Journal of Contemporary History* 22, no. 1 (January): pp. 21–44.

Darwazah, Hakam. 1961. *al-Shuyu'iyah al-Mahalliyah* (Local Communis). Beirut: Dar al-Fajr al-Jadid.

Darwazah, Muhammad 'Izzat. 1971. *The Emergence of the Modern Arab Movement* (Nash'at al-Harakah al-'Arabiyyah al-Hadithah). Beirut: al-Maktabah al-'Asriyyah.

———. 1984a. *One Hundred Palestinian Years: Notes and Recordings: (1305–1404/1887–1984)* (Ma'at 'Amm Falastiniyyah: Mudhakarat wa-Tasjilat [1305–1404/1887–1984]). Damascus: Palestinian Society for History and Archeology.

———. 1984b. *The Palestinian Issue in Its various Stages: History, Memoirs and Comments* (al-Qadiyya al-Filistimiyya fi Mukhtalf Marahilha: Tarikh wa-Mudhakirat wa-Ta'liqat). Beirut: Dar al-I'lam w-l-Thaqafah.

———. 1993. *Mudhakarat Muhammad Izza Darwazah, 1305–1404/1887–1984* (Memoirs of Muhammad 'Izzat Darwazah, 1305–1404/1887–1984). Beirut: Dar al-Gharb al-Islami.

Davis, Uri. 1977. *Zionism: Utopia Incorporated*. London: Zed Press.

Dawn, C. Ernest. 1960. "The Amir of Mecca Al-usayn Ibn-Ali and the Origin of the Arab Revolt." *Proceedings of the American Philosophical Society* 104, no. 1 (February 15): pp. 11–34.

Dhadha, Hasan alt. 1971. *World Zionism and Israel* (al-Sahyuniyyah al-'Alamiyya wa-Isra'il). Cairo: al-Hay'ah al-'Ammah lil-Kutub.

Do'ar, Jarban Ghasan. 2004. *Arabists: Israeli Death Squads* (al-Musta'ribun: Firaq al-Mawt al-Isra'iliyyah). Amman: Dar al-Shuruq.

Druks, Herbert. 2001. *The Uncertain Friendship: The U.S. and Israel from Roosevelt to Kennedy*. London: Greenwood Publishing Group.

Edmunds, June. 2000. "The British Communist Party and Israel: From the Establishment of the Jewish State to the Invasion of Lebanon." In *The Left and Israel: Party-Policy Change and Internal Democracy*, pp. 111–133. London: Palgrave Macmillan.

Egremont, Max. 1980. *Balfour: A Life of Arthur James Balfour*. London: Collins.

Eliav, Yaakov "Yashka." 2016. *Among the Files of Zionist Terrorism: The Crimes of Irgun and Lehi, 1937–1948* (Min Malafat al-Irhab al-Sahyuni: Jara'im al-Irgun wa-Lihi). Translated by Ghazi al-Sa'di Amman. Amman: Dar al-Jalil.

Elpeleg, Z., and Shmuel Himelstein. 2012. *The Grand Mufti: Haj Amin al-Hussaini, Founder of the Palestinian National Movement*. London: Routledge.

Erickson, Edward J. 2021. *The Turkish War of Independence: A Military History, 1919–1923*. Santa Barbara, CA: Praeger.

Essaid, Ada. 2013. *Zionism and Land Tenure in Mandate Palestine*. London: Routledge.

Etheredge, Laura. 2011. *Historic Palestine, Israel, and the Emerging Palestinian Autonomous Areas*. New York: Rosen Publishing Group.

Fahmy, William. 1975. *Zionist Settler Colonialism in Palestine* (al-Isti'mar al-Istitani al-Sahyuni fi Falastin). Cairo: Ma'had al-Buhuth wa-l-Dirasat.

Fahum, Zuhir 'Abd al-Majid. 2012. *Palestine: Victim and Executioners, Palestine in the Late Ottoman Period* (Falastin: Zahiyah wa-Jaladun, Falastin fi Awakhir al-'Ahd al-'Uthmani). Cairo: Shams lil-Nashir.

Farsakh, 'Awni Farsakh. 2008. *The Challenge and Response in the Arab-Zionist Conflict: The Roots of the Conflict and Its Control Laws, 1799–1948* (al-Tahadi wa-l-Ijabah fi al-Sira' al-'Arabi al-Sahyuni Judhur al-Sira' wa-Qawaninuhu al-Dhabitah 1799–1949). Beirut: Markiz Dirasat al-Wahdah al-'Arabiyya.

Farsoun, Samih K., and Nasser H. Aruri. 2018. *Palestine and the Palestinians: A Social and Political History*. New York: Routledge.

Farsun, Samih. 2003. *Palestine and the Palestinians* (Falastine wa-l-Falastiniyun). Translated by 'Atta 'Abd al-Wahab. Beirut: Markas Dirasat al-Wahdah al-'Arabiyya.

Faruqi, Hamza A. al-. 2003. *Dhaya' Falastine* (The loss of Palestine). Beirut: Dar al-Hadatha.

Fathi, Nasar. 2003. *Palestine Documents: From the Age of Custody to the Balfour Declaration, 637–1917* (Watha'iq Falastin min al-'Uhdah al-'Umariyyah 'la wa'id Balfour 637–1917). Cairo: Dar al-Thaqafah.

Fawaz, Leila Tarazi. 2014. *A Land of Aching Hearts: The Middle East in the Great War*. Cambridge, MA: Harvard University Press.

Fawcett, Louise. 2013. *International Relations of the Middle East*. Oxford: Oxford University Press.

Fawzi, Tariq. 2002. *Isra'il Dawlah Sana'ataha al-Mukhabarat* (Israel is a state created by the intelligence). Cairo: Dar al-Ahmadi.

Fieldhouse, D. K. 2006. *Western Imperialism in the Middle East, 1914–1958*. Oxford: Oxford University Press.

Fierro, Maribel. 2009. "Muslims and Jews in Al-Andalus: Some Historical and Historiographical Considerations." *Al-Qantara* 30, no. 2: pp. 297–315.

Fisher, John. 1988. "Syria and Mesopotamia in British Middle Eastern Policy in 1919." *Middle Eastern Studies* 34, no. 2 (April): pp. 129–170.

Fitzgerald, Edward Peter. 1994. "France's Middle Eastern Ambitions, the Sykes-Picot Negotiations, and the Oil Fields of Mosul, 1915–1918." *Journal of Modern History* 66, no. 4 (December): pp. 697–725.

Flapan, Simha. 1979. *Zionism and the Palestinians*. London: Croom Helm.

———. 1987. *The Birth of Israel: Myths and Realities*. New York: Pantheon Books.

Fraser, Ronnie. 2022. *British Trade Unions, the Labour Party, and Israel's Histadrut*. London: Palgrave.

Friesen, Aileen E. 2020. *Colonizing Russia's Promised Land: Orthodoxy and Community on the Siberian Steppe*. Toronto: University of Toronto Press.

Fromkin, David. 1990. *A Peace to End All Peace: The Fall of the Ottoman Empire and the Creation of the Modern Middle East*. New York: Avon Books.

———. 2010. *A Peace to End All Peace: The Fall of the Ottoman Empire and the Creation of the Modern Middle East*. New York: Henry Holt and Company.

Galnoor, Itzhak. 2012. *The Partition of Palestine: Decision Crossroads in the Zionist Movement*. New York: State University of New York Press.

Gerber, Jane S. 1998. "Jewish-Muslim Relations in Al-Andalus: Literature and Culture in the Golden Age." *Jewish Social Studies* 4, no. 2: pp. 24–50.

Ghafani, Sayyid Husain al-. 2001. *Reminding the Soul of the Narrative of Jerusalem and Its Sanctifying* (Tadhkir al-Nafs bi-Hadith al-Quads wa-Aqdasihi). Cairo: Maktabat Mu'adh ibn Jabal.

Ghani, 'Abd al-Rahman 'Abd al-. 1995. *Nazi Germany and Palestine, 1933–1945* (Almanya al-Naziyyahwa-Falastin, 1933–1945). Beirut: Mu'asassat al-Dirasat al-Falastiniyah/Institute for Palestine Studies.

Gharib, 'Isam. 2014. *Al-Hajj Muhammad Amin al-Husseini and His Role in the Palestinian National Movement (1897–1974)* (Al-Hajj Muhammad Amin al-Husseiniwa dawruhu fi al-Harakah al-Qawmiyyah al-Falastiniyyah (1897–1974). Beirut: Markiz al-Hadarah lil-Tanmiyyah al-Fikir al-Islami.

Gharibah, Bahjat Abu. 1989. "Pages from the History of the Palestinian Issue until the Year 1949: Historical Vision and Features of a Personal Experience." In *The Palestinian Cause in Forty Years: Between the Ferocity of Reality and the Aspirations of the Future*, edited by Ahmad Sa'id Nawfal, pp. 80–81. Beirut: Markaz Dirasat al-Wihdah al-'Arabiyya.

Gharibieh, Bahjat Abu. 1993. *Amidst the Arab-Palestinian Struggle: Memoirs of the Fighter, Bahjat Abu Gharibieh, 1916–1949* (Fi Khidhim al-Nidhal al-'Arabi al-Falastini: Mudhakarat Bahjat Abu Gharibieh, 1916–1948). Beirut: Institution of Palestinian Studies.

Ghunaym, 'Adil Hasan. 1980. *The Palestinian National Movement, from the Revolution of 1936 to the Second World War* (al-Harakah al-Wataniyyah al-Falastiniyyah min Thawrat 1936 hata al-Harb al-'Alamiyyah aThaniyyah). Cairo: Maktabat al-Khanji.

Ghuri, Emile al-. 1972. *Palestine over Sixty Years* (Falastin'abir sitin 'aman). Beirut: Dar al-Nahar.

Gibbons, Herbert Adams. 1919. "Zionism and the World Peace." *Century* 97: pp. 369–374.

Gilmour, David. 1980. *The Dispossessed: The Ordeal of the Palestinians, 1917–1980*. London: Sidgwick and Jackson.

Glick, Edward Bernard. 2020. *The Triangular Connection: America, Israel and American Jews*. New York: Routledge.

Goitein, S. D. 1967. *Jews and Arabs: Their Contacts through the Ages*. New York: Schocken Books.

Goldmann, Nahum. 1994. *The Memoir of Nahum Goldmann* (Mudhakirat Nahumm Goldmann). Translated by Dar al-Jalil, Shakhsiyat Sahyuniyyah. Amman: Dar al-Jalil lil-Nashir wa-l-Dirasat wa-l-Abhath al-Falastiniyyah.

Hadi, 'Abd al-Hasim, and Anis Sayigh. eds. 1990. *Palestinian Encyclopedia* (al-Mawsua'h al-Falastiniyyah). Beirut: Hay'at al-Mawsua'h al-Falastiniyyah.

Hadi, 'Awni 'Abdel. 2002. *'Awni 'Abdel Hadi's Diary* (Mudhakirat 'Awni 'Abdel Hadi), edited by Khayriyyah Qasimiyyah. Beirut: Markaz Dirasat al-Wahdah al-'Arabiyya.

Ḥakīm, Yūsuf. 1983. *Suriyya w-al-Intidab al-Faransi* (Syria and the French Mandate). Beirut: Dar al-Nahar.

Halderman, J. 1968. "Some International Constitutional Aspects of the Palestine Case." *Law and Contemporary Problems* 23: pp. 78–109.

Halevi, Yossi Klein. 1995. *Memoirs of a Jewish Extremist: The Story of a Transformation.* Boston: Little, Brown and Company.

Hall, Duncan. 1948. *Mandates, Dependencies and Trusteeship*. Dordrecht: Martinus Nijhoff.

Halul, Jabir. 2004. *al-Mawathiq w-al-'Ahud fi Mumarast al-Yahud* (Covenants and covenants in Jewish practices: A reading of contemporary Jewish religious and political thought). Beirut: al-Mu'asassah al-Jami'iyya lil-Dirasat.

Hamad, Jawad al-. 2004. *Geography of Palestine and Its History* (Gughrafyat Falastin wa-Tarikhuha). Beirut: Center for Middle Eastern Studies.

Hamadih, Sa'id. 1937. *The Economic System in Palestine* (al-Nizam al-Iqtisadi fi Falastin). Beirut: American University.

Hamdan, Badr. 1985. *The Role of the Haganah Organization in Establishing Israel* (Dawr al-Haganah fi Insha' Isra'il). Amman: Dar al-Jalil.

Hamudi, Sana' Muhammed. 2008. *Mafhum al-Qiyadah al-Siyasiyah fi Falastin fi al-'Ahd al-Britani: Qiyadat al-Hajj Amin al-Husseini* (The concept of political leadership in Palestine during the British mandate: The leadership of Hajj Amin al-Husseini). Beirut: al-Shabakah al-Arabiyya lil-Abhath.

Harvey, A. D. 1993. *Collision of Empires: Britain in Three World Wars, 1793–1945*. London: Bloomsbury Publishing.

Hassani, Muhammad ibn 'Ali al-. 2013. *History of the Great Arab Revolution* (Tarikh al-Thawrah al-'Arabiyyah al-Kubra). Beirut: al-Dar al-'Arabiyyah lil-Mu'asassat.

Hazmawi, Muhammad Majid al-. 1998. *Land Ownership in Palestine, 1918–1948* (Mulkiyat al-Aradi fi Falastin, 1918–1948). Acre: Mu'asassat al-Aswar.

Hazony, Yoram. 2001. *The Jewish State: The Struggle for Israel's Soul*. New York: Basic Books.

Heikal, Mohamed Hassanein. 1996. *Secret Negotiations between the Arabs and Israel* (al-Mufawadat al-Siriyyah bayn al-'Arab w-Isa'il). Cairo: Dar al-Shuruq.

Henig, Ruth. 2001. "New Diplomacy and Old: A Reassessment of the British Conception of a League of Nations, 1918–1920." In *The Paris Peace Conference, 1919: Peace without Victory?*, edited by M. Dockrill and J. Fisher, pp. 157–174. London: Palgrave.

Herremans, Brigitte. 2013. "Belgium and the Israeli-Palestinian Conflict: The Cautious Pursuit of a Just Peace." Studia Diplomatica 66, no. 4: 77–94.

Hertzberg, Arthur. 1969. *The Zionist Idea: A Historical Analysis and Reader*. New York: Atheneum.

High Arab Authority for Palestine. 1954. *Facts on the Question of Palestine: Statements by Mr. Muhammad Amin al-Husseini*. Cairo: Salafi Press.

Hirst, David. 2003. *Gun and the Olive Branch: The Roots of Violence in the Middle East* (al-Bunduqiyyah wa-Gusn al-Zaytun: Judhur al-'Unf fi al-Sharq al-Awsat). Translated by 'Abdul Rahman Ayas. Beirut: Riyad al-Rayis.

Hodgson, Godfrey. 2006. *Woodrow Wilson's Right Hand: The Life of Colonel Edward M. House* New Haven, CT: Yale University Press.

Hout, Bayan Nuwihid. 1979. *Documents of the Palestinian National Resistance, 1918–1939: From the Most Honorable Paper of Akram Zu'atir* (Watha'iq al-Muqawamah al-Wataniyyah al-Falastiniyyah, 1918–1939: min Awarak Akram Zu'atir). Beirut: Palestinian Institute for Studies.

———. 1981. *Political Leaders and Institutions in Palestine, 1917–1948* (al-Qiyadat wa-l-Mu'asassat al-Siyasiyyah fi Falastin, 1917–1948). Beirut: Institute for Palestine Studies.

———. 1991. *Palestine—the Cause, the People, the Civilization: The Political History of the Canaanites until the Twentieth Century* (Falastin al-Qadiyyah, al-Sha'b al-Hadarah: al-Ta'rikh al-Siyasi min 'Ahd al-Kin'aniyyin 'ila al-Qurn al-'Ashrin). Beirut: Dar al-Istiqlal.

Howard, Harry N. 1931. *The Partition of Turkey: A Diplomatic History, 1913–1923*. Norman: University of Oklahoma Press.

————. 1963. *The King-Crane Commission: An American Inquiry in the Middle East.* Beirut: Khayats.

Hughes, Matthew. 2016. "Lawlessness Was the Law: British Armed Forces, the Legal System and the Repression of the Arab Revolution in Palestine, 1936–1939." In *Britain, Palestine and Empire: The Mandate Years*, edited by Rory Miller, pp. 141–156. New York: Routledge.

————. 2019. *Britain's Pacification of Palestine: The British Army, the Colonial State, and the Arab Revolt, 1936–1939.* New York: Cambridge University Press.

Hunidi, Sahar al-. 2003. *British Founding of the Jewish National Home: Herbert Samuel's Period, 1920–1925* (al-Ta'sis al-Britani lil-Watan al-Qawmi al-Yahudi: Fatarat Hirbirt Samu'il). Translated by 'Abd al-Fatah al-Subhi. Beirut: Mu'asassat al-Dirasat al-Falastiniyya.

Hussein, 'Abd al-Rahim Ahmed. 1984. *Zionist Activity during World War II, 1939–1945* (al-Nashat al-Suhyuni khilal al-Harb al-'Alamiyyah al-Thaniyya, 1939–1948). Beirut: al-Mu'asasah al-'Arabiyyah lil-Dirasat.

Hyamson, Albert Montefiore. 1942. *Palestine: A Policy.* London: Methuen & Co.

Ingrams, Doreen. 1972. *Palestine Papers, 1917–1922: Seeds of Conflict.* London: J. Murry.

Izzeddin, Nejla M. Abu. 1981. *Nasser of the Arabs: An Arab Assessment.* London: Third World Centre for Research and Publication.

Jabbar, 'Abbas 'Atiyyah. 2017. *Al-Iraq wa-l-Qadiyyah al-Falastiniyyah, 1932–1941* (Iraq and the Palestinian question, 1932–1941). Jerusalem: Dar al-Jundi.

Jabareen, Yosef. 2017. "Controling Land and Demography in Israel: The Obsession with Territorial and Geographical Dominance." In *Israel and Its Palestinian Citizens: Ethnic Privileges in the Jewish State*, edited by Nadim N. Rouhana and Sahar S. Huneidi, pp. 238–265. New York: Cambridge University Press.

Jabbour, George. 1970. *Settler Colonialism in Southern Africa and the Middle East.* Khartoum: University of Khartoum.

Jadir, 'Adil Hamid al-. 1976. *The Impact of British Mandate Laws on Establishing the Jewish National Home in Palestine* (Athar Qawanin al-Intidab al-Britani fi iqamat al-Watan al-Qawmi al-Yahudi fi Falastin). Baghdad: Center for Palestinian Studies.

Jana, Tawfiq. 1938. *Collection of Arab Testimonies in Palestine before the British Royal Commission* (Majmu'at Shahadat al-'Arab fi Falastin amam al-Lajnah al-Malakiyyah al-Britaniyya). Damascus: Matba'at al-'I'tidal.

Jarrar, Hosni Adham. 2011. *Scholars and Preachers in Jerusalem and Its Surroundings* ('Ulama' wa-Du'at Bayt al-Maqdis wa-Aknafihi). Amman: Dar al-Ma'mun.

Jeffery, Keith. 2014. "The British Army and the Creation of Israel." *Journal of Military History* 78, no. 1: pp. 105–124.

Jeffries, Joseph Mary Nagle. 2000. *Palestine: The Reality/Palestine: Here's the Truth.* Translated by Ahmed Khalil al-Hajj. Sharjah: Department of Culture and Information.

Jiryis, Sabri. 1977. *History of Zionism* (Tarikh al-Sahyuniyyah). Beirut: Markiz al-Abhath.

———. 1995. "Establishment of the Jewish National Home in Palestine (1917–1923)" (Ta'sis al-Watan al-Qawmi al-Yahudi fi Falastin (1917–1923). *Palestinian Affairs*, no. 95 (October): pp. 37–59.

Johnson, Gaynor. 2016. *Lord Robert Cecil: Politician and Internationalist*. London: Routledge.

Juha, Shafiq. 2004. *Al-Harakah al-'Arabiyya al-Sirriyyah* (The Arab underground movement: The Red Book Group, 1935–1945). Beirut: al Furat.

Kamal, Aftab Pasha. 2000. *Arab-Israeli Peace Process: An Indian Perspective*. New Delhi: Manas Publications.

Kamil, Mahmud Kamil. 1858. *The Great Arab State* (al-Dawlah al-'Arabiyya al-Kubra). Cairo: Dar al-Ma'arif.

Karsh, Efraim. 2010. *Palestine Betrayed*. New Haven, CT: Yale University Press.

Katz, David S. 2016. *The Shaping of Turkey in the British Imagination, 1776–1923*. New York: Palgrave McMillan.

Katz, Samuel. 1988. *The Night Raiders: Israel's Naval Commandos in the Second World War*. London: Arms and Armour Press.

———. 1992. *The Elite*. New York: Pocket Books.

Kayali, 'Abd al-Wahab al-. 1968. *Documents of the Palestinian Arab Resistance against the British and Zionist Occupation, 1918–1939* (Watha'iq al-Muqawamah al-'Arabiyyah al-Falastiniyya did al-Ihtilal al-Britani wa-l-Sahyuniyyah, 1918–1939). Beirut: Institute for Palestine Studies.

———. 1985. *Modern History of Palestine* (Tarikh Falastin al-Hadith). Beirut: al-Mu'asassah al-'Arabiyya lil-Dirasat.

———. 1990. *Encyclopedia of Politics* (al-Mawsu'ah al-Siyasiyyah). Beirut: Arab Foundation for Studies and Publishing.

Keith, Berriedale. 1922. "Mandates." *Journal of Comparative Legislation and International Law*, 3rd series, vol. 4: pp. 71–83.

Kessler, Oren. 2023. *Palestine 1936: The Great Revolt and the Roots of the Middle East Conflict*. London: Rowman & Littlefield.

Khadduri, Majid. 1960. *Independent Iraq, 1958–1932: A Study in Iraqi Politics*. London: Oxford University Press.

———. 1970. *Political Trends in the Arab World: The Role of Ideas and Ideals in Politics* Baltimore: Johns Hopkins Press.

Khadir, Bisharah. 2003. *Europe and Palestine: From the Crusades to This Day* (Uruba wa-Falastin: min al-Hurub al-Salibiyyah 'ila al-Yawm). Beirut: Markaz Dirasat al-Wahda al-'Arabiyya.

Khalaf, 'Issa. 1991. *Politics in Palestine: Arab Factionalism and Social Disintegration, 1939–1948*. Albany: State University of New York Press.

Khalaf, Noha. 2019. "The Secret of the King-Crane Report 1919: The Important Document Hidden" (Sirr Taqrir King-Crane 1919: al-Wathiqah al-Hamah al-lati tama Ikhfa'iha). *al-Ra'y al-Yaum/Today's Opinion*. January 15.

Khalah, Kamel. 1982. *Palestine and the Mandate, 1922–1939* (Falastin wa-l-Intidab al-Britani, 1922–1939). Tripoli: al-Mansha'ah al-'Ammah lil-Nashir.

Khalidi, Rashid. 1997. *Palestinian Identity: The Construction of Modern National Consciousness*. New York: Columbia University Press.

————. 2007. *The Iron Cage: The Story of the Palestinian Struggle for Statehood.* Boston: Beacon Press.

————. 2020. *The Hundred Years' War on Palestine: A History of Settler Colonialism and Resistance, 1917–2017.* New York: Metropolitan Books.

Khalidi, Walid. 1977. "The Arab Revolt and the Palestine Problem." *Journal of Palestine Studies* 6, no. 3: 44–60.

————. 2001. "The Palestinians and 1948: The Underlying Causes of Failure." In *The War for Palestine: Rewriting the History of 1948*, edited by Eugene L. Rogan and Avi Shlaim, pp. 21–44. Cambridge: Cambridge University Press.

————. 2006. *Before Their Diaspora: A Photographic History of the Palestinians, 1876–1948.* Washington, DC: Institute for Palestine Studies.

Khalidi, Walid al-. 1971. *From Haven to Conquest: Readings in Zionism and the Palestine Problem until 1948.* Beirut: Institute of Palestine Studies.

————. 1998. *Zionism in a Hundred Years: From Crying Ruins to Domination over Levant, 1998–1897.* Beirut: al-Nahar Publishing House.

————. 1998. *Fifty years since the Partition of Palestine (1947–1997)*, Khamsun 'Aman 'ala taqsim Falastin) Beirut: Dar Al-Nahar, p. 13; Najjar, 'Ayida. 2005. *Sahafi Falastin wa-l-Harakah al-Wataniyya fi Nisf Qarn, 1900–1948* (The Palestinian press and the national movement in half a Century, 1900–1948). Beirut: al-Mu'asassah al-'Arabiyya lil-Dirasat, pp. 234–235.

Khalifa, Ahmed, and Samir Jabbour, trans. 1989. "Palestine War 1947–1948." In *The Great Arab Revolt in Palestine, 1936–1939: An Official Israeli Account.* Introduction by Walid al-Khalidi. Beirut: Institute for Palestine Studies with Kuwait University.

Khalifah, Ijlal. 1973. *al-Harakah al-Nisa'iyya al-Hadithah: Qiaat al-'Imar'ah al-'Arabiyyah 'ala Ard Masir*) Modern women's movement: The story of Arab women in the land of Egypt). Cairo: al-Matba'ah al-'Arabiyya al-Haditha.

Khalil, Muhsin 'Issa. 1998. *Falastin wa-Samahat al-Mufti al-Akbar: al-Hajjj Amin al-Husseini* (Palestine and his eminence, the Grand Mufti, Hajj Amin al-Husseini) .N.a: I. Kh. Muhsen.

Khilah, Kamil Mahmud. 1974. *Palestine and the British Mandate, 1922–1923* (Falastin wa-l-Intidab al-Britani, 1922–1939). Beirut: Markaz al-Abhath.

Khuli, Hasan Sabri al-. 1973. *The Policy of Colonialism and Zionism towards Palestine in the First Half of the Twentieth Century* (Siyasat al-Isti'mar wa-l-Sahyuniyy itijah Falastin fi al-nisf al-awal min al-qarn al-'Ushrin). Cairo: Dar al-Ma'arif.

Kimmerling, Baruch. 2005. *The Invention and Decline of Israeliness: State, Society, and the Military.* Berkeley: University of California Press.

Kimmerling, Baruch, and Joel S. Migdal. 1993. *Palestinians: The Making of a People.* Cambridge, MA: Harvard University Press.

Knock, Thomas J. 1992. *To End All Wars: Woodrow Wilson and the Quest for a New World Order.* Princeton, NJ: Princeton University Press.

Kobler, Franz. 1956. *The Vision Was There: A History of the British Movement for the Restoration of the Jews to Palestine.* London: Lincolns-Prager.

Koestler, Arthur. 1949. *Analyse d'un miracle, traduction de Dominiaue Aury.* Paris: Calmann Levy.

Kolinsky, Martin. 1993. *Law, Order and Riots in Mandatory Palestine, 1928–35.* London: Springer.

———. 2016. *Britain's War in the Middle East: Strategy and Diplomacy, 1936–42.* New York: Palgrave.

Kolsky, Thomas. 1992. *Jews against Zionism: The American Council for Judaism, 1942–1948.* Philadelphia: Temple University Press.

Kumar, Ram Narayan. 2012. *Martyred but Not Tamed: The Politics of Resistance in the Middle East.* New Delhi: Sage Publications.

Kupferschmidt, Uri M. 1987. *The Supreme Muslim Council: Islam under the British Mandate for Palestine.* Leiden: E. J. Brill.

Lachman, Shai. 2015. "Arab Rebellion and Terrorism in Palestine, 1929–1939: The Case of Shiekh 'Izz al-Din al-Qassam and His Movement." In *Zionism and Arabism in Palestine and Israel,* edited by Elie Kedourie and Sylvia G. Haim, pp. 52–99. New York: Routledge.

Laqueur, Walter. 1972. *A History of Zionism: From the French Revolution to the Establishment of the State of Israel.* New York: Holt, Rinehart and Winston.

———. 1976. *A History of Zionism.* New York: Schocken Books.

Laqueur, Walter, and Dan Schueftan. 2016. *The Israel-Arab Reader: A Documentary History of the Middle East Conflict.* New York: Penguin.

Lehn, Walter, and Uri Davis. 1988. *The Jewish National Fund.* London: Kegan Paul International.

Lieshout, Robert H. 2016. *Britain and the Arab Middle East: World War I and Its Aftermath.* London: Bloomsbury Publishing.

Luciani, Giacomo. 2016. "Oil and Political Economy in International Relations of the Middle East." In *International Relations of the Middle East,* edited by Louise Fawcett, pp. 105–130. Oxford: Oxford University Press.

MacMillan, Margaret. 2007. *Paris 1919: Six Months That Changed the World.* New York: Random House Publishing Group.

Mahjoubi, 'Ali. 1990. *Juzur al-Isti'mar al-Sahyuni bi-Falastin* (The roots of Zionist colonialism in Palestine). Tunisia: Dar Saras Publishing.

Mahmud, Shakir. 1968. "The Legal Problems Concerning the Juridical Status and Political Activities of the Zionist Organization/Jewish Agency." *William and Mary Law Review* 9: pp. 556–578.

———. 2002. *Encyclopedia of the History of the Jews* (Mawsu'at Tarikh al-Yahud). Amman: Dar Usamah.

Mallison, W. Thomas. 1968. "The Legal Problems Concerning the Juridical Status and Political Activities of the Zionist Organization/Jewish Agency." *William and Mary Law Review* 9: p. 556.

Mallison, W. Thomas, and Sally V. Mallison. 1986. *The Palestine Problem in International Law and World Order.* London: Longman Group Ltd.

Mangold, Peter. 2016. *What the British Did: Two Centuries in the Middle.* London: I. B. Tauris.

Manual, Frank E. 1949. *The Realities of American-Palestine Relations.* Washington, DC: Public Affairs Press.

Mardor, Munya M. 1964. *Haganah.* New York: New American Library.

Marlowe, John. 1946. *Rebellion in Palestine*. London: Cresset Press.

———. 1954. *A History of Modern Egypt and Anglo-Egyptian Relations: 1800–1956*. London: Cresset Press.

———. 1959. *The Seat of Pilate: An Account of the Palestine Mandate*. London: Crescent Press.

Marston, Daniel, and Carter Malkasian. 2011. *Counterinsurgency in Modern Warfare*. London: Bloomsbury Publishing.

Masalha, Nur. 1999. "A Critique on Benny Morris." In *The Israel-Palestine Question: Rewriting Histories*, edited by Ilan Pappé, pp. 184–211. New York: Routledge.

Massad, Joseph. 2006. *The Persistence of the Palestinian Question: Essays on Zionism and the Palestinians*. London: Routledge.

Masud, Muhammad Khalid. 1993. "Conclusion: The Limits of 'Expert' Knowledge." In *Russia's Muslim Frontiers: New Directions in Cross-Cultural Analysis*, edited by Dale F. Eickelman, pp. 190–200. Bloomington: Indiana University Press.

Mattar, Philip. 1988. *The Mufti of Jerusalem: Al-Hajj Amin al-Husayni and the Palestinian National Movement*. New York: Columbia University Press.

McDonalf, James G. 1951. *My Mission in Israel, 1948–1951*. London: Victor Gollancz.

Menuhim, Moshe. 1965. *The Decadence of Judaism in Our Time*. New York: Exposition Press.

Messiri, 'Abd el Wahab. 1977. *Zionism, Nazism and the End of History: A New Cultural Vision* (al-Sahyuniyyah w-al-Naziyyah wa-Nihayat al-Tarikh). Forward by Mohamed Hassanin Heikal. Cairo: Dar al-Shuruq.

———. 1999. *Encyclopedia of Jews, Judaism and Zionism: A New Model of Interpretation* (Mawsu'ah al-Yahud w-al-Yahudiyya w-al-Sahyuniyya). Cairo: Dar al-Shuruq.

Miller, Rory. 2010. *Britain, Palestine and Empire: The Mandate Years*. Surrey, UK: Ashgate Publishing.

Misiri, 'Abd al-Wahab al-. 1997. *Zionism and Nazism and the End of History: A New Civilized Vision* (al-Sahyuniyya wa-l-Naziyyah wa-Nihayat al-Tarikh: Ru'yah Hadariyyah Jadidah). Forward by Mohamed Hassanein Heikal. Cairo: Dar al-Shuruq.

Morris, Benny. 1999. *Righteous Victims: A History of the Zionist-Arab Conflict, 1881–1999*. London: John Murray.

———. 2008. *1948: A History of the First Arab-Israeli War*. New Haven, CT: Yale University Press.

———. 2012. *The Birth of the Palestinian Refugee Problem Revisited*. New York: Cambridge University Press.

Morsy, Laila. 1984. "The Military Clauses of the Anglo-Egyptian Treaty of Friendship and Alliance, 1936." *International Journal of Middle East Studies* 16, no. 1 (March): pp. 67–97.

Mu'awiyyah, Ibrahim. 1990. *Palestine from the Earliest Times to the Fourth Century BC* (Falastin min Aqdam al-'Usur 'ila al-Qurn al-Rabi' qabl al-Milad). In *al-Mawsu'ah al-Falastiniyyah*. Beirut: al-Dirasat al-Tarikhiyyah. pp. 1–138.

Mufarej, Fu'ad Khalil Mufarej. 1937. *The Arab Conference in Bloudan* (al-Mu'tamr al-'Arabi al-Qawmi fi Bouladan). Damascus: al-Maktab al-'Arabi al-Qawmi lil-Di'ayah wa-l-Nashr.

Muhafazah, 'Ali. 1980. *German-Palestinian Relations from the Establishment of the Protestant Archdiocese of Jerusalem to the End of World War II, 1841– 1945* (al-'Iliqat al-Falastiniyya al-Almaniyya min Insha' Mutraniyat al-Quds al-Brutustaniyya wa hata nihayat al-Harb al-'Alamiyyah al-thaniyyah, 1841– 1945). Beirut: al-Mu'asassah al-'Arabiyyah lil-Dirasat.

———. 1985. *Mawaqif al-Duwal al-Kubra min al-Wahdah al-'Arabiyyah* (The position of France, Germany and Italy on Arab unity, 1919–1945, the positions of the great powers on Arab unity). Beirut: Markaz al-Wahdah al-Arabiyya.

———. 1989. *Political Thought in Palestine from the End of the Ottoman Rule to the End of the British Mandate, 1918–1948* (al-Fikir al-Siyasi fi Falastin min Nihayat al-Hukum al-'Uthmani hata Nihayat al-Intidab al-Britani, 1918–1948). Amman: Markaz al-Kutub al-Urduni.

———. 2009. *Al-'Arab w-al-'Alam al-Mu'asir* (Arabs and the contemporary world). Amman: Dar al-Shuruq.

Muharib, 'Abd al-Hafiz. 1981. *Relations between Armed Zionist Organizations, 1937–1948* (al-'Ilaqat byan al-MunaÐamat al-Sahyuniyyah al-Musalahah, 1937– 1948). Beirut: Markaz al-Abhath.

Musa, Suliman. 1973. *Historical Correspondence, 1914–1918: The Great Arab Revolt* (al-Murasalat al-Tarikhiyyah, 1914–1918: al-Thawrah al-'Arabiyyah al-Kubra). Amman: Matba'at al-Quwat al-Musalahah.

Muslih, Muhammad. 1981. "The 1939 Arab Conference in Cairo and the Palestinian National Movement." *Journal of Palestine Studies* 10, no. 4 (summer): pp. 3–22.

Muslih, Muhammad Y. 1988. *The Origin of Palestinian Nationalism.* New York: Columbia University Press.

Mustafa, Nadiya Mahmud, Sha'ban, Ahmed Baha' al-Din. 2004. *Ma ba'da 'Amaliyyat al-Taswiyya?*)What after the collapse of the peace settlement process?(Beirut: Research and Discussions of the Center for Arab Unity Studies, 147.

Nafa,' Sa'id 'Ali. 2009. The Druze Arabs and the Palestinian National Movement until 1948 (Arab al-Duruz wa-l-Harakah al-wataniyyah al-Falastiniyya hata 1948). Amman: Dar al-Jalil.

Nafi, Basheer M. 1997. "The Arabs and the Axis: 1933–1940." *Arab Studies Quarterly* 19, no. 2 (spring): 1–24.

Nafi,' Bashir Musa. 1999. *Imperialism, Zionism and the Palestinian Cause* (al-Imbiryaliyya w-al-Sahyuniyya w-al-Qadiyya al-Falasiniyya). Cairo: Dar al-Shuruq.

Najjar, 'Ayida. 1997. "The Arabs and the Axis: 1933–1940." *Arab Studies Quarterly* 19, no. 2 (Spring): pp. 1–24.

———. 2005. *Sahafi Falastin wa-l-Harakah al-Wataniyya fi Nisf Qarn, 1900–1948* (The Palestinian press and the national movement in half a Century, 1900–1948). Beirut: al-Mu'asassah al-'Arabiyya lil-Dirasat.

Nashashibi, Nasir al-Din. 1990. *Jerusalem's Other Voice: Ragheb Nashashibi and Moderation in Palestinian Politics, 1920–1948.* London: Ithaca Press.

Newberg, Eric Nelson. 2012. *The Pentecostal Mission in Palestine: The Legacy of Pentecostal Zionism*. Eugene, OR: Wipf and Stock Publishers.

Newsinger, John. 2016. *British Counterinsurgency*. London: Palgrave MacMillan.

Nicosia, Francis R. 2015. *Nazi Germany and the Arab World*. New York: Cambridge University Press.

Northedge, S. 1986. *The League of Nations: Its Life and Times, 1920–1946*. New York: Holmes and Meier.

Nuwar, Ma'n Abu. 2000. *The Development of Trans-Jordan, 1929–1939: A History of the Hashemite Kingdom of Jordan*. Reading, UK: Ithaca Press.

Nuwihid, 'Ajaj. 1981. *Rijal min Falastin* (Men of Palestine). Beirut: Occupied Palestine Publications.

Odeh, Ziad. 1984. *'Abd a- Rahimm al Hajj Muhammad Champion and Revolution of Bright Pages from the History of the Palestinian Struggle during the 1936–1939 Revolution* ('Abd a- Rahim al Hajj Muhammad Batal wa-Thawrah: Safahat Mushriqah min Tarikh al-Nidal al-Falastini 'aban Thawrat 1936–1939). Zarqa: al-Wikalah al-'Arabiyyah lil-Tawzi.'

Ofuatey-Kodjoe, W. 1977. *The Principle of Self-Determination in International Law*. New York: Nellen Publishing Co.

Ovendale, Ritchie. 1984. *The Origins of Arab-Israeli Wars*. London: Longman.

Palumbo, Michael. 1987. *The Palestinian Catastrophe: The 1948 Expulsion of a People from Their Homeland*. London: Quartet Books.

Panayi, Panikos. 2020. *Migrant City: A New History of London*. New Haven, CT: Yale University Press.

Pappe, Ilan. 2006. *The Ethnic Cleansing of Palestine* Oxford, UK: Oneworld Publications.

———. 2010. *The Rise and Fall of a Palestinian Dynasty. The Husaynis, 1700–1948.* London: al-Saqi.

Parisien, Pierre. 2010. *Blood and the Covenant: The Historical Consequences of the Contract with God*. Bloomington, IN: Trafford Publishing.

Parsons, Laila. 2016. *The Commander Fawzi al-Qawuqji and the Fight for Arab Independence, 1914–1948*. New York: Hill and Wang.

———. 2019. "The Secret Testimony to the Peel Commission (Part 1): Underbelly of Empire." *Journal of Palestine Studies* 49, no. 1 (autumn): 7–24.

———. 2020. "The Secret Testimony to the Peel Commission (Part 1): Partition." *Journal of Palestine Studies* 49, no. 2 (winter): 8–25.

Patai, Raphael. 1960. *The Complete Diaries of Theodor Herzl*. New York: Herzl Press and Thomas Yoseloff.

———. 1986. *The Seed of Abraham: Jews and Arabs in Contact and Conflict*. Salt Lake City: University of Utah Press.

Patai, Raphael, and Jennifer Patai Wing. 1975. *The Myth of the Jewish Race*. New York: Charles Scribner's Sons.

Pearlman, Moshe. 1965. *Ben-Gurion Looks Back*. London: Weidenfeld and Nicolson.

Polley, Gabriel. 2022. *Palestine in the Victorian Age: Colonial Encounters in the Holy Land*. London: Bloomsbury Publishing.

Porath, Yahosha. 1974. *Palestinian Arab National Movement: From Riots to Rebellion, 1929–1939*. Vol. 2. London: Frank Cass.

Pressman, Jacob. 2002. *Dear Friends: A Prophetic Journey through Great Events of the 20th Century*. Brooklyn, NY: KTAV Publishing House.

Qaddurah, Jamal Muḥammad. 1993. *Al-Qadiyyah al-Falastiniyyah wa-Lijan al-Tahqiq, 1937–1948* (The Palestinian Cause and Commissions of Inquiry, 1937–1948). Beirut: Dar al-Hamra House.

Qarqut, Dhawqan. 2006. *In the Modern History of the Arab Nation* (Fi Tarikh al-'Ummah al-'Arabiyyah al-Hadith). Cairo: Maktabt Madbuli.

Qasimiyah, Khayriyah. 1974. *'Awni 'Abdel Hadi Awraq khasah* (Awni Abdel Hadi: Private papers). Beirut: Research Center of the Palestine.

Qasimiyyah, Kahyriyyah. 1973a. "Najib Nassar in His Newspaper Karmil (1909–1914): One of the Pioneers of Anti-Zionism" (Najib Nassar fi Jaridatuhu al-Karmil [1909–1914]: Ahad Ruwad Munahadat al-Sahyuniyyah). *Shu'un Falastiniyyah/Palestinian Affairs*, no. 23 (July 1973): pp. 101–123.

———. 1973b. *Zionist Activity in the Arab East and Its Impact* (al-Nashat al-Sahyuni fi al-Sharq al-'Arabi wa-Sadahu, 1908–1918). Beirut: Dar al-Thaqafah al-Jadidah.

———. 1975. *Palestine in al-Qawuqji Diary: 1936–1948* (Falastin fi Mudhakarat al-Qawuqji: 1936–1948). Beirut: Markaz al-Abhath.

Qatan, Henry. 1970. *Palestine in the Light of Right and Justice* (Falastin fi Dhaw' al-Haqq wa-l-'Adil). Translated by Wadi' Falastin. Beirut: Maktabat Lubnan.

Quandt, William Baver, Fuad Jabber, and Ann Mosely Lesch. 1973. *The Politics of Palestinian Nationalism*. Berkeley: University of California Press.

Quigley, John. 1990. *Palestine and Israel: A Challenge to Justice*. Durham, NC: Duke University Press.

Rabinowicz, Oskar K. 1960. *Winston Churchill on Jewish Problems*. New York: Thomas Yoseliff.

Rafiq, 'Abdul Karim. 1974. *The Arabs and the Ottomans, 1516–1916* (al-'Arab wa-l-'Uthmaniyun, 1516–1916). Damascus: Maktabat Atlas.

Rashid, Madawi Ùalal al-. 1991. *Politics in an Arabian Oasis: The Rashidis of Saudi Arabia*. New York: I. B. Tauris.

Rashidat, Shafiq. 1991. *Palestine: A History, a Lesson, and a Destiny* (Falastin: Tarikhan, wa-'Abrah, wa-Masiran). Beirut: Markaz Dirasat al-Wahda al-'Arabiyya.

Raugh, Harold E. 2013. *Wavell in the Middle East, 1939–1941: A Study in Generalship*. Norman: University of Oklahoma Press.

Regan, Bernard. 2018. *The Balfour Declaration: Empire, the Mandate and Resistance in Palestine*. London: Verso Books.

Report of the King-Crane Commission. 1947. *Foreign Relations of the United States: Paris Peace Conference 1919*. Vol. 12. Washington, DC: Government Printing Office.

Riq, As'ad. 1968. *Zionism and Arab Human Rights* (al-Sahyuniyyah wa Huquq al-Insan al-'Arabi). Beirut: Markiz al-Abhath.

Roberts, Priscilla. 2018. *The Cold War: Interpreting Conflict through Primary Documents*. Santa Barbara, CA: ABC-CLIO.

Roberts-Zauderer, Dianna Lynn. 2019. *Metaphor and Imagination in Medieval Jewish Thought: Moses ibn Ezra, Judah Halevi, Moses Maimonides, and Shem Tov ibn Falaquera*. New York: Palgrave McMillan.

Rogan, Eugene. 2009. *The Arabs: A History*. New York: Basic Books.

———. 2015. *The Fall of the Ottomans: The Great War in the Middle East, 1914–1920*. New York: Basic Books.

Rogan, Eugene L., and Avi Shlaim. 2001. *The War for Palestine: Rewriting the History of 1948*. New York: Cambridge University Press.

Roosevelt, Kermit. 1948. "The Partition of Palestine: A Lesson in Pressure Politics." *Middle East Journal* 2: pp. 1–16.

Rose, Jacqueline. 2007. *The Question of Zion*. Princeton, NJ: Princeton University Press.

Rossetto, Luigi. 1982. *Major-General Orde Charles Wingate and the Development of Long-Range Penetration*. Lawrence, KS: Sunflower Press.

Rossides, Eugene R. 1977. "The League of Nations Mandate for Palestine: A Legal Analysis." *Journal of Palestine Studies* 6, no. 2: 70–91.

Sa'd, Ahmad. 1985. *The Economic and Social Development in Palestine* (al-Tatawr al-Iqtisadi al-Ijtima'i fi Falastin). Haifa: Dar al-Itihad.

Sa'dun, Salih ibn Mahmud al-. 2010. *The Anglo-Jewish Union for the Control of Palestine, 1299–1340/1882–1922* (al-Itihad al-Anglu-Yahudi lil-Saytarah 'ala Falastin, 1299–1340/1882–1922). Amman: Dar Kunuz al-Ma'rifah.

Sa'id, Amin. 1997. *Great Arab Revolt: A Detailed History of the Arab Cause in a Quarter of a Century: The Struggle between Arabs and Turks* (al-Thawra al-Kubra: Tarikh Mufasal lil-Qadiyya al-'Arabiyya fi Rubi' Qarn: al-Sira' bayn al-'Arab w-al-Atrak). Cairo: Maktabt Madbuli.

Saab, Hassan. 1956. *The Arab Federalists of the Ottoman Empire*. Amsterdam: Djambatan.

Sabbagh, Karl. 2006. *Palestine: A Personal History*. London: Atlantic.

Sadaqah, Najib. 1946. *The Palestinian Cause* (al-Qadiyyah al-Falastiniyya). Beirut: Dar al-Kutub.

Safari, 'Issa al-. 1937. *Arab Palestine between the Mandate and the Zionist* (Falastin al-'Arabiyyah bayn al-Intidab wa-l-Sahyuniyyah). Jaffa: Maktabat Falastin al-Jadidah.

Sakhnini, 'Isam. 1985. *Palestine, the State: The Roots of the Issue in Palestinian History* (Falastin al-Dawlah: Judhur al-Mas'alah fi al-Tarikh al-Falastini). Beirut: Markaz al-Abhath.

Salih, 'Abd al-Qudus Abu. 2005. *Diary of Dr. Ma'ruf al-Dawalibi* (Mudhakarat Ma'ruf al-Dawalibi). Riyadh: Maktabt al-'Abikan.

Salih, Muhsin. 1985. *Population of Palestine Demographically and Geographically* (Sukan Falastin Dimughrafiyyan wa-Jughrafiyyan). Amman: Dar al-Shuruq.

———. 2012. *The Palestinian Issue: Historical Background and Contemporary Developments* (al-Qadiyyah al-Falastiniyyah: Khalifyatuha al-Tarikhiyyah wa-Tatawuratiha al-Mu'asirah). Beirut: Markaz al-Zaytunah lil-Dirasat wa-l-Istisharat.

Salim, Muhammed 'Abdel-Ra'uf. 1982. *The Jewish Agency Activity for Palestine from Its Inception until the Establishment of the State of Israel, 1922–1948* (Nashat al-Wikalah al-Yahudiyyah li-Falastin mindh Insha'iha hata qiyam al-Dawlah, 1922–1948). Beirut: al-Mu'asassah al-'Arabiyyah lil-Dirasat.

Sanagan, Mark. 2020. *Lightning through the Clouds: 'Izz al-Din al-Qassam and the Making of the Modern Middle East*. Austin: University of Texas Press.

Sayigh, Yazid. 2002. *Armed Struggle and the Search for a State: The Palestinian National Movement, 1949–1993*. Beirut: Institute for Palestine Studies.

Sayigh, Rosemary. 1979. *The Palestinians: From Peasants to Revolutionaries*. London: Zed Press.

Sayigh, Yezid. 1997. *Armed Struggle and the Search for a State: The Palestinian National Movement, 1949–1993*. Oxford: Oxford University Press.

Schechtman, Joseph B. 1956–1961. *The Vladimir Jabotinsky Story*. New York: Thomas Yoselloff.

———. 1961. *Fighter and Prophet: The Valdimir Jabotinsky Story the Last Years*. New York: Thomas Yoseloff.

Schiff, Ze'ev. 1985. *A History of the Israeli Army*. New York: MacMillan.

Schneer, Jonathan. 2011. *The Balfour Declaration: The Origins of the Arab-Israeli Conflict*. London: Bloomsbury.

Scholoch, Alexander. 1985. "The Demographic Development of Palestine, 1850–1882." *International Journal of Middle East Studies* 17, no. 4 (November): pp. 485–505.

Segev, Tom. 1986. *1949: The First Israelis*. New York: Free Press.

———. 2000. *One Palestine, Complete: Jews and Arabs under the British Mandate*. New York: Metropolitan Books.

Shafir, Greshon. 2016. "Theorizing Zionist Settler Colonialism in Palestine." In *The Routledge Handbook of the History of Settler Colonialism*, edited by Edward Cavanagh and Lorenzo Veracini. London: Routledge.

Shahabi, Mustafa al-. 1961. *Arab Nationalism: Its History, Strength, and Goals* (al-Qawmiyyah al-'Arabiyyah: Tarikhuha wa-Qawamuha wa-Maramiha). Cairo: Ma'had al-Dirasat al-'Arabiyyah al-'Aliyyah.

Shahin, Ahmad. 1985. "For Palestine to Be a First Arab Issue" (Kai Takunu Falastin Qadiyya 'Arabiyya 'Ula). *Shu'un Falastiniyyah/Palestinian Affairs*, no. 144–145 (March-April): pp. 3–9.

Shaqra, Ibrahim Abu. 1999. *Mufti Falastin al-Hajj Amin al-Husseini wa-Thawrat 1936–1939* (The Mufti of Palestine, Hajj Amin al-Husseini, and the 1936/1939 Revolution). Damascus: Dar Al-Numeir.

Sharett, Moshe. 2019. *My Struggle for Peace: The Diary of Moshe Sharett, 1953–1954*, edited by Neil Caplan and Yaakov Sharett. Bloomington: Indiana University Press.

Sharif, Regina. 1985. *Non-Jewish Zionism: Its Roots in Western History* (al-Sahyuniyya ghayr al-Yahudiyyah: Juduraha fi al-Tarikh al-Gharbi). Translated by 'Ahmad 'Abd al-'Aziz. Kuwait: al-Majlis al-Watani lil-Thaqafah wa-l-Funun.

Shindler, Colin. 2011. *Israel and the European Left: Between Solidarity and Delegitimization*. New York: Bloomsbury Publishing.

Shlaim, Avi. 1988. *Collusion across the Jordan: King Abdullah, the Zionist Movement, and the Partition of Palestine*. New York: Columbia University Press.

———. 1993. "The Rise of Jewish Immigration to Palestine in the 1930s." *Middle Eastern Studies* 29, no. 4: 593–617.

———. 2000. *The Iron Wall: Israel and the Arab World*. New York: W. W. Norton & Company.

———. 2001. "The Rise of Arab Nationalism." Chapter 4 of *The Iron Wall: Israel and the Arab World*, pp. 82–105. New York: W. W. Norton & Company.

———. 2015. *The Iron Wall: Israel and the Arab World*. London: Penguin.

Shufani, Ilyas. 2002. *Isra'il fi khamsin 'aman: al-Mashru' al-Sihyuni min al-mujarrad 'ila al-Malmus* (Israel in fifty years: The Zionist project from the abstract to the tangible). Damascus: Dar Jafra lil-Dirasat.

———. 2003. *Abridgment in the Political History of Palestine since the Dawn of History until 1949* (al-Mujaz fi Tarikh Falastin al-Siyasi mindh Fajr al-Tarikh hata sinat 1948). Beirut: Mu'asassat al-Dirasat al-Falastiniyya.

Shuqiri, Ahmad al-. 1970. *Dialogue and Secrets with Kings and Presidents* (Hiwar wa-Asrar ma' al-muluk wa-l-Ru'sa') Beirut: Dar al-'Awdad.

Simpson, John Hope. 1932. *Report on Immigration, Housing Projects and Urbanism* (Taqrir 'an al-Hijrah wa-Mashari' al-Iskan wa-l-Imran). Jerusalem: Matba'at Dar al-Aytam al-Islamiyyah/Islamic Orphan Press.

Sinanoglou, Penny. 2019. *Partitioning Palestine: British Policymaking at the End of Empire*. Chicago: University of Chicago Press.

Smuts, Jan Christiaan. 1918. *The League of Nations: A Practical Suggestion*. London: Hodder and Stoughton.

Snyder, Louis Leo. 1960. *The War: A Concise History, 1939–1945*. New York: Simon & Schuster.

Sokolow, Nahum. 1919. *History of Zionism, 1600–1918*. London: Longmans, Green and Co.

Stein, Kenneth. 1984. *The Land Question in Palestine, 1917–1919*. Chapel Hill: University of North Carolina Press.

Stein, Leonard. 1961. *The Balfour Declaration*. London: Simon & Schuster.

Stevens, Richard. 1971. "Zionism as a Phase of Western Imperialism." In *The Transformation of Palestine: Essays on the Origin and Development of the Arab-Israeli Conflict*, edited by Ibrahim Abu Lughod, pp. 27–59. Evanston, IL: Northwestern University Press.

Stevenson, David. 2017. *1917: War, Peace, and Revolution*. Oxford: Oxford University Press.

Stillman, Norman. 1979. "The Jews of Arab Lands: A History and Source Book." Philadelphia: *Jewish Publication Society*.

Stråth, Bo. 2016. *Europe's Utopias of Peace: 1815, 1919, 1951*. London: Bloomsbury Publishing.

Sulaymah, 'Āyidah. 1986. *Masir wa-l-Qadiyyah al-Falastiniyya* (Egypt and the Palestinian cause). Cairo: Dar al-Fikr.

Swedenburg, Ted. 1995. *Memories of Revolt: The 1936–1939 Rebellion and the Palestinian National Past*. Minneapolis: University of Minnesota Press.

Sykes, Christopher. 1965. *Cross Roads to Israel*. London: Collins.

Sykes, Christopher Simon. 2016. *The Man Who Created the Middle East: A Story of Empire, Conflict and the Sykes-Picot Agreement*. London: HarperCollins UK.

Tahat, Muhammad 'Abdullah. 2015. *al-Faluti* (al-Faluti). Beirut: Dar al-Kitab al-Thaqafi.

Talim, Ephraim, and Menahem Talim. 1988. *Lexicon of Zionism* (Mu'jam al-Mustalahat al-Sahyumiyyah). Translated by Ahmad Barakat al-'Ajrami. Amman: Dar al-Jalil.

Tamimi, 'Abd al-Rahman al-. 2018. *Iraq's Official and Popular Position on Arab-Israeli Clashes, 1947–1979* (Mawqif al-Iraq al-Rasmi wa-l-Sha'bi min Muwajahat al-'Arabiyya, al-Isra'iliyya). Amman: Dar al-Mu'taz.

Tamraz, Sa'id Jamil. 2018. *Tard al-Falastiniyyin fi al-Fikir w-al-Mumarasah al-Sahyuniyah, 1882–1949* (The Expulsion of the Palestinians in Zionist Thought and Practice, 1882–1949). Amman: Durub Dar al-Yazuri.

Tarbin, Ahmad. 1990. *Palestine during the British Mandate* (Falastin fi 'Ahd al-Intidab al-Britani): Beirut: *The Palestinian Encyclopedia* Part 2, Volume 2, pp. 997–998.

Tarbush, Mohammad A. 2015. *The Role of the Military in Politics: A Case Study of Iraq to 1941*. New York: Routledge.

Taylor & Francis Group. 2003. *The Middle East and North Africa*. London: Psychology Press.

Tessler, Mark. 2009. *A History of the Israeli-Palestinian Conflict*. Bloomington: Indiana University Press.

Teveth, Shabtai. 1987. *Ben Gurion and the Arabs.* Translated by Ghazi al-Sa'di. Zionist Personalities. Amman: Dar al-Jalil.

Ther, Philipp. 2014. *The Dark Side of Nation-States: Ethnic Cleansing in Modern Europe*. New York: Berghahn Books.

Thomas, Baylis. 2011. *The Dark Side of Zionism: The Quest for Security Through Dominance*. Lanham, MD: Lexington Books.

Thompson, Elizabeth F. 2022. *How the West Stole Democracy from the Arabs: The Syrian Arab Conference of 1920 and the Destruction of Its Historic Liberal-Islamist Alliance*. Translated by Muhammad M. Arna'ut. Beirut: Arab Center for Research and Policy Studies.

Thompson, John A. 2018. "Woodrow Wilson and 'Peace without Victory': Interpreting the Reversal of 1917." *Federal History Journal*: 10/1, pp. 9–25.

Tibawi, 'Abd al-Latif. 1969. *A Modern History: Including Lebanon and Palestine*. London: MacMillan.

Touma, Emile. 1978. *Sixty Years of Palestinian Arab Nationalism* (Situn 'Amman 'ala al-Harakah al-Qawmiyya al-'Arabiyyah al-Falastiniyya). Beirut: Dar Ibn Rushd.

Tulloch, Derek. 1972. *Wingate in Peace and War*. London: Macdonald.

Turbin, Ahmad. 1968. *Qadiyat Falastin* (The case of Palestine, 1897–1948). Damascus: Matabi' al-Hilal.

'Ubaydi, Fakhri al-Din al-, and Muhammad Hamid al-Tai.' 1948. *Falastin: Wad'uha al-Jughrafi wa-Tatawuruha al-Tarikhi* (Palestine: Its geographical status and historical development). Baghdad: Matba'at al-Ma'arif.

'Udah, Butrus 'Udah. 1975. *The Palestinian Cause in the Arab Reality* (al-Qadiyya al-Falastiniyyah fi al-Waqi' al-'Arabi). Tripoli: Dar al-Fikir.

'Umar, 'Abd al-Karim al-. 1999. *Memoirs of al-Haj Muhammad Amin al-Husseini* (Mudhakirat al-Haj Muhammad Amin al-Husseini). Damascus: al-Ahali.

'Umari, Subhi. 1969. *Lawrence as I Knew Him* (*Lawrence kama 'Araftuhu*). Beirut: Dar al-Nahar.

'Uthman, Ahmad. 1963. *The Principle of the International Organization of Colonial Administration and Its Applications in the Mandate and in the International Guardianship System* (Mabda'al-Tanzim al-Duwali li-Idarat al-Musta'mrat wa-Tatbigihi fi al-Intidab wa-Nizam al-Wasaya al-Duwaliyya). Cairo: Dar al-Nahdah.

'Uwaisi, 'Abd al-Fatah al-. 1992. *The Roots of the Palestinian Cause, 1799–1922* (Jidhur al-Qadiyyah al-Falastiniyyah, 1799–1922). Hebron: Dar al-Hassan.

Wallance, Gregory J. 2018. *The Woman Who Fought an Empire: Sarah Aaronsohn and Her Nili Spy Ring*. Lincoln, NE: Potomac Books.

Wasserstein, Bernard. 2001. *Divided Jerusalem: The Struggle for the Holy City.* New Haven, CT: Yale University Press.

Watson, James. 2014. *Religious Thoughts*. Bloomington, IN: iUniverse.

Watts, Martin. 2004. *The Jewish Legion during the First World War*. New York: Palgrave McMillan.

Weinstock, Nathan. 1979. *Zionism: False Messiah*. London: Inklinks Ltd. and Pluto Press.

Weizmann, Chaim. 1945. "Palestine in 1936: Address Given at Chatham House, London, on June 9th, 1936." In *Chaim Weizmann: A Tribute on His Seventieth Birthday*, edited by Paul Goodman, pp. 235–243. London: Victor Gollancz.

———. 1949. *Trial and Error: The Autobiography of Chaim Weizmann*. New York: Harper.

Wilson, Mary Christina. 1987. *King Abdullah, Britain and the Making of Jordan*. New York: Cambridge University Press.

Woodward, Ernest L., and Rohan Butler, eds. 1946–1985. *Documents on British Foreign Policy, 1919–1939*. London: H. M. Stationary Office.

Wright, Quincy. 1972. "The Palestine Conflict in International Law." In *Major Middle Eastern Problems in International Law*, edited by Majid Khadduri, pp. 13–36. Washington, DC: American Enterprise Institute for Public Policy Research.

Yassin, 'Abd al-Qadir. 1980. *History of the Palestinian Working Class* (Tarikh al-Tabaqah al-'Amillah fi Falastin). Beirut: Markaz al-Abhath.

Yassin, Sweid. 1992. *Mu'amarat al-Gharb 'ila al-'Arab: Mahatat fi Marahil al-Mu'amara w-Muqwamatuha* (The West's conspiracy against the Arabs: Stations in the stages of the conspiracy and its resistance). Beirut: Arab Center for Research and Documentation.

Yassin, Subhi. 1967. *The Great Arab Revolt in Palestine, 1936–1939* (al-Thawrah al-'Arabiyyah al-Kubra, 1936–1939). Cairo: Dar al-Katib al-'Arabi.

Yisraeli, David. 1975. *Germany and Zionism, Germany and the Middle East, 1835–1939*. Tel Aviv: Tel Aviv University, Institute of German History.

Za'im, Ibrahim Saqir Isma'il. 2019. *al-Ta'ayush al-Silmi bayn al-Muslimin w-al-Masihiyin fi bayt al-Maqdis* (Peaceful coexistence between Muslims and Christians in Jerusalem between 1897–1994). London: E-Kutub Ltd.

Zaken, Mordechai. 2011. *Jews and Arabs in the Ottoman Empire: Two Worlds Collide*. Bloomington: Indiana University Press.

Zamili, Ibrahim Salim al-. 2016. *Falastin fi al-Taqarir al-Britaniyya, 1919–1947* (Palestine in British reports, 1919–1947). Cairo: Dar Ibn Rushd.

Zaquq, Nahid. 2003. *Documents of the Palestinian Cause* (Watha'iq al-Qadiyya al-Falastiniyya). Gaza: al-Markaz al-Qawmi lil-Dirasat wa-l-Tawthiq.

Zayadah, Nicola. 1990. "Palestine from Alexander to the Arab Islamic Conquest" (Falastin min Alexander 'ila al-Fatih al-'Arabi al-Islami). In *al-Mawsu'ah al-Falastiniyyah*, Special Studies, Volume 2, part 2, pp. 2:144–145. Beirut: al-Dirasat al-Tarikhiyyah.

Zebel, Sydney Henry. 1973. *Balfour: A Political Biography*. Cambridge: Cambridge University Press.

Zu'itir, Akram. 1955. *Palestinian Cause* (al-Qadiyyah al-Falastiniyyah). Cairo: Dar al-Ma'arif.

———. 1979. *Documents of Palestinian National Movement, 1918–1939* (Watha'iq al-Harakah al-Wataniyyah al-Falastiniyyah, 1918–1939). Beirut: Mu'asassat al-Dirasat al-Falastiniyyah.

Zua'iter, Akram. 1958. *The Palestine Question*. Beirut: Palestine Arab Refugees Institution.

Zweig, Ronald W. 1987. *Britain and Palestine during the Second World War*. London: Royal Historical Society.

Arab League, Jerusalem, no. 1335, July 5, 1929, issued by the Arab League.

al-Karmel, Haifa, January 29, 1928; no. 1404, and November 26, 1929; no. 1405, April 30, 1930, no. 1406.

Falastin, Jaffa, October 13, 1933.

Mir'at al-Sharq, Jerusalem, November 7, 1933.

New York Times, May 30, 1939, p. A11; June 1, 1939, p. A17; June 3, 1939, p. A3; June 20, 1939, p. A4; July 4, 1939, p. A4.

Palestine Post, October 22, 1936.

Palestine, December 24, 1936.

Palestine, Jaffa, nos. 659–662, March 4–14, 1924.

Palestine Post, May 15, 1935, and August 17, 1936.

Index

About the Author

Labeeb Ahmed Bsoul has been a professor in the Department of Humanities and Social Sciences at Khalifa University since 2009. He speaks several languages and edits academic journals. He has published thirty-eight peer-reviewed articles, six books, three book chapters, and several encyclopedia entries. He received his BA and MA in international relations from San Francisco State University and his PhD from McGill University. He taught at Canadian and Gulf universities. He is conducting research for a project to investigate the causes of the ongoing conflict in the Middle East. His research interests include international relations, Middle East and Islamic studies, science in Islam, Palestine affairs, and Orientalism.

Milton Keynes UK
Ingram Content Group UK Ltd.
UKHW012218141123
432582UK00002B/15